CHINA'S GREAT TRAIN

CHINA'S
GREAT TRAIN

BEIJING'S DRIVE WEST AND THE CAMPAIGN TO REMAKE TIBET

ABRAHM LUSTGARTEN

TIMES BOOKS

HENRY HOLT AND COMPANY   NEW YORK

To Jodie

Times Books
Henry Holt and Company, LLC
Publishers since 1866
175 Fifth Avenue
New York, New York 10010
www.henryholt.com

Henry Holt® is a registered trademark of
Henry Holt and Company, LLC.

Library of Congress Cataloging-in-Publication Data
Lustgarten, Abrahm.
China's great train : Beijing's drive west and the campaign to remake Tibet/Abrahm
Lustgarten.—1st ed.
    p. cm
Includes bibliographical references and index.
ISBN-13: 978-0-8050-8324-8
ISBN-10: 0-8050-8324-3
1. Railroads—China—Tibet—History—20th century. 2. Transportation policy—
China. 3. Tibet (China)—Relations—China. 4. China—Relations—China—Tibet.
I. Title.
HE3289.T53L87 2008
385.0951'5—dc22

                                                                    2008004165

Henry Holt books are available for special promotions and
premiums. For details contact: Director, Special Markets.

First Edition 2008
Designed by Kelly S. Too

Printed in the United States of America
1 3 5 7 9 10 8 6 4 2

In [the game of] Go, when your goal is to improve, you don't treat each game as the end all and be all; each game is but a step on a long path. The particulars of your emotional investment don't matter in this longer-term perspective. . . . The winner in Go is not the player who wins the most spectacular battle somewhere, but the player who wins the war. . . .

At the beginning of Go, the board is completely empty. One's initial moves can only be effective if they are seen for what they are—options or probes of a potential future, which one can trade, use, or sacrifice later.

The middle game starts as the two opponents develop differing opinions about who gets what. This stage taxes the frames and sketches developed in the opening through multiple skirmishes, all-out brawls, and chaos of the worst kind. Here, one's ability to read many moves ahead can make the difference. . . . Every move counts. The middle game is a razor-sharp tightrope. One slip to either side or just resting on the wire and you'll be either falling fast or cut in two. . . . Things and territory that at first were mere potential may now be actually mapped. . . .

Toward the end of the game, the feeling is analytical, bureaucratic. The later stages of the end game have no room for intuition; in this, its final throes, a mathematical science dictates the absolute best way to play. While not sexy, the end game is about sealing the deal. Ratcheting up the global perspective of things, you can look beyond the game you are playing now.

—Troy Anderson, *The Way of Go*

CONTENTS

CONTENTS

CHINA'S GREAT TRAIN

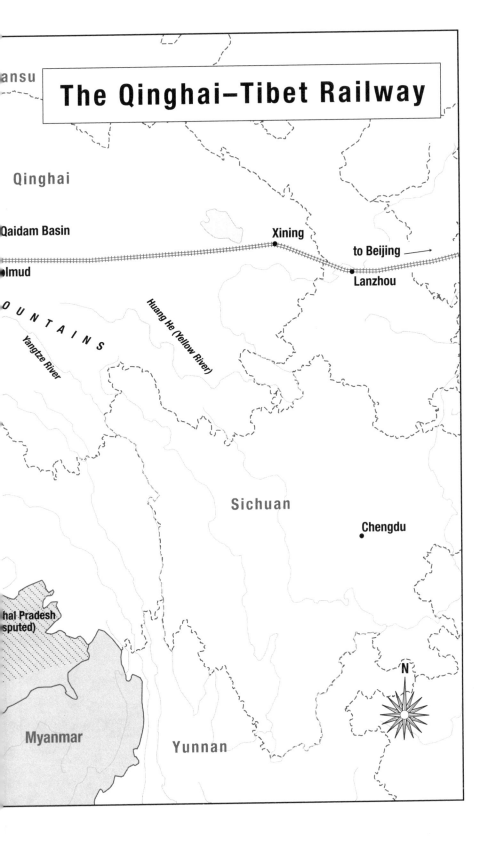

The Qinghai–Tibet Railway

ansu

Qinghai

Qaidam Basin

Xining

to Beijing →

Imud

Lanzhou

O U N T A I N S

Yangtze River

Huang He (Yellow River)

Sichuan

Chengdu

hal Pradesh
sputed)

Myanmar

Yunnan

N

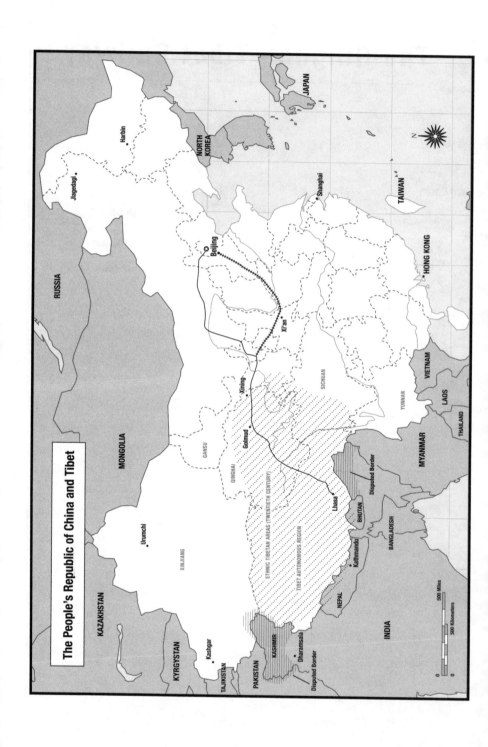

The People's Republic of China and Tibet

PART I

A FIFTY-YEAR AMBITION

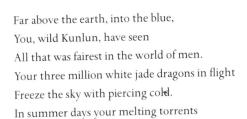

Far above the earth, into the blue,
You, wild Kunlun, have seen
All that was fairest in the world of men.
Your three million white jade dragons in flight
Freeze the sky with piercing cold.
In summer days your melting torrents
Flood the streams and rivers,
Turning men into fish and turtles . . .

To Kunlun now I say . . .
Could I but draw my sword o'ertopping heaven,
I'd cleave you in three:
One piece for Europe,
One for America,
One to keep in the East.
Peace would then reign over the world,
The same warmth and cold throughout the globe.
—Mao Zedong, "Kunlun," 1935

1

NOW IS THE TIME

DIMLY LIT CORRIDORS SNAKE THROUGH IMPERSONAL AND inconspicuous government buildings in downtown Beijing. These are China's true halls of power, remnants of a twentieth-century China that is increasingly becoming outdated—an architecture of communism, of pale, outsized bureaucracies. Inside, voices and cigarette smoke ricochet off the cold polished granite. Fluorescent lights accentuate the faded lichen-colored paint. Behind the doors, endless and unceremoniously numbered, the big decisions about China's future are made.

Outside, the city of Beijing has moved on. It buzzes with the optimistic temperament of 15 million people and its pole position in China's breakneck race for economic greatness. In just one short decade, its streets have been transformed into broad avenues packed not with bicycles and rickshaws but with hundreds of thousands of cars driven by newly affluent and unabashedly proud middle-class workers. There is little of the developing-world chaos of Delhi or Kathmandu. Audis and Ferraris zip past the Cartier store on Beijing's main shopping avenue. Overpasses and exit ramps are lined with green and purple neon strips of light, lending a tacky but futuristic feel. Across downtown, mammoth plates of polished glass encase brightly lit storefronts—designer leather handbags (real ones), flat-screen TVs. The lines outside the Kentucky Fried Chicken, Pizza Hut, and Starbucks franchises swamp the occasional corner noodle shops. This is the new China.

Old hutongs, the quaint thin alleyways full of traditional courtyard homes, have mostly been torn down to make way for the new. Those that haven't are being restored with a vigor grown from a newfound sense of tourist-market potential rather than of valued heritage. This urban, and for the most part eastern, China has already made the leap into the twenty-first century global economy and is joyously consuming the goods its factories once only exported for the rest of the world. The booming middle class, with its cars and skyscrapers, is self-perpetuating, a ravenous appetite that energizes the breakneck Chinese economy. This cycle demands fuel on a level unprecedented in world history—more land as well as grander cities, a politically willing citizenry, ever more consumer hunger, and a still larger middle class. It also, of course, demands the natural resources to construct it all.

Fortunately for those piloting the vast experiment, China today is nouveau riche. Mao Zedong's iron-fisted Great Leap Forward and Cultural Revolution drained Beijing's government accounts, but Deng Xiaoping's "capitalist road" has brought China back to solid financial footing and economic growth through a paradoxical jumble of expansion and Communist-era ideals and social policies. While most of China's 1.3 billion people still struggle in poverty, the nation's coffers are finally overflowing—much at the expense of western regions that provided the labor and resources for the east.

It's that cash that has emboldened China's leaders to think they can extend prosperity by simply manufacturing more growth on a massive scale, and financing it all from their hive of offices in Beijing. Across the country, whole cities are being rebuilt with seeming disregard for demand; dozens of sky-rises are erected almost overnight with no clear indication of who will inhabit them. The western outposts are linked by an expanding transportation infrastructure—roads, power transmission lines, pipelines, and railways—built at a rate that makes Dwight Eisenhower look lazy. China is in the throes of an industrial revolution that can only be compared to America's great expansion in the late nineteenth century.

By the year 2000, the construction of the unprecedented Three Gorges Dam was well under way, the country had launched spacecraft and planned to send astronauts into orbit, the World Trade Organization was preparing to open its door, and Beijing was on track to win the equivalent of international knighthood, an Olympic bid. It looked clear that China could do almost anything it wanted. Its momentum appeared unstoppable. Social unrest and environmental catastrophes, the makings of what China expert Bruce Gilley fears will be a "metastatic crisis," lurked in the remote and destitute agricultural provinces, but these were far from the eastern megalopolises that were driving the country's emergence in the global economy. China's leaders were taking full advantage of a historic opportunity to reinvent itself as an economic wonder and bring its full society into the fold of success. Its continuing growth simply depended on making smart strategic decisions that would bring business and investment while maintaining stability and control.

So it was especially curious in the fall of 2000 when a seemingly obscure development puzzle emerged from inside Beijing's halls of power to become a paramount national priority: how could a train be built to Tibet?

WINTER WAS DESCENDING UNDETECTABLY THROUGH THE THICK ATMO-
spheric haze of soot and sand that obscures Beijing's seasons on the
day in October 2000 when the conversation again turned to Tibet, the
far-flung and controversy-riddled region in China's westernmost frontier. Behind one of the anonymous doorways inside the Ministry of
Railways compound, thirty or so scientists, engineers, and politicians
were assembled around a stately wooden conference table to talk about
the possibility of laying rails to the capital of the Tibet Autonomous
Region (TAR) of China, the fabled city of Lhasa. Among them was a
fifty-four-year-old junior career engineer, Zhang Luxin. Soft-spoken
and slightly built, and with his dark wispy hair combed over a thin-
ning top, he physically embodied the lack of authority he possessed
in a room full of more senior technocrats.

Zhang had spent a career on China's railways, much of it in Tibet.
But he had not yet made a mark in the railway bureaus' vast hier-
archies. His involvement in the meeting was owed to his solid engineering skills rather than any sort of political agility. In fact, he was
among the lowest-ranking men in attendance, and therefore the least
likely to speak up. Ministerial-level officials and regional leaders who
had traveled cross-country from Qinghai, Sichuan, Yunnan, and Gansu
provinces crowded the room with a heady mixture of power, ego,
and scientific knowledge. They had been bandying around ideas about
a railway to Tibet over the previous year, but with little headway. A
senior scientist present at many of the ministry's meetings on Tibet
could not recall Zhang being present at any of the previous con-
ventions; he mostly sat quietly off to the side and listened. Yet by the
end of the day, Zhang would speak out boldly, even inappropriately
given China's strict etiquette for respecting authority, giving shape

to what would become the distinctive first project of China's new century.

Tibet accounts for more than an eighth of the land mapped today within China's borders, yet in 2000, it was the only region in the country without a rail link to connect it to the east. Almost as soon as the Chinese army entered Lhasa in 1951, building a railway became a top goal. But at the time there was no money to pursue the project, which required the invention of new engineering tactics for crossing the lofty mountains and unstable frozen tundra. In many ways, Tibet's infrastructure in the decades since had remained more tied to India and Nepal than to Beijing—something Chinese nationalists found excruciatingly untenable.

For many people in the boardroom that day, this in itself was the motivation to finally get the railway done. The vast 1-million-square-mile plateau that makes up most of the TAR is an ecological wonderland, but it held little obvious value for China as a nation. Tibetans did not have much industry or trade to offer—they dealt in yak tails, fur, and salt—and were mostly engrossed in their own cultural values. China had made scant investment in elevating Tibetan society—through education, health care, or an improved standard of living—never reaching a point where the people there were interested in or able to engage fully in China's economic machine. Yet China was suddenly willing to invest years and billions to lay railroad tracks into what many eastern Chinese view as a wasteland of formidable desert and mountains. Of course, there was the strategic military importance of Tibet, which borders China's economic and political rival, India, and had been used as a base for Allied air operations during World War II. But modern defense technology seemed to make Tibet less essential as a staging ground than as an old-fashioned natural buffer.

The Chinese hoped there were mineral resources to be discovered under the Tibetan Plateau, the highest region on Earth, but the number-crunching bureaucrats had determined that the cost of bringing anything over the rough land to China's eastern industrial centers, even on a train, was financially impractical. One large copper deposit had been found years earlier, but its development had lagged because it was many rugged miles from a viable road. A single railway line that would overcome such obstacles, it seemed, could not be drawn. Beijing's last great railway extension to China's remote provinces, to Kashgar in the Xinjiang Uighur Autonomous Region in the northwest, had been completed a year earlier. Xinjiang, however, boasted extensive lands fit for agriculture and forestry and large mineral lodes and water resources. It also was predicted to deliver 37 percent of China's internal coal supplies and 25 percent of its oil and natural gas.

A train to Lhasa had defied fifty years of efforts to build it for good reasons. Tibet, which stakes the full southwest corner of China, is bounded by the world's largest mountains on all sides: in addition to the Himalayas and the Karakoram on the borders with India, Pakistan, and Nepal, the Kunlun Mountains divide the Tibetan Plateau from the lowlands of the northeastern province of Qinghai, and the jagged Nyenchen Tangla range separates it from Yunnan and Sichuan to the east. At the heart of this geographic sanctuary is the Chang Tang, a formidable plateau region four times the size of France, stretching fifteen hundred miles east to west and five hundred miles north to south. The plateau is home to the largest subarctic permafrost region on the planet, a delicate frozen soil that becomes treacherous when it melts. The geographic difficulties defied the best science and railway engineering China could devise. International experts said the railway simply could not be built, and China's railway engineers were considered by many to be the most capable in the world.

No matter how a visitor enters Tibet, the roads climb to altitudes higher than any mountain in the continental United States. They twist and wind through steep gorges loaded like cannons with unstable rock and snow at their peaks and flushing with torrents of interminable water in their troughs. Passersby must weave somewhere in between, on paths frequently swept out of existence by the mountains' hazards. One route from the north, from Qinghai, offers the only exception. There are the usual deep gorges and glacier-capped mountain ranges rising out of China's hinterland into Tibet's northern steppe, but they span a short distance compared to any other gateway. Once you breach the first main pass of the Kunlun, the plateau extends for hundreds of miles in what seems at first glance to be docile flatlands and rolling hills, a relief from the violently savage protrusions and peaks of the region's other borders. But then the route crosses the Chang Tang and presents other problems. The flatlands are congested with huge expanses of intermittently frozen marshes, lakes, and soggy permafrost that heave and shift more actively than almost any other geologic environment on Earth. In places it is wrought with quicksand deep enough to swallow a tank. As if to add insult to the injuries of the trek, the endless fields sustain an elevation of around fifteen thousand feet—an altitude that would require pressurization in an airplane and where a breath of air contains half the oxygen it does at sea level.

Yet, the Chang Tang was the path of least resistance should a railway ever be built. Starting from the northern outpost of Golmud in Qinghai, it is nearly a straight 710 miles south to the Lhasa Valley. It was roughly the route Tibetan traders and dignitaries had used for centuries to reach the Mongols and the Chinese via foot and on horseback, the first route the Chinese army pounded into a road in 1951, the route Mao had hoped to turn into a railway before the Cultural

Revolution crippled China and made such an effort impossible. It was also the place in which Zhang had spent much of the three previous decades, stationed in tents and a forlorn metal trailer, virtually banished from China's mainstream scientific community, researching the frozen soil and preparing the country for a railway that until that October morning looked like it would never happen.

In the decades since the army's capture of Lhasa, discussions of a railway had proceeded in fits and starts. More often than not, plans were abandoned—sometimes for the lack of money and technology, sometimes for the lack of political will, even once for the lack of food. But the underlying problem was always the ability to engineer a system that could cross either the mountains or the endless plain of frozen soil, a puzzle that had fallen in a small way to Zhang, among others. He had been jerked through most of the false starts—on the verge of conducting breakthrough research, with nowhere to go and nothing to do when work was stopped. By the 1990s, he no longer believed he would ever have a chance to ride an engine into Lhasa, to prove himself as an engineer.

An old Chinese cadre who had been stationed in Tibet since the start of the occupation, and who had at one point risen to become the TAR's party secretary, was, however, pushing a plan. In 1951, Yin Fatang had been assigned by Mao to serve as a secretary of the working committee in what was called, before the creation of autonomous prefectures, the Tibet Military District. It was likely then that his portrait was taken in front of the revered Potala Palace wearing his government-issue canvas uniform and cap with the trademark red star, a spindly beard hanging from his chin to his sternum in a combination of Fu Manchu and Fidel Castro. Yin built his career as a party cog in Tibet. (His whereabouts during the Cultural Revolution remain a mystery.) During much of his time as a bureaucrat in the region, Tibetans suffered under ruthless policies. When reform-minded Secretary-General Hu Yaobang visited the region in early 1980, he was appalled by what he saw. "We feel very bad. We have worked for nearly thirty years, but the life of the Tibetan people has not notably improved. Are we not to blame?" Hu's reign was widely seen as sympathetic to Tibet, a brief window of liberal-leaning policy, and when he came to power one of the first corrective measures he took was the installation of Yin as secretary-general—the province's first leader to speak Tibetan. Yin had been an underling and loyalist of Deng Xiaoping, and Deng reportedly had recommended him for the post. In 1981, Yin proposed to restart the stalled Lhasa railway construction at a working meeting of the central government in Beijing. A railway would tie Tibet more closely with the rest of the nation, he suggested, and it would make it possible for the industrial machinery needed for the development of minerals and resources to be brought to Tibet. As he would summarize in later interviews, the "reason was politics and economics."

Yin soon grew frustrated. "The constant changes and delays in the decision making had greatly harmed the Tibetan people's confidence and enthusiasm in the railway," he wrote in a high-profile 1982 letter circulated to, among others, Secretary-General Hu Yaobang and Deng Xiaoping. "We feel now that everything is ready." Despite a series of personal conversations with Deng on the costs and routing, Yin's arguments were unheard. By the mid-1980s, the party leaders had decided to connect Tibet to the rest of the country in less ambitious ways. Money was flowing to building roads and, eventually, a flurry of airports.

Then, in 1999, President Jiang Zemin launched a monumental campaign to develop China's west, and prospects shifted. His deputy, Hu Jintao, was a former secretary of Tibet, and momentum for projects seemed to grow in earnest. As talks about World Trade Organization membership unfolded, U.S. president Bill Clinton warned China that its chances ultimately hinged on the country's ability to equalize standards of living between those in the eastern cities and those in the western rural provinces. The political opportunity seemed ripe.

THE LONG JOURNEY FROM BEIJING TO LHASA AT THE TIME OFFERED A miniseminar on Jiang's ambitions. The Xi'an line toward Tibet—the railway link that swerved closest to the TAR and ended abruptly in the wasteland province of Qinghai—originated in Beijing's western train station. There, monumental twin towers sheathed in bronze-tinted stone and glass are joined by an elevated bridge and a hundred-and-fifty-foot archway that evoked awe from a full mile away. The trains lined on its platforms were far less noteworthy. Many of the cars were at least twenty years old, a green paint fading on their walls. A small red scrawl, *Xian,* in both pinyin and Mandarin characters, marked the line west. The rush to boarding was mayhem, with throngs of people dragging duffels and sacks and boxes, pushing and shoving their way to the mouth of the funnel—a shoulder-width door. There was a frantic sense that those who did not fight their way onboard within seconds would simply be left behind.

Inside, the interiors were utilitarian, and uncomfortably bare, like a jail cell. The numbered bunks, thin slabs of sparsely padded steel, were stacked three to a side, six to a cabin, and braced on clunky steel triangles anchored to the wall. When it wasn't time to sleep, travelers assumed that the upper beds would be folded up and all six passengers in the car would cozy up on the bottom bench to chat. As the train rolled lazily toward Beijing's suburbs, the soot-coated window displayed a stream of monochromatic freeways, transformer stations, and shabby condominiums, and the jolt and clink of hundreds of track intersections ricocheted through the car. The midafternoon sun disappeared into atmospheric haze, beginning a roughly six-hour period of dusk. Everyone sipped black tea from plastic mugs and played mah-jongg, filling the cramped cabin with raucous noise and cigarette smoke. The men chewed the skin off the roasted knuckles of chicken feet and spat the wet remnants onto the floor by their beds. A woman scraped at the wax inside her ear with a small metal spoon attached to her keychain.

Gradually, over three nights, the train crossed a thousand miles, traversing the provinces of Hebei, Shanxi, Shaanxi, and Gansu. As urban Beijing sprawled into the countryside, the landscape was converted to a procession of midsized towns and big cities, all apparently covered in a thin layer of ash. Near Xi'an, a city of 6 million people, the train passed the giant cooling towers of a nuclear power plant, surrounded by huge apartment blocks that stretched for miles. Farther west, a group of people sat around the rim of a decrepit Olympic-size swimming pool while a man fished from its earth-brown water. In Beijing, the trains seemed dilapidated, antique. But with every rhythmic rotation of the locomotive's giant steel wheels, the wealthy east slipped away, and the train transformed into an ever more modern icon against the panorama of China. China's railways, if you take them west, are a time machine.

Jiang's development initiative—"Go West"—was plain to the naked eye. As you headed west, the obvious dilution of wealth coincided with a sharp increase in construction: new roads, factories, airports, cities. In places, earth-moving equipment seemed to outnumber people, and the pace of change left much of the countryside looking ravaged and raked over. Poorer villages were being razed so that cheap modern buildings—blocky, dormitory-style structures with identical tinted glass and generic white tile work—could take their places. At Lanzhou, which in thirty years had bloomed from a poor village to a teeming city almost the size of Chicago, the construction, with the look of temporary solutions, nudged up against the shoreline of the polluted Huang He, or Yellow, River.

On a map, Lanzhou is scarcely halfway across China, yet it flirts in the periphery of ethnic Tibet, an area twice the size of the TAR. A few hours' drive southwest of the city is the Chinese town of Xiahe, home to the head of the Geluk order of Tibetan Buddhism and Labrang Monastery, the sixth most important in the faith. Grasslands begin, a rolling carpet of lush, gentle green dotted with roaming herds of yak and the black tarpaulin tents of the nomadic Tibetans who have lived there for centuries. As you gaze over the slopes, it seems as though Lhasa, still many hundreds of miles and a rugged mountain range west, is just over the next rise.

But to get there from Lanzhou, travelers to Lhasa first had to take the train to the end of the line, in Golmud, a bleak city in the forlorn west of Qinghai Province, and then continue over the plateau by bus on a notoriously slow and uncomfortable journey. For foreigners, this rarely used route was the only legal overland way to get to Tibet from China, and it subjected them to fleeting changes in permits and restrictions that tended to vary like the plateau's weather and could suddenly shut them out of Tibet altogether. Most travelers, except for the poorest, preferred to fly from Chengdu or safari past Mount Everest from Nepal.

If the rural expanse of Gansu and southern Qinghai are idyllic, the reaches of Qinghai past the provincial capital of Xining—three hundred square miles—are not. The rivers and mountains, and the infamous tunnels through them, give way to nothingness. Somewhere to the north lie the colossal prisons that at one time housed as many as 10 million Chinese and Tibetan prisoners—a "black hole," in the words of a 1979 *Time* magazine article, "from which little information ever reached the outside world or even the rest of China"—and then the ancient Silk Road and the towering dunes of the Gobi Desert. The monotonous view from the train was peppered with backhoes scraping the caked surface of salt-crusted plains and dumping it into waiting trucks. After six hundred miles of desolation, the train passed a coal mine, followed shortly by the flaring towers of a distant refinery that lit up the night sky, and finally reached Golmud station.

Golmud, which was founded in the early 1960s as a forced labor prison for Tibetans, had grown into a small city. On the west end of the town, where most of the commerce took place, pavement gave way to potholed dirt streets and a poor shantytown centered on a large mosque. Hui men, wearing white skullcaps and long goatees, worked as traders and drivers. As the highway portal to Tibet, Golmud had a thriving trucking industry. Construction materials, clothing, grain, and manufactured Chinese goods, ranging from PVC piping to cooking woks, were stacked in teetering piles and roped to the beds of an endless string of big rigs, which coughed black clouds of diesel smoke as they sputtered up into the mountains to Tibet. Trucks coming down were usually empty, or loaded with minerals and Nepali goods. A tsunami of imports headed to the TAR, but not much was brought back out.

Golmud's bus station consisted of yet another muddy lot on the south end of town, the kind of place that, were it in the Bronx, you would avoid even in daylight. Three to four beat-up buses served the town. A crowd milled around a long purple one, with worn tires and a dashboard altar of colorful Buddhas and silk cloth, headed to Lhasa. Han Chinese men dressed in torn pants and bad shoes heaved burlap sacks to a man on the bus's roof. A couple of tough-looking young Tibetan men with cowboy boots and thick leather motorcycle jackets smoked cigarettes and kicked at the tires. Several Tibetan nomad families, identifiable as being from the region of Kham because of their traditional dress and long horsetail-like hair adorned with quarter-size sparkling turquoise and amber beads, crammed themselves into their seats for the chilling thirty-two-hour ride on the Qinghai-Tibet Highway.

A dust storm kicked up the plains above town, and as the bus started its four-hour climb onto the plateau, the air hung thick and oppressive. The blanket of earthy brown sky draped a fine layer of silt over the dead hills so that they looked like books that had been shelved and forgotten for thousands of years. The bus weaved through a constricted canyon and then navigated the fifteen-thousand-foot Kunlun Mountain pass, at which point the plateau opened into a glorious panorama befitting the "roof of the world" and the uninhibited infinity of heaven. Here, the highway diminished into an insignificantly thin strip of pavement, a line of thread strung across the wide-open tundra that looked as though it might easily be whisked away—by the wind, the harsh land, or man himself. In places, the permafrost-riddled highway, which had been rebuilt perhaps a half dozen times since the 1950s, was broken and cracked. It heaved up and crashed down in naturally formed speed bumps and was deeply rutted. The road was the only sign of humanity. This portion of the high plateau, the vast Chang Tang, is one of the least populated places on Earth. But it may also contain, China hoped, the richest untapped resources on the planet.

JIANG S GO WEST CAMPAIGN WOULD GUIDE MUCH OF CHINA S DEVELOPment for a decade. In the early stages, it was little more than a vague set of guidelines, left to dissipate slowly through the seemingly bottomless layers of staff, authority, and corruption with each mile it traveled from Beijing. China formally recognized the need to address the unstable poverty that existed outside the modernized east, but while fixing the imbalance was declared a priority, making specific plans to do so was not. Self-interested proposals began to matriculate from the far provinces, and local officials jockeyed for pet projects, seeking a share of Beijing's wealth. By the early spring of 2000, when Yin circulated another letter about the railway to Tibet, it was clear that the train stood its best chance if it made it onto the amorphous Go West project list. Meetings of the Ministry of Railways were called to evaluate the options for connecting Lhasa to Beijing by train, and if one was marginally suitable, to recommend the train, along with a plan and a budget, by the winter.

To reach consensus, though, the Ministry of Railways had to determine which of its experts had the most persuasive case for grabbing some of China's development money. Zhang and his fellow engineers at the ministry's First Railway Institute had focused forty years of research on the route south from Qinghai, but special interests were lobbying hard to earn the chance for the railway to be laid through their districts. Five proposed routes for a train to Tibet—all varying greatly in difficulty, estimated cost, and practicality—were competing for the shot to be built. Zhang had a stake in only one.

The rival plans had their own appealing and quixotic qualities. The Gansu route would lead from the club-shaped territory wedged neatly between Xanxi in the east and Qinghai and Tibet on the west. Its largest city was Lanzhou, an established base for railway and scientific research and an easy starting point for the line. Tracks from Lanzhou would cover more than thirteen hundred miles, following the Yellow River into the idyllic grasslands and ethnically Tibetan areas before climbing through the Qilian Mountains to the plateau. Eventually, this route would intersect with Zhang's north-south route from Qinghai at the dusty outpost of Nagqu, a tiny blip on the map of Tibet where truckers filled up on gas and food and where the Northwest Military Command kept a foothold and operated China's largest nuclear facility. The cost estimates were five years old—from 1995—but pegged at roughly $8 billion.

Running a railway along the existing Sichuan highway, from Dujiangyan station near Chengdu, was another tantalizing alternative but, at a cost of nearly $10 billion, impractical almost from the start. The highway's winding curves reached stratospheric heights amid glaciers and rocky peaks, and it had been difficult to keep the route open since it had been built in the 1950s. Indeed, though two highways to Tibet had existed since then, people tended to remember mostly the road from Qinghai. A more fantastic route would circumvent the mountains entirely by looping around China's far west border, meeting the Silk Road in Kashgar, and heading south along the Indian and Pakistani borders before tracing the northern flank of the Himalayas to Lhasa—an eight-day trip. If anything, the design showed how strong was the desire to find an alternative to crossing Tibet's main ranges.

The most serious contender with Zhang's Qinghai route was a path from Yunnan Province, in China's south, that would branch off the Guangdong-Dali Railway and cut west, at times along the Mekong River north of the Myanmar border. Twice as long as the link from Golmud and estimated to cost $7.5 billion, the railway would provide crucial transportation and communication infrastructure to a bustling province and had substantial lobbying support behind it. But Zhang's route straight south from Qinghai, by comparison, was only half the length, seven hundred miles, and was estimated to cost just $2 billion. If the permafrost issue could be solved—a huge "if" in any scientific judgment—the Qinghai route was shorter, cheaper, far better studied, and generally the most attractive—at least to Zhang Luxin.

As the argument unfolded around the conference table, the political and power maneuverings were set aside. The ultimate question was whether building on permafrost would be easier and cheaper than bringing a train through ragged mountains. The central committee would not spend its entire Go West development budget on one project. The Ministry of Railways' no. 2 bureau battled for the mountainous Yunnan route, citing the reputed fact that at least once when Yin Fatang had met with Deng Xiaoping about the Tibet railway connection, Deng had said it was his preferred path. Far less work had been spent developing a Yunnan plan, but at the meeting, according to Zhang, "very strangely, a majority supported the Yunnan-Tibet route."

On the face of it, a route into Tibet from the southwest seemed more strategically useful to China. Running along the region's disputed border with India, it would give the military added transportation access and flexibility, and it would draw near the headwaters of the Brahmaputra River (a great rugged gorge in Tibet, where it is called the Yarlung Tsangpo), which was suspected to hold undiscovered mineral resources of its own. And while it was not an open topic of discussion among the scientists and engineers that day, any southwest route would undoubtedly appeal to the Chinese army's powerful Southwest Command, which though still based in Chengdu had recently expanded its base in Lhasa and had been locked in a power feud with the Northwest Command ever since the Long March, five decades earlier. The swell of professional evidence was bolstered, perhaps even overshadowed, by deep personal and political desires that had little to do with the best route, or even Tibet's development. "Look, we try to base our arguments on technical terms, but underneath, inevitably," said Zhang, "everyone wished the project was in his own area so that he can be involved. This is so important."

As Zhang listened, he felt threatened. If the Yunnan route

was chosen, he would be relegated to the life of an impoverished researcher in some dank hallway of a remote Lanzhou University office complex. After a lifetime of wishing beyond his wildest hopes for acceptance into the Communist Party's power structure, he would remain unknown and unacknowledged. For all the sacrifice—years spent away from his wife, a skeletal relationship with his son—he would have nothing to show for it. He had given his life to building the Qinghai-Tibet Railway. If a train to Tibet never happened, he would lose all pride. If it happened somewhere else, that would be even worse: his ambitions would be hijacked by someone else's success.

As the supporters of the Yunnan-Tibet Railway became more vocal and aggressive, Zhang saw the Qinghai-Tibet route slithering away from him like a rope coil falling over a precipitous edge. "These experts," Zhang said, "most of them had never been to the Qinghai-Tibet Plateau. Many had not even traveled through the Yunnan-Tibet route that they proposed. Their arguments were not based on experience. They were based on theory." Opponents to Zhang's route were loudly mulling over a disturbing letter from an engineer Zhang had never met named Wong. The letter had been circulated—through some unique access or influence of Wong's—to the highest levels of the Chinese government, not just the Ministry of Railways but to the State Council directly. Wong argued that attempting a railway on the Tibetan Plateau was a huge mistake.

"It is impossible to solve the permafrost problem," read the letter, recited aloud according to Zhang's recollection. Wong asserted that the science for dealing with permafrost terrain was not suitable for investing billions of dollars in, and added that the altitude and harsh conditions made the plateau inhospitable for construction. "And more importantly, workers could not survive the building of the railway on the plateau." That last claim struck a nerve because when the first leg of the Tibet railway, connecting Xining with the ramshackle outpost of Golmud, had been attempted in the late 1970s, more than a hundred people had died building the infamous Guanjiao tunnel alone. The railway to Lhasa would entail dozens more tunnels, all on that impossible terrain. Wong's reminder eroded support for the Qinghai option immediately—the construction would be tough enough, but what if workers succumbed to the fatigue and illness caused by altitude, and then after all the effort, the railway broke down because the experimental permafrost engineering was faulty? All good questions, but they endangered Zhang's future.

WITH THE QINGHAI ROUTE IN JEOPARDY, ZHANG GRABBED WHAT SEEMED a last opportunity to adjust fate in his favor. He took the platform from his colleagues and engaged the senior officials in debate. He does not remember how he managed it, just that at some point after he stood, the room grew startlingly quiet, and he began to speak. "The route from Yunnan," he began, "many parts of it, no one has ever been there. We don't know anything about it. But the Qinghai-Tibet Plateau, we've been traveling it for forty years, we know every inch of it." For forty-five minutes, Zhang, the unknown but ambitious engineer poised at the door of old age, explained that scientists had studied the plateau's permafrost for years. "Among all those experts, I was the only person who had actually worked on the plateau for almost thirty years," said Zhang, "so I was the one who had the right to say something in this dispute." Yet, that wasn't quite true. Hundreds of engineers had worked hard on the plateau, but Zhang would readily inflate his own persona if it would save his pride, and his career. He explained that the work of these researchers, among whom he proudly if not accurately depicted himself as quite senior, had become renowned worldwide for their understanding of frozen soil and arctic conditions—even more advanced than the Russians, who had built some of the earliest pipelines and the Trans-Siberian Railway on frozen ground. He methodically countered the criticisms heard that day: people died in the 1970s because there was little food, because the machinery was primitive; the tunnel collapsed because it was dug by hand. But in twenty-first-century China, he promised, "we have made great progress. Now is the time." Technology, machinery, and other equipment were now advanced; not only could the economy feed its workers, it would pay them well enough to attract an overflow of labor.

As the room grew restless and tired, Zhang's fervor intensified. He leaned forward, bracing both palms on the table, paused, and sought eye contact with his peers and his critics. "Wong says that no one can work at such high altitude because people can hardly breathe," he told the silenced group. "I just came down from five thousand meters [sixteen thousand feet] yesterday. I not only live there, but I work there, and I have for thirty years. I am fifty-four years old, and I am healthy as I stand here. I promise you that we have solved the problems relating to permafrost on the plateau, and I have proved that people can work at such altitude."

When he finished and returned to his seat, the silence continued uninterrupted. Then a single person slowly started clapping his hands.

By the next meeting of the Ministry of Railways, the Qinghai route had been named the presumed choice. Zhang's impassioned speech seemed to have convinced the senior officials. With the debate dispelled, the ministry group focused on the details of making the railway proposal attractive to the State Council, which was considering Go West projects by year's end. A few days before the New Year, officials from the Ministry of Railways approached Zhang during a break as he was delivering a conference lecture to fellow engineers. "Did you know that President Jiang has approved the project?" they asked a breathless Zhang. "He has signed the documents."

Like most people of his generation, Zhang thought of Tibet as a backward place populated by desperately poor people who could not muster the intellect or the technology to bring their province into the modern age. They seemed barbaric in their centuries-old costumes, and their preoccupation with religion and custom was often interpreted as a lack of motivation and work ethic. This was an embarrassment, not because Zhang cared particularly how a Tibetan lived his days but because he considered the region as much a part of China as Louisiana is to the United States. Tibet reflected poorly on him, and on modern China as a whole.

So Zhang, like so many of the nationalistic—and often blindly idealistic—men who drove China's push for a railway to Lhasa, saw the project as a paternalistic mission of great generosity, a philanthropic endeavor to give Tibetans a fighting chance in China's new economy. "*Xibu Dake Fa:* the great develop the west," explained Charlene Makley, a professor of anthropology at Reed College, of the mission of twenty-first-century China. "Some people want to translate it as *Kai Fa,* as 'exploit the west,' but really it means to open up and unleash potential." Zhang believed his work was making the social enterprise possible, even if the larger questions of what a Tibetan economy—based in a fruitless wilderness—could contribute remained unanswered.

On the morning of March 5, 2001, Premier Zhu Rongji convened the Fourth Session of the Ninth National People's Congress in Beijing. Before an audience of 1,100 officials from throughout the country, he outlined China's Tenth Five Year Plan. The decree articulated China's goals in only slightly less obtuse terms than the Go West campaign's announcement, offering mostly platitudes and optimism.

Prosperity will sweep across the western regions. Poverty will be diminished. Water and energy should be conserved. Oil is of special importance—more is required. And so on. Anchoring the wispy rhetoric were a series of more than a thousand minuscule development projects grounded in four major initiatives to address the most crucial needs of the nation. They provided a map forward, but also a window into the otherwise illusive strategies of the State Council in shaping the future of a modern China.

The projects were lofty and in most cases reflected red-tagged development issues. Possibly the largest irrigation project in world history was hatched to supply water to the northern half of the country, where nearly half of China's farming is based and desertification is gobbling land at an alarming rate. Nearly 50 billion cubic meters—roughly equivalent to the annual flow of the Yellow River—would be diverted from the south in a project one Chinese scientist said would "break the bottleneck hampering economic and social development in China." A pipeline and transmission lines would be run, at an estimated cost of roughly $15 billion, to carry natural gas and power from the Tarim Basin in the western Xinjiang region to Shanghai. A modern Japanese-style high-speed railway would be built between Beijing and Shanghai, an artery deemed essential to consolidating and strengthening China's eastern economic hub.

The fourth project on the list of national priorities—and illogically so, in the view of those members of the People's Congress who wanted measurable economic benefits from the plan—was Zhang's train to Tibet. The purpose of such a train, Zhu and the State Council declared, was economic well-being and equality for the Tibetan people, hardly a policy goal consistent with China's treatment of the region in the preceding decades. Zhang would have known better.

2

A SOMETIME BUDDHIST

RENZIN TASHI ISN'T A FERVENT BUDDHIST—MANY TIBETANS aren't. He may be guided by the four noble truths, and he rests superstitious importance on the icons of deities representing the Buddha and his teachings toward enlightenment—they line the walls of his home and business. But his meditations on the suffering of existence are fleeting, not all-consuming, and Buddhist concerns fall second to the tasks of commerce and a secular lifestyle. The festivals, the few times each year marked by holy significance, are what bind him to his spiritual self, to his heritage, and remind him of what it means to be Tibetan.

In June 2001, Renzin headed to the monastery at Tsurphu, the main seat of the Karma Kagyu order of Tibetan Buddhism. The previous year, the sect had been thrown into disarray when its most important lama, the Seventeenth Karmapa, a fourteen-year-old baby-faced boy named Ogyen Trinley Dorje, daringly escaped to India through Nepal to join the Dalai Lama's government-in-exile in Dharamsala. The First Karmapa had sited the monastic center at Tsurphu in 1189, and the 1992 enthronement of Ogyen Trinley Dorje as the reincarnated Karmapa was the first state-approved enthronement of a legitimate high lama allowed in the Tibet Autonomous Region since the Dalai Lama fled in 1959. On February 19, the Seventeenth Karmapa had explained his decision to leave Tibet to the international media. "Tibetan religion and culture have reached the point of complete destruction," he said, according to an account published by the Tibetan Center for Human Rights and Democracy. The boy's claim followed a year of some of the most severe crackdowns on religion in Tibet in a decade, and boosted the West's scrutiny of China's treatment of Tibetan Buddhist leaders.

Following the Karmapa's escape, Tsurphu had been temporarily shut down. According to the U.S. State Department's report on religious freedom, at least two high-ranking monks at the monastery had been arrested, and many more were interrogated. In March 2000, authorities began to enforce a ban on possession of the Dalai Lama's picture and prohibited any government employee from taking part in religious practice. In May, a monk at Thenthok Monastery, in the eastern Chamdo region, was forcibly removed from a temple by a Chinese "work team" intent on searching his quarters for photographs of the Dalai Lama. A short time later, the monk was found dead, having "fallen" from the third story. Chinese authorities declared that anyone implying a government role in the monk's death would be thrown in jail.

Now, the fate of Tsurphu Monastery hung in the balance. Would the Chinese government allow celebrations at the monastery, which had been razed during the Cultural Revolution but largely rebuilt since 1992, to continue, now that the Karmapa had left? Would this year's festival to usher in the Saga Dawa, the great celebration of the Buddha's birth and enlightenment, but also, in part, to honor the bold young Karmapa, carry even a fraction of the importance placed on it since the Karmapa's seating?

These thoughts rolled through Renzin's mind as his Toyota Land Cruiser bucked its way up the rough twin-track road that shoots off the main Qinghai-Tibet Highway and the Tolung Valley into the snaking Dowo Lung Valley, fourteen thousand feet high and ninety minutes from Lhasa. It had taken just half an hour to traverse the twenty-five miles of modern paved highway out of Lhasa's busy downtown and thin film of suburban sprawl. But when Renzin turned onto the ancient mountain road, he steered into Tibet as it had been centuries before, and the going was slow, just a few miles per hour as the truck's knobby tires negotiated basketball-size boulders and a series of small streams bridged by hand-cut logs. Renzin braked to a stop. The small dirt lot was crowded with cars and a few old dented minibuses. Outside the festering development ringing Lhasa, the searingly crisp spring morning had ascended, along with the blunt brown hills, from the freeze-dried night. His engine shut, the stillness of the vast valley and its mountains washed over Renzin, clearing away the thrum of city life, the drone of diesel engines, and the carbon-heavy air of trucks and generators. The silence of Tibet's wilderness engulfed him. Then he heard the drumming.

Behind the monastery's old stone walls—in places, twelve feet thick—a crowd had gathered. When the Tsurphu complex was destroyed by the Chinese in 1966, its one thousand resident monks were banished or killed. The Sixteenth Karmapa, who had fled Tibet in 1959, had established a new monastery in the Sikkim region of northern India. As the Cultural Revolution receded, modest reconstruction began, and the main temple was the first project, in 1980. A pyramid of stone steps rose to the portico and tall entry of the burnt sienna cube of a building. Heavy blood-hued curtains hung in the doorway, stained at shoulder level by the oily prints of the thousands of hands that had pushed them aside to enter the temple's cool, dark recesses. Inside, dozens of the sect's Black Hat monks were dressing in elaborate masks and costumes for celebration.

Renzin joined the crowd of other Tibetans outside who settled on the steps as they poured into the courtyard from thin tributary alleyways like sand leaking into a buried box. Many of the women lining the steps looked ancient, their wrinkled faces creased with years of sun and work. They wrapped themselves in silk-lined coats whose saffrons and golds somehow shimmered through the dirt, and spun prayer wheels, each rotation of the wheels' spindles a symbolic recitation of the scrolled mantras tucked inside them. Some of the men also wore the traditional dress of their regions; they were engulfed by chubas, the Tibetans' oversized woolen robes, an arm hooked through one sleeve while the other sleeve was tied around the waist. Others simply wore leather jackets or pin-striped sports coats over their dust-embedded shirts. Many stared through cheap, oversized sunglasses, entirely modern devices that they hoped would better protect their eyes from the high-intensity ultraviolet rays. Renzin recognized the spirited contingent of men from Kham—an industrious region in the northeast of Tibet—by their sharp cheekbones and the bindings of bright red wraps and green turquoise beads on their flowing hair. All of the men sat, and smoked, and talked. The children ran about, amusing themselves, exposing glimpses of their hand-me-down Western T-shirts with their iron-ons of Oscar the Grouch and Mickey Mouse.

They were assembled in a full-blown celebration of Tibetan customs. The Tsurphu Monastery itself encapsulated the evolutionary nature of tradition. Through the centuries, the Karmapa belief that a lama received prophecies of and thus could identify his future reincarnated self was widely accepted among Tibetans. But when the Sixteenth Karmapa died in 1981, he had not specified his successor, and the management of the Black Hat sect passed to four fractious regents who held different visions for the future. The religious issues were complicated, but the political entanglements were clear: with the Dalai Lama leading the Tibetan government-in-exile, from which side of the border would future incarnations of the most revered lamas be found? When in 1990 an old letter from the Sixteenth Karmapa was "discovered" that designated Dorje, then a five-year-old living in western Tibet, as his reincarnate, the Chinese as well as a majority of Tibetans eagerly embraced him—and the opportunity to retain Tibetan religious authority inside of Tibet along with it. A similar situation had arisen over the Panchen Lama, the second-highest figure in Tibetan Buddhism, when the Dalai Lama's designate was kidnapped by the Chinese and replaced with their own chosen Panchen Lama, a figure now widely discredited. With the Karmapa, China had avoided such controversy, but that did not mean the Tibetans were all in agreement. One of the dissenting regents—who believed a different boy, living in India and independent of the Chinese state, was the real Karmapa incarnate—was mysteriously killed in a car accident. Though Dorje's ascension had always had most Tibetans' support, the lingering resistance to his seating evaporated when he arrived at Tsurphu, where twenty thousand Tibetans recognized him as the Seventeenth Karmapa. In the following years, he was educated by the Chinese, and there was a risk that Dorje, like the young Panchen Lama, would become another figurehead to benefit the state. His flight to join the Dalai Lama and his traditional Tibetan teachers in exile came as a massive political blow to the Chinese, and as an invigorating reinforcement of the boy's spiritual authority for the Tibetans, who had feared a descent of the Karmapa to superficiality.

At one end of the courtyard, under a wooden overhang that kept the burning sun at bay, five monks were cushioned on gold and rust-tinted pillows. Nearby, a small man with a shaved head beat the taut leather of a circular drum four times his size. The crowd at the doorway of the main building spread as dancing monks spilled down the temple's steps onto the courtyard's flat dirt. They wore huge, brilliantly painted masks, depicting deities that represented dharma and the Buddha, which the monks had cast in molds following stringent guidelines. They bounced and spun and whirled amid billowing smoke. Renzin leisurely took in the scene—breathed in the burning juniper and laughed at the needle-mustached man who poked and prodded the audience like a Chinese clown. Renzin's gaze wandered, and as he looked over his left shoulder he saw a Tibetan man snapping his picture.

A chill ran down his spine. Police were everywhere after the Karmapa incident. But why him? The man wore a dark leather jacket, dark sunglasses, and dark short-cropped hair. He stood ten feet away. Nothing was out of the ordinary, except that he seemed just a little more methodical than the rest of the crowd. The camera was a 35-millimeter film model—not new, but not a toy, not for a Tibetan. Renzin was distracted for a moment. When he looked again, the man was gone. A friend had recently warned him he was being watched. Out of instinct, he immediately thought of the picture files the Chinese state security was said to still keep of Tibetans, especially those like Renzin who also held a Nepali passport and owned a business. The files had been set up after Tibetans rioted against the government in 1989. Spies were recruited and dispatched to identify troublemakers before more dissent fomented; they would mingle undercover in crowds to nab potential offenders before anything political got out of hand. Often the agents were Tibetans—and their pervasive, if invisible, presence had established an air of tightened control and paranoia that still weighed down the rising rhetoric about how twenty-first-century reforms would improve everyone's lives.

Renzin surveyed the crowd for the rest of the morning, half enjoying the show, half wanting to catch sight of this man to have his wild imagination proven wrong. It wasn't that Renzin, a boyish and slight forty-six-year-old with puffy cheeks that belied his soft city life, had anything to hide; he was honest and apolitical, and had little taste for trouble. But over the years—going back to his difficult boy-hood in Lhasa, his own flight over the border to Nepal, and his even-tual return—he had been warned to keep one eye open over his shoulder. As he returned to Lhasa that afternoon, he made another note to watch his back. It's when you are most relaxed in this place, he said, "when you can get yourself into trouble."

The road back to the Tolung Valley, and then the larger Kyichu Valley, went easier on the return; gravity helped the truck on its amble. Where the Dowo Lung (wheat) Valley spills into the Tolung, yaks pulled wooden-handled steel plows as men and women sowed their fields along the river. By autumn, the fertile valley floor—a broad plain interrupted only by the steel-gray glacial rush of the Tol-ung River and the thin strip of paved highway—would have a full crop of golden barley. Interspersed among the fields are small vil-lages, some with clusters of as many as forty earth-colored homes, much as Lhasa itself looked when Renzin was a young boy.

LHASA SITS AT THE WIDEST SECTION OF THE EIGHTY-FIVE-MILE-LONG ⅜yichu Valley, a pupil in the eye of Tibet. Near its center, the three-hundred-foot Red Hill juts out of the valley floor, propping the seventh-century Potala Palace, the traditional residence of the Dalai

Lama, on its shoulders. From the time the palace was first built through the Chinese occupation, the small village of Shol hummed within its walls, separated from the rest of Lhasa by pastureland, gardens, and forest. A little more than a mile away, in what used to be a neighboring village, is the Barkhor—a maze of alleyways cutting between stone and mud adobe buildings distinguished by their broad black windowsills and thick-based, pyramid-like walls. These traditional Tibetan homes and businesses, selling everything from yak butter to padlocks, surround the Jokhang Temple, Tibet's holiest site.

The Barkhor's dual identity—part religious mecca, part marketplace—has made it Tibet's beating heart. This was where Renzin lived as a boy, and where he returned to run a small shop catering to tourists—in 2000, half a million of them visited Lhasa—and to the nomadic Tibetans eager to take mementos back into the grasslands each spring. Renzin passed his days on a stool in the corner of his cozy shop, behind a glass case full of turquoise and amber beads and silver jewelry. The walls were draped with a rainbow of scarves made from wool or silk—mostly imported from Nepal, like the rest of the Buddhist artifacts and statues around him.

Outside his doorway, an endless river of people streamed by, most walking in the same clockwise direction, following the holy kora, or perambulation, circuit around the Jokhang Temple of the old city. The Barkhor is where the nomads and rural pilgrims come when the winter winds push them off the plateau, where the monks migrate to chant and solicit donations, where the tourist groups stop first, and where the entrepreneurial, like Renzin, have established their trades. Over the last half century, the Barkhor, at least superficially, has changed the least.

The Barkhor embodies much of what people find magical about Tibet. The Jokhang is Tibet's holiest temple, turning the Barkhor into

Tibet's spiritual nucleus. The central temple was built in the seventh century by the Tibetan king Songtsen Gampo, apparently in honor of a Chinese bride princess—a story showcased by the Chinese as evidence of long-standing relations between their regions. It inherited from a nearby temple a sacred statue of Jowo Sakyamuni, a relic thought to have been blessed by Buddha himself, which is the single most revered image in Tibet. It alone inspires hundreds of monks and pilgrims to travel to Lhasa, some of whom repeatedly prostrate themselves over hundreds of miles. Inside the temple's sprawling compound, there are a few dozen sub-temples, nothing more than cramped chapels, many too small to accommodate the throngs of worshippers filing through in devotion to Jowo Sakyamuni as well as Maitreya, the Buddha of the future, Avalokiteshvara, the Buddha of compassion, and other Buddhas and protector deities in each shrine. The rooms are dimly lit by rows of dripping yak butter candles. The stone floors are slick with spilled butter, the thresholds worn by hundreds of years of foot traffic. Outside these dark, cool temples, the Tibetan Buddhists pray at the front gate, where their full-body prostrations have left the cobblestones worn similarly shiny and smooth. On the half-mile Barkhor kora itself, they encircle the complex in its entirety, walking clockwise, or sometimes prostrating every inch, to purify negative afflictions and to show their respect for the Buddha. On the way, they pass Renzin's shop.

The Barkhor circuit doubles as the city's central market, and always has. Side by side with the burning juniper and prostrating monks are endless stalls of goods for sale. There are piles of religious and cultural trinkets, like the ones Renzin sells, including the iconic prayer flags rolled tightly into colorful, cigarlike bundles. More pragmatic, a row of burlap sacks expose the dried, stonelike curdled cheese inside for buyers stocking up on rations. A goat's stomach, dried and hard as leather, serves as a bag for yak butter. The utensils for sale convey the market's crossroads heritage: there are the tin pots and giant hammered-copper ladles traditionally used to stew thugkpa noodle soup, the sawed top of a human skull for use as a bowl in religious rituals to purge wrathful deities, and knives—some glinting freshly manufactured steel and others dull and rusted above bone- and jewel-encrusted handles that have served perhaps hundreds of years of work. The tourist items are thrown in among the rest: audiotapes of Tibetan chanting and Indian pop songs; small copper Buddhas soiled through intentional burial and unearthing to make them look older than they really are; singing bowls—iron bowls monks use to elicit a meditative unearthly humming—manufactured cheaply and stamped with the curled, omnipresent eyes of the Bodinath stupa, in Kathmandu. Dressed in a *chuba,* an elderly Tibetan man stops by Renzin's shop to buy a new watch shortly after praying at Jokhang and picking up some sugar in the market. Somehow the mad rush of the bazaar is calming and otherworldly. The tourist markets are new—as are the restaurants and tea stalls—but otherwise, according to Renzin, the place remains much the way it was when he was a young child.

Everything inside the Jokhang appears ancient, but it is difficult to know exactly what artifacts date back to the temple's origins, if any do at all; much of it, like the other temples of Tibet, was destroyed following the brutal crackdown in 1959 and, later, during China's Cultural Revolution. What wasn't destroyed was repurposed. One section of the temple was transformed into a People's Liberation Army barrack, another into a pigsty, where meat would be raised for the imported political and military officials.

The modernizing incursions of the Chinese often were not subtle. Officially, most of the 250,000 people living in Lhasa in 2000 were Tibetans, but a large shadow community of Chinese, counted as transient residents, had been settling for some time, and those numbers did not reflect the more than one hundred thousand soldiers stationed in and around the city. Some years earlier, the city's prominent road running in front of the Potala atop the Barkhor, Dekyi Shar Lam, had been repaved with four lanes, though there were few private cars in Lhasa. By the late 1990s, it had been renamed Beijing Dong, or Beijing Happiness, Road and bustled with green and white Volkswagen taxis that were introduced by the Chinese. Outside the Potala, a Tiananmen-like People's Square, anchored by a massive, swooping concrete monument, had been built in place of the Dalai Lama's former Throne Garden to commemorate the "peaceful liberation of Tibet" and Communist China. At the south end of town, a pastoral island in the river, called Gomulinka, had once been a favorite Tibetan picnic ground; the Chinese had renamed it Dream Island and the spot soon brayed with a collection of karaoke bars and malls selling counterfeit Tommy Hilfiger jeans and Louis Vuitton bags. The foreign tourists, many of whom had trekked for days to get a glimpse of the ancient Tibetan kingdom, complained that Lhasa showed inklings of becoming unremarkable, like so many Chinese cities.

At the west end of Beijing Dong Road, a Han enclave had emerged: strips of Sichuan restaurants, brightly lit coffee shops and more karaoke bars, and hair salons where young Chinese girls not-so-discreetly offered massages to officers and businessmen. The Chinese sector sported the blocky, uncreative architecture of quick construction, all cheap stone and glass. Ugly storefronts, with the charm of industrial garages, were popping up with the persistence of weeds, in Lhasa and along the dusty roads of otherwise quaint villages across Tibet and all of rural China. The quick assembly of such thoughtless structures was part of what Beijing meant by "development." In Lhasa, the border between east and west, old and new, could not have been clearer if it had been drawn with a bold black line on the city's map.

THE MODERN TINGES OF LHASA'S URBAN LANDSCAPE ARE ON THE WEST side of town in part because that is where the highway from Golmud connects the rest of China with Tibet. From Qinghai Province, it snakes south, up onto the plateau and down again into the TAR, then slides east to Lhasa, and for fifty years it was one of China's few reliable breaches into Tibet's geographic defenses. Now the change seeps off the end of the road like silt settling off a river delta, and as the flow of development hastened, it seemed bound to fan out from "Chinatown" to the rest of the city.

The Qinghai-Tibet Highway, the shortest route from anywhere into Tibet, was no easy trip. A bus ride from Golmud to Lhasa usually took more than two days, figuring in vehicle breakdowns, foul weather in the mountain passes, and accidents. Driving yourself required at least fifteen hours behind the wheel with no place to stop save for the occasional dingy motel or Mongolian hot pot café. The truckers who provided the only means for goods and materials to flow between Tibet and interior China complained about heaving potholed roads and treacherous conditions. In places, as recently as the 1980s, the road just faded away to faint tire tracks in the grassy tundra. "It was difficult, just dirt," said one driver. "When they paved it, well, it was always broken." Hauling a shipment to Golmud to meet the train east was entirely unpredictable—taking anywhere from twenty to forty hours, and often enough, the trucks never got there at all. Of the thousands of trucks that plied the route each day, at least two would slide off the road, roll over mountainous embankments, or slam into one another as drivers battled ice, fog, and fatigue.

And this was in "modern" times. As recently as the 1960s, even after the highway was completed, Chinese officials who could not fly into the military airstrip that was in Damxung, ninety miles north of Lhasa, at the time would fly to India and then make their way by truck up the Friendship Highway from Nepal. When Renzin first visited Nepal in 1970, he bounced along in the back of a flatbed truck for nearly two weeks to get there. That's how Lhasa became known to Westerners as the "Forbidden City"; it wasn't simply that the Chinese, and before them, the Tibetans, had so restricted travel access through its gates, but because geography too had kept outsiders at bay. In describing the British invasion of Tibet, from India, in 1904, Peter Fleming notes that for the previous ninety-four years, no Englishman had reached Lhasa, despite the empire's command of the southern half of the Asian continent. "Lhasa represented for the adventurous a goal as unique, in its own way, as the peak of Everest was to become for mountaineers," Fleming wrote. It was "a sparsely inhabited no-man's-land which, to the west, to the north, and to the northeast, formed a huge desolate glacis masking the closely guarded passes which alone gave access to the heart of the country and its capital." The number of foreigners who had set foot in front of the Potala Palace at the turn of that century could be counted on one hand. In his epic tome about his flight to Tibet, escaping the Nazis' collapse to the Allies, Heinrich Harrer noted upon walking through the gates of Lhasa: "Nobody stopped us, or bothered about us. We could not understand it, but finally realized that no one, not even a European, was suspect, because no one had ever come to Lhasa without a pass."

Long one of the most isolated corners of the world, Tibet had been protected until recently from the rushing tides of globalization. After four sustained decades of investments, by the late 1990s China was anxious to finally revolutionize Tibet's economy and upend its unsophisticated ways, if only it could conquer the mountains. This natural Great Wall had for decades denied the Chinese real success. Even among the modernity of western Lhasa, Tibet felt far, far away from Beijing Dong Road's namesake city. In its simplest form, the essence of Tibet's mystique, its very identity, was its remoteness. It was the greatest thing Tibet stood to lose to the Chinese. And to the Chinese, this geographic separation, and how it sustained Tibet's political separation too, was an embarrassing reminder of the limitations of the nation's progress.

From the moment that Communist China came into existence, Beijing had determined that closing this distance was key to claiming and controlling Tibet. Mao Zedong immediately clumped the remote region alongside Taiwan, where Chiang Kai-shek's national forces had retreated, as an essential part of securing Chinese territory under the Common Program of 1949. On September 2 of that year, a government editorial in the *Hsin Hwa Pa* newspaper bluntly asserted, "Even an inch of Chinese land will not be permitted to be left outside the jurisdiction of the People's Republic of China." In a May 6, 1950, broadcast that the Tibet historian and author Tsering Shakya identifies as China's final warning to Tibetans of the imminent invasion, the announcer promised that the Tibetan region would never be considered too remote for the Chinese to access. "If anyone should doubt the ability of the [People's Liberation Army (PLA)] to overcome geographical difficulties they need only remember the Long March or the recent liberation of Hainan," warned the broadcaster, echoing across the short-wave radios in Tibetans' primitive homes. Tibet's "liberation" was assured.

When the Chinese army attacked later that year, on October 7, it was forced to do so via the arduous route that traced its way into the mountains toward Chamdo, in the southeast corner of what is now the Tibet Autonomous Region. Eighty-four thousand PLA eviscerated the Tibetan force of roughly eight thousand men, killing half of them.

The Tibetans were caught ill-prepared to defend this critical eastern stronghold. Political strife within Tibet further distracted the government in Lhasa. Weeks before the invasion, Tibetan leaders carelessly replaced Chamdo's regional governor-general, who was prepared to defend the border but whose term limit had expired, with an aristocrat, Ngabo Ngawang Jingme. Ngabo, fearful of the approaching Chinese, fled Chamdo by mule in the middle of the night. On his retreat, he passed Tibetan reinforcements and ordered them to surrender without a fight. One Tibetan, reminiscing on the situation in an interview with the journalist John Avedon, said, "If we Tibetans had fought together from the first day of the Chinese attack, we could never have lost. Our mountains are impregnable. There were no roads. The Chinese had no supply lines. Their soldiers were helpless for days, marching snow-blind one behind another. No army on earth could have conquered that country with the people united against it, but, because of our own confusion, they just walked in." Soon Chamdo fell, and the Chinese army settled to a halt.

The Chinese waited, for almost a year, hoping to force Lhasa to negotiate. The Tibetans spent the next ten months pleading for help from the United States, Britain, and the United Nations. On the consult of an oracle, they invested fifteen-year-old Tenzin Gyatso, the Fourteenth Dalai Lama, as the supreme ruler of Tibet, hoping to consolidate power. But later that year, the Dalai Lama was forced across the Indian border when warning came of a plot on his life. He dispatched four officials, led by Ngabo, to Beijing to begin negotiations. It was on that trip that, without authority from the Dalai Lama and apparently under duress, Ngabo signed the infamous Seventeen-Point Agreement formalizing Tibet's subservience to China and giving up control of its external affairs.

For the Chinese, it was time to push to Lhasa. It took the fantastically emboldened PLA, fresh from their victory over the nationalists, six weeks to fight the weak, understaffed Tibetan regiments that rose up along their path. The PLA slowly shifted its troops and matériel through the mountain passes, the altitudes transforming the disciplined advance into an alternately lugubrious and treacherous forced march. Lhasa maintained radio contact with its eastern outposts, but otherwise communication and travel were limited—another testament to the region's isolation and lack of infrastructure. In a final Tibetan retreat, fighters traveled on scruffy donkeys and camels back to Lhasa, sending word ahead by foot in a frantic attempt to warn the city of the PLA's approach. On September 9, 1951, three thousand Chinese troops took Lhasa.

The Chinese foothold in Tibet, which had been varyingly sturdy and absent over the preceding six hundred years, could not fully take root as long as getting to Lhasa entailed the kind of expedition the PLA had just endured. At the time, Lhasa boasted only two cars; they had been disassembled in Nepal and carried in pieces on the backs of porters and yaks through the Himalayas, and because paved roads were scarce in Lhasa, they were limited to short two-mile sprints between the Potala Palace and the Norbu Linka summer palace grounds. Among the first projects undertaken by the Chinese was the painstaking construction of roads back to the hinterland from which they had invaded.

Beginning immediately in 1951, Mao set his own army and tens of thousands of conscripted Tibetans to work shoveling out the two roadways from Lhasa. One meandered east, winding up over the mountains to Chengdu, in what became Sichuan Province. The other struck north over the Tibetan Plateau, a hellishly rough expedition through mud and marsh and mountains with altitudes of almost seventeen thousand feet, to Qinghai Province. The construction, the central focus of the Chinese military in the region, took three years. More than 110,000 poorly shod soldiers and forced laborers—there was only a slight distinction between the Chinese and the Tibetans—moved tens of millions of tons of earth by hand and built some four hundred bridges. Many Tibetans were paid for their work, the first introduction of wage labor in Tibet. But for every half mile of cleared and graded dirt, one worker fell dead—usually of exposure in the driving winds and snow, altitude sickness, exhaustion, or the desperate lack of food. A gaudy stone monument in the west end of Lhasa commemorates the more than three thousand "martyrs" who died building the two highways, while at the other end of the Qinghai road, six miles outside Golmud, a lonely black granite tombstone stands in a forlorn military cemetery. "In 1954 an Army came and they fought against the life-forbidding Tibetan Plateau and endured great hardship," the poetic inscription reads in chiseled Chinese characters. This particular stone memorializes 680 of the PLA soldiers who died on the project. When the highways were completed—the Qinghai-Tibet route opened on December 15, 1954—motorized vehicles rolled into Lhasa under their own power for the first time.

The introduction of twentieth-century transportation to Tibet quickly enabled Mao to extend his policies and aggressive development programs west. Suddenly Lhasa was twenty days' travel from Beijing. The militarization and consolidation of China's physical control triggered the Dalai Lama's flight to asylum in India in 1959. It ushered in the attempt at a great agricultural revolution, whose mechanized farming, communal living, and central planning led to mass starvation. It allowed armed troops to enforce the cultural geno-cide of the "Democratic Reforms" of 1959–60 and then the Cultural Revolution and enabled the Tibetan Plateau to become the site of China's primary nuclear research and weapons development facility. Later, it opened the plateau to the nuclear Cold War, as the remote regions of the Kunlun Mountains became sites for missile silos and other defense infrastructure. Systematically, thousands of Tibet's monasteries and temples were blown up, burned down, demolished, and repurposed for the storage of grain or animals. Religious artifacts were destroyed or shipped out of the region, to be sold on the black market to Western art collectors. Monks, the cultural and intellec-tual core of Tibetan society, were forced to disavow their beliefs or suffer torture, imprisonment, or execution. An estimated 1 million Tibetans died fighting in resistance or at the hands of the Chinese military, police, or work bosses. Still, Tibet never folded completely under China's wing. Debate persisted among many Tibetans and the watchful international community, including the Tibetan government-in-exile in Dharamsala, India, about Tibet's sovereignty. China didn't trust its political hold in Tibet either. Violence and oppres-sive policies continued in tandem with modernization through the 1990s. Mao knew soon after entering Tibet that he wanted a railway connection to Lhasa, but despite all of his power, it could not yet be done. What China had learned in the ensuing years was that the highways would never be enough.

THOUGH THERE WAS A LONG LIST OF GRIEVANCES AGAINST THE CHINESE to complain about, Renzin believed he was lucky. The toughest years—those of the Democratic Reform, the Great Leap Forward, and the Cultural Revolution—were in the past, and he had his own taste of progress. His Land Cruiser trek to Tsurphu, for instance—it was a sign of some wealth that Renzin had friends who owned their own vehicle. His government-supplied flat had water and electricity; he no longer had to haul kettles to the public well in an apartment courtyard (though the average Tibetan in Lhasa did). Business was steady, if not booming. There was a comeback in the tourism industry now that China had begun to let foreigners back in; following the 1989 uprising, his trinkets had been hard to sell. And he had not failed to notice that the wealthy Chinese were fascinated with Tibet and Buddhism. There was just more money in Lhasa. The enthusiasm among the Chinese middle class was rallying preservationist sentiments that, despite a raging government crackdown in 2000, was encouraging the rebuilding of temples and monasteries. Plus, the freshly paved highways cut Renzin's biannual trip to Kathmandu down to two days of travel.

Outside Lhasa, change had been less tangible. The term *Tibet* has largely been defined by China, and adopted by the West, to refer to the TAR, the autonomous region that includes Lhasa, much of the plateau, and the far west. It is where the tourists travel to and where almost all of the political attention is focused. But Tibet, as populated by Tibetan people, is an area twice as large that spills north and east into twelve prefectures and counties, including Amdo in the northeast and Kham in the east, that cover another four hundred thousand square miles, roughly the same area as the TAR itself. Taken together, the Chinese-government areas that are classified as "Tibetan autonomous" regions comprise a quarter of all the land within China's borders, yet Tibetans make up less than half of one percent of China's population. More Tibetans live in these mostly rural outlying provinces than in the TAR.

The villagers throughout the larger, sparsely populated Tibet lived a simple pastoral existence off their animals and their land. After the Chinese arrived, many were corralled into work crews—forced or later hired to build the roads, bridges, and dams—and then forced to live on agricultural communes. Their land and resources were pooled, and each person worked the fields to produce food not just for their collective, but for the Chinese army and the governmental bureaucracy that managed it. The most progress came for rural Tibetans in the 1980s, when they were allowed to return to "private" land ownership and live independently. The little roadside shacks and strip-mall storefronts stocked with instant noodle soup, liquor, and snacks wrapped in plastic were convenient during trips to Lhasa or monasteries. But schools and health care remained underfunded, and roads tended to be improved only if there was something valuable—like coal or metals—at the other end. Across China, development happened in cities; in Tibet, the government's focus was no different.

WITH EXPECTATIONS SO LOW, THE SUBTLE BUZZ OF ACTIVITY THE PREVIous October went almost unnoticed. The barley had grown head-high in the small villages at the intersection of the Dowo Lung and Tolung valleys, where the road turns south to Tsurphu. Life in Tolung-Dechen County in 2000 was a lot like life in 1985.

Kalden—a sixteen-year-old boy with shoulder-length black hair, high cheekbones, and the ruddy good looks that might cast him as a model for Benetton—had only known the years after the Great Leap Forward. And life, though full of blistering work, wasn't half bad. He was the youngest boy in a large family of four brothers and three sisters. Most of his siblings lived at home, together caring for their crops, grazing land, and yaks. The tight-knit community of the family's village would help one another in the fields.

Three acres of the barley crops belonged to Kalden's family. They lived on the south edge of the village, on a majestic plot of leveled terraces nestled inside a swooping oxbow of the Tolung River, which ran cold and strong in light whitewater through its little canyon about seventy feet below. Because their home sat at the edge of this pronounced little ridge, Kalden enjoyed a commanding view of the wilderness east, into the widening Lhasa Valley, and south, up the drainage to Tsurphu and the snow-doused rocky peaks above it. If you wanted to sit and take in the silence and austerity of Tibet's landscape, a perch by the rippling irrigation canal that ran by Kalden's gate might have been the place to do it.

His home itself was modest—but it was also new and he felt immensely proud. In the summer of 1996, the boys, with their father, poured themselves into a wholesale renovation, building the house with their bare hands. It was comfortable, but also a symbol of their stature in the village and their sophistication. Stones from the river, worn round from glacial torrents, had been meticulously stacked and cemented with a mixture of grass and clay earth to form a wall that would contain their goats and chickens. The house, a large room with a kitchen and living area, a prayer room full of Buddhas, and several sleeping rooms, was built of the same material, smoothed over with clay and whitewashed. In the summer, the earthen walls kept the house cool despite the piercing, high-altitude sun that baked everything beneath it; in the winter, they insulated the radiated heat from a small steel stove that burned wood and yak dung. The family had spent some of its savings on several glass windows, in wooden panes, which helped to brighten things. From the perspective of developers in Beijing, or, for that matter, Kansas City, it was a third-world, almost ancient building, but in the valleys of the Himalayas, it was eminently efficient, and even pretty.

Outside Kalden's gate—a small wooden-hinged door with a latch—thirty similar homes sprawled across the village. Kalden's house was on the edge of town, with the fields stretching from behind his home, so he was consumed with monitoring the barley harvest. One of the few crops that grow naturally in the central region's shallow rocky topsoil and arid climate, the barley would feed the village through the long, cold winter and would be toasted for *tsampa,* the grainy, doughlike meal that Tibetans take for hearty sustenance and also brew to make beer and ferment to make *raksi,* a sour wine. When it came time to cut the barley down, Kalden and his family would head to the fields with scythes or machetes to methodically mow the tall grasses, hand-collect and pile the cuttings, and then bundle them into manageable packages for carrying and stacking. During breaks, they would pull a few sips of water or *raksi* from a beat-up plastic jug.

It was during such a day of harvest that Kalden recalls, perhaps as the tall crop was cleared from his view, a small Chinese work crew walking into the village. Three or four men had crossed the highway bridge a few hundred yards away and then descended the mild grade down to the homes above the river. They were dressed in bright orange jumpsuits, and one of them carried a large, industrial-strength tripod. The sight was a strange intrusion. Kalden knew nothing about plans to build in the village, which was far enough from the city to be untouched by its rabid development.

The men stopped on a slight incline, just fifty feet from Kalden's home, and opened their wooden contraption. While one man took notes, another peered through the small scope attached to the tripod's top, as if he were lining up the full length of the countryside. They worked this way for perhaps an hour and then, by foot, continued across the field and up the valley, in the direction of Lhasa.

3

A BIGGER STAGE

CHINESE PREMIER ZHU RONGJI STOOD ON A LARGE PILE of dirt, fresh from the bulldozer. It was June 29, 2001—the official start of construction on the Qinghai-Tibet Railway. Perhaps a thousand workers, engineers, and officials had been trucked in to the nothing desert town of Nanshankou, up nine miles from the city of Golmud or down from several established labor camps farther south along the highway to Lhasa, and they gathered to watch Zhu, the country's third-ranking official, officiate over the prototypical Communist Party ribbon-cutting ceremony. His appearance made one thing especially clear: the train to Tibet was a priority for Beijing.

Zhu wore a black suit that seemed out of place against the ceaseless copper-colored rock around him. The sun radiated uninhibited from the cloudless sky, but a brisk wind cut the chill, as it is bound to do at elevations ten thousand feet above sea level. Zhu stood at the crown of a half circle of similarly uniformed officials. Each held a shovel, garnished at the handle with a bright red ribbon, and at the dictated moment, sometime around 11:00 A.M., they chucked a symbolic load of dirt into a hole containing a concrete foundation block inscribed with Chinese characters for good fortune. But for that, the scene could have been mistaken for the burial of some forgettable provincial party official.

In 1979, when China last abandoned its plans to construct a railway line to Lhasa, Nanshankou had been the spot that marked the failure. The station in Golmud, just down the ramping dirt plain, had technically been named the end of the line, though the tracks extended to this short spur. Golmud was not much of a city, but it made Nanshankou, 710 miles northeast of Lhasa, look like a truck stop.

Before the train, Golmud was known mostly as a forsaken town surrounded by sand dunes, dry craggy peaks, and high-altitude plains—not as high as the plateau, but, at an altitude of seven thousand to nine thousand feet, shockingly inhospitable to the lowlander Chinese. Salt flats stretched into shimmering mirages that obscured the horizon, except where an occasional ridge pierced it like a shark fin on the sea. It was a place very few people wanted to be in. It had one main street—just five hundred yards long—a post office, a government hotel, and a restaurant or two. Ethnically, Golmud was very much Tibetan, though it also contained large Uighur and Mongolian populations from the north. There were some, but very few, Chinese living there, many of whom had either served time in or staffed the enormous prisons that had been built in the 1960s. Others had been posted to Qinghai during Mao's Third Front campaign to develop coal and mineral mines. Golmud, along with the nearby saltwater Qinghai Lake, the largest in China, was (and still is) rich in minerals; the Tibetans called it Tsaidam (salt) Basin—a name preserved by the Chinese in their version, Qaidam—and the salt was a large reason the original railway to Tibet was planned through Qinghai Province's capital city, Xining, when construction first started in 1959.

Xining then was a small but bustling trade city, home to a significant Tibetan population, and nearby Kumbum Monastery, a sixteenth-century center for learning. It was a crossroads of western China, connecting southern Gansu and Sichuan cities like Lanzhou and Chengdu with the northern Gobi Desert and Inner Mongolia. The railway began its path west to Golmud in 1959, when the No. 10 Division of Railway Troops—an army division kept busy in peacetime through hardy development and labor projects—was set to work on the 396-mile-long track. Tibetan prisoners from Amdo were also forced into manual labor, digging and grading the line, often barely sustained by starvation rations consisting of low-grade barley flour mixed with sawdust. Thousands perished in the camps. Tunnels were dug near Golmud, and the steel was laid from Xining as far as the town of Haiyan, about sixty miles to the west. But the work was interrupted by government bankruptcy and what the Chinese slyly refer to as the Three Year Disaster, a period of drought and "natural" circumstances during which an estimated 40 million Chinese and Tibetans died, mostly of starvation that resulted directly from Mao's misguided agricultural policies under the Great Leap Forward.

By 1974, the Chinese had gathered the material and the will to try again. A colossal force of Chinese army crews set to work extending the railway from Xining to Golmud, hoping they could eventually push all the way to Lhasa. "This railway will do a lot to develop the Qaidam basin," the then vice chief engineer Chen Wan Wu explained, quickly adding that national defense was as important as mineral riches in the planning. The Chinese government media reports focused instead on the economic opportunity a new rail line would bring to the nomadic people of Qinghai. In 1961, a railway was built to nearby Urumchi, the capital of Xinjiang Uighur Autonomous Region, a development that would bring 2 million Han Chinese to the city. A train had recently reached north of Xining to Haxai Mongolian Autonomous Prefecture. Before that railroad had been built, traders would herd their healthy animals on foot for weeks to markets in Xining, and their animals would go from fat to thin over the course of the journey. The more weight they lost before they could be slaughtered, the less cash earned by the owners from selling the meat. With the new train, the animals could be killed at their fattest and shipped in refrigerated cars to market almost overnight. This was exactly the kind of local economic benefit the Chinese touted in the Golmud rail development.

Striking west to Golmud was tougher than pushing a train north to Mongolia, however, and the first phase of the 1974 construction was as challenging to the Chinese engineers' technological limits as the twenty-first-century railway to Lhasa would be. Though not as cold or as extreme as the conditions in Tibet, the terrain in Qinghai pushed the workers to the limits of their endurance. One laborer told a Chinese documentary crew that workers survived with little water; stingy rations were trucked in from Golmud, with an entire unit expected to share a single barrel of gray water for two weeks' worth of washing and cooking. There was little portioned out for drinking. The earth-moving and steel laying went slowly, with bare hands and hammers— a methodical march past the great Qinghai Lake.

One of the division's first obstacles would become the most notorious: the construction of the 2.5-mile Guanjiao tunnel, which at the time was the highest tunnel in China. Tunnel building requires some of the heaviest lifting in railway construction and has always been the most dangerous. An entrance to the Guanjiao tunnel had been partially dug in 1959, but work was stopped midway and the roughly chiseled bore was sealed in 1961. It sat, leaking groundwater and slowly deteriorating, for another thirteen years before workers entered it again to try to finish the job in 1975. The tunnel was dark and oxygen-deprived, the air so thick a match would not light. "It felt suffocating," one soldier recalled. "Sometimes you just fainted." On April 5, a 150-foot section of rock collapsed and sealed off the tunnel's single entrance, trapping 127 soldiers inside. Their situation was desperate. "The vent pipe was not destroyed in the collapse and wind could still be blown into the cave," Liang Yuanzhang, a former soldier with the No. 10 Division of Railway Troops told China Television in a 2006 interview. "We called into the cave from the pipe and the soldiers in it could answer us." According to Liang, it took fourteen hours to clear the debris. What happened then depends on which version of history you believe: either all 127 soldiers were found dead, as was stated in the Ministry of Railways meeting before Zhang Luxin had argued that tunnel-boring technology had improved so much that building a new railway would be safe, or all 127 were heroically saved, as more recent propaganda about China's railways assert. Regardless, many subsequent incidents in the Guanjiao tunnel and others on the Xining-Golmud line exacted a discerning death toll.

When the railway reached Golmud in the summer of 1979, it was billboarded as the highest train in China and feted for the project's perseverance against extreme conditions. On July 28, Tibetan and Mongolian nomads decked out in traditional garb galloped on horseback into the central square of the new station and poured barley wine and milk tea into the cups of the celebrating soldiers and laborers. Golmud was China's new end-of-the-line, the western frontier of central China. The tracks were used exclusively for military transport and development for the next four years, during which the industrial development of the Tsaidam Basin surged, right to where the tracks petered out in the desert around Nanshankou. Although researchers, among them Zhang, were working full-bore on preparations for construction farther south on the plateau and into Tibet, Beijing faced a fiscal crisis. The central leaders decided, for the second time, that they could not afford the risky construction project to Lhasa.

The push to begin construction anew in 2001 thus held special significance; the zealous ambitions of 1959 and the late 1970s were finally backed by science and by money. The Tenth Five Year Plan would be different. In many ways, the international profile of problems in Tibet had diminished. China would be working with the luxury and stability of peacetime, and the consent, it seemed, of an international community that, with a few notable exceptions, had proven its willingness to cede the argument over Tibet's sovereignty to China.

After all the decades of waiting, as Zhang Luxin surveyed the crowd and watched Zhu toss his ceremonial shovelful of dirt that June 2001 morning, he found himself in tears. He stood for the festivities beneath a long line of poles that had been set up to triumphantly wave dozens of red pennants emblazoned with China's golden star. The crowd erupted with applause and drumming and song in an echo of the ceremony at Golmud twenty-two years earlier. Zhang had been hoping for this moment for a very long time.

ZHANG LUXIN WAS BORN IN TIANJIN, A CITY OF 10 MILLION PEOPLE SOUTH-east of Beijing, on November 9, 1947. His childhood coincided directly with Mao Zedong's dramatic remaking of the People's Republic of China, and as the great-grandson of a landlord, the grandson of a banker, and the son of a factory owner, Zhang did not exactly have a covetous pedigree in the newly emboldened proletariat Communist nation. "In the 1950s and '60s, in which family you are born decides what kind of person you are," Zhang said. His uncle, having spent years in the Soviet Union, had joined the Communist Party in 1946. Zhang's parents decided it would be best for the boy to live with him.

Zhang's childhood "was like the old Soviet films—all sunny days and everything was good." Beneath the superficial recollections of straight As and self-congratulatory professions to love hard work was a darker memory, of a boyhood in the shadow of Mao's early policies. When he was ten, he arrived at school to find his teacher, whom he admired very much, engrossed in the diminutive task of sweeping the courtyard's dirt floor. "He had been denounced," Zhang said. "The school taught us to hate the rightists, but I could never hate anyone who taught me." Zhang's family too was in a perilous position. His father had switched jobs and become a teacher, but their capitalist background remained a vulnerability. His father and uncle established a family policy of keeping their mouths shut. Zhang called it "prudent," but it meant he learned that survival was born of political caution and fear. "As long as you don't speak, you are safe," he said.

The next year, as the Great Leap Forward began in earnest, Mao's work edicts ran roughshod over Zhang's childhood. His school was closed, and the children were put to work hauling bricks from the kiln of a nearby factory. Zhang was the youngest in his class by two years, and the smallest. "The bricks had just come out and were very hot," he recalled. "I couldn't carry six, so I made a wooden board and hung it on my neck. I had to walk that way for five kilometers [three miles]." Again the following year, when the area suffered a drought, the children were put to work, that time hauling water, walking several miles with as many gallons as their weight could bear. Only when the day was over, once he was home, did Zhang have a chance to study. He was exhausted and afraid.

In one significant way, Zhang was fortunate. Since he started primary school at a young age, he finished ahead of schedule, heading to college at the Southwest Communications University—a place he described as "China's Cornell"—in 1964. Two years later, with the start of the Cultural Revolution, Mao closed the nation's universities entirely. Zhang slipped in, and out, just in time, barely escaping the persecutions of students by the Red Guards. But he didn't get out with the education he had wanted. From childhood, Zhang had pinned his aspirations on becoming a nuclear engineer. "It was the most important thing for an ambitious young person to do," he said. His family background haunted his hopes. Existing in the realm of state secrets, the study of nuclear science was reserved for the most trusted. In addition to his capitalist ancestry, Zhang had uncles in Chicago and Taiwan, both dangerous places to have connections, in Mao's view. Zhang was forced instead to study what he says was the least popular major offered, engineering geography. "It wasn't my choice," he lamented. "I was made to do it."

For a salve on the wounds to his pride, and despite his bitter memories of the Great Leap Forward, Zhang sought membership in the Communist Party. That, he hoped, would allow him a token of acceptance in a career dedicated to such an obscure and unimportant science. But again, the family file was opened, and what was found inside led only to setbacks. "That file goes back to ask what does your father do? What does your grandfather do?" Zhang said. "I tried to state that my family background was in teaching. But somebody did not agree. They said, 'No, your grandfather was a landlord.'" His application to the party was denied.

So upon graduation in 1966, Zhang found himself rejected by the mainstream in the blurry first days of the Cultural Revolution, entering a profession he did not choose at a time when intellectualism and professionalism were disdained. Throughout China, scientists, scholars, and officials who had fallen from favor were ripped of their credentials and put to work as manual laborers. Deputy Prime Minister Deng Xiaoping was assigned to a tractor factory in southeast China. Zhang, afraid of ruffling the party officers after his rejection, was shipped without protest to a job with the Ninjiang Railway Bureau in Jiagedaqi, a brutally cold northern Chinese outpost beyond the city of Harbin, in Inner Mongolia, near North Korea. He might as well have been banished to Siberia; his posting was just a hundred miles or so south of the Russian border.

Zhang's first assignment in Jiagedaqi was to mix concrete. He lasted a few weeks before he grew disillusioned and restless, and begged for a real job on the railway. Though he didn't know quite what he was asking for, he got it. A new rail extension was being punched through the Xianan Mountains in the rugged northern forest, and the army was in need of more labor. All the work was done by hand, especially in the mountains, and the work was hard. A steel section of rail ran about forty feet long and weighed nearly thirteen hundred pounds. Half a dozen men would hoist the bar onto their shoulders and walk it to the end of the track, where it would be set on hand-positioned wooden ties and hammered down with fat iron nails. Winter temperatures dropped to minus fifty Farenheit, and frostbite was common. Workers' hands and feet would freeze solid and twist into useless black stumps. Zhang earned a handsome fifty-five yuan, or seven dollars, a day in today's money, but made few friends. "The local workers despised college graduates," he said, referring not just to the blue-collar work camps but to the Cultural Revolution's relegation of intellectuals to the bottom of the societal hierarchy. "They challenged me constantly—said I couldn't do it."

It was the intellectual repression that Zhang felt the most. Across the country, scientists and scholars—a cohort that Zhang, perhaps

prematurely, included himself in—were laboring in farms and factories. The Chinese government called it an "overthrow," crowing that
society would "step on their backs" to reach new heights. China's glory
would be renewed by elevating the common man to control of his
own destiny, albeit through communes and political party member-
ships. Zhang was shocked by the intellectual resources being wasted.
"Everyone knew this was not right, but no one dared to criticize,"
Zhang said. "If a country wants to develop, to prosper, it needs knowledge. I just hoped this would not last forever." He waited. He lived in
a camp packed with canvas army tents. Each had a coal stove, for heat
and cooking, around which were arranged beds composed of a sheet
laid over a board with four posts. To keep up with his studies, Zhang
would sit on a stack of bricks, piled at the foot of his bed, and use his
wooden trunk as a desk. He read railway engineering textbooks, trying to unravel the construction of a water supply system for a new
two-mile coal-mine extension on which he had been promoted to
work. He played his violin, read Chinese poetry, learned the Russian
language, and read old Soviet literature. He never saw a fresh fruit or
vegetable; the rations were mostly a soupy, frozen cabbage that, "when
it was cooked, smelled like pig food." Years went by. Zhang eventually found a mentor in a senior engineer, and also increasingly important engineering assignments on the railway expansion. In 1972, he
was given a slide rule, a gift he remembered as symbolizing his rise
from laborer to engineer. Later that year, he was sent to learn about
construction on frozen soils, a problem that challenged the engineers in Inner Mongolia's icy climate. But still he lived in the camp,
in the desolate isolation of the north.

The freezing evenings were punctuated by news broadcasts
from Beijing. Throughout the camp, megaphones were mounted on

wooden poles and woven together by sagging wires, and the camp's activity would slow to a crawl for each transmission. The sound that came out was scratchy at first—static piped through the makeshift city's primitive electric grid. One evening in February 1973, the announcer droned, "Our great leader Chairman Mao, today he met with the visiting king of Nepal." Zhang and his bunkmates crowded around the open door of their glowing furnace for warmth while they listened. Mao had met earlier that day, February 10, with Nepal's newly instated King Birendra. The topic was distant and obscure to most of the laborers in this northeast outpost of China, but it immediately caught Zhang's interest. In the meeting, Mao had wooed the tiny Himalayan nation, seeking to play it against the neighboring region of Tibet. Even with the Himalayas, the border with Nepal had always been the most porous route into, and out of, Tibet. Mao was promising to link China and Nepal economically and physically, to support the fledgling and impoverished country with China's girth and power. He hoped to gain greater control over Tibet and greater influence below the Himalayan steppe and beyond, onto the plains of South Asia. What Mao dangled in the bargain, and what captured Zhang's imagination, were the makings of a diplomatic coup: China would finally build a railway to Tibet, and it would reach all the way to Nepal.

Nepal was not insignificant in the great chess game of South Asia. Its longtime authoritarian monarch, Mahendra, had traditionally aligned himself with India and had been sympathetic to the Tibetan plight, allowing many people to migrate south past Mount Everest to reside in Nepal when China rolled into Tibet. When the Tibetans had organized an armed resistance to the Chinese in the late 1950s, with the feeble but symbolically significant aid of the American CIA, many of their attacks were launched from the Mustang region of far west Nepal. Following Mahendra's death in 1972, his son Birendra immediately struck a more conciliatory tone with China, hoping to negotiate a stronger position against India. Mao seized the opportunity wholeheartedly.

That year, China built two major road projects in Kathmandu, and financial aid to Nepal jumped from 3 to almost 20 percent of the Himalayan country's total budget. By the time Birendra made a winter visit to Beijing, he had closed the Tibetan base in Mustang and begun confiscating arms from and arresting Tibetans inside Nepal. At Mao's urging, Birendra fired the largely Tibetan staff of Nepal's Lhasa-based consulate—long known to be a center for Tibetan resistance—and moved the offices to the outskirts of town. For Mao, in the context of a quarter century's struggle to tame the Tibetan region, the new relationship with Nepal was working quite well. Promising the railroad, though far-fetched at the time, seemed the least he could do.

Zhang too knew an opportunity when he saw one. "When I was a child I had already heard that the lands of Qinghai and Tibet were so mysterious and spiritual," he said. "It was the roof of the world, a prohibited zone for human beings because one can't live there." Zhang, like many Chinese, barely knew where Tibet lay on a map. He had only the barest preconceptions. When he was nine years old, the school choir had performed a song about the People's Liberation Army. Dressed vaguely like a Tibetan boy, he had danced across the stage while belting out the lyrics that remained in his memory fifteen years later: *A red sun rises over the snow mountains.* Those lyrics were his first and lasting impression of Tibet, a place he always knew as a part of China. Books and films celebrated Mao's "liberation" of Tibet but also, in the spirit of propaganda for the Great Leap Forward and the Cultural Revolution, the Tibetans' agrarian lifestyle. The maps, he remembered, always showed Tibet inside China's borders and always colored it a drab brown. "I always imagined Tibet was kind of terrible, a harsh desert," he said. "I imagined Tibetans were a very spiritual people, but they lived in a very primitive way."

Preparations to construct the extension from Xining to Golmud began swiftly, and researchers were dispatched to the plateau later that year to begin mapping a route. But it wasn't until about October 1974, as a fall chill set on China's northernmost reaches, that Zhang's bureau was summoned to a meeting inside one of the cavernous, dimly lit army tents. His supervisor marched in with a printout from the Ministry of Railways clenched in his fist and announced the details of the Tibet train project. The ministry was seeking two technicians from the Jiagedaqi branch bureau, who would be shipped out almost immediately.

Perhaps the only posting less desirable than Harbin and its far north forests, Tibet was a hard sell. Even today—with grocery stores and fiber-optic cable and wireless Internet—the Chinese bureaucracy categorizes Tibet as "a hardship post," entitling government employees to receive double wages for being stationed there. The far-off region had little to offer but more cold, more pain, more isolation. Lhasa, a small town of just thirty thousand people, was a social and military battleground of sorts. On the plateau, there was simply nothing at all.

Zhang had a sense of adventure that surely guided his attraction to the assignment on the Tibetan plateau, but even more so, he was ambitious and pragmatic. He had heard about the challenges of the plateau's permafrost and the harsh environment; he had even heard that some thought the project impossible. Every time Zhang had sought to follow a conventionally respectable path—as a nuclear engineer or as a member of the party—he had been rejected. He was tired of rejection. And he was quick to recognize that though Tibet might not be a desirable place to work, the railway project had attention from the highest levels of the Chinese government. That no one else wanted the job suddenly seemed to open so many doors that had closed when bureaucrats flipped through his family's file. If there was ever a chance for him to emerge from among the ranking masses, Zhang thought, this was it. "The Qinghai-Tibet railroad would be the miracle of the history of railroad construction. I wanted to overcome this global obstacle," he said. "I never wanted to spend my whole life in Jiagedaqi. I wanted more people to know me. I wanted a bigger stage for myself—something that was almost impossible for someone with my background." Two days later, he volunteered for the post. "Everyone thought I was a fool."

Zhang had a girlfriend of six months—a young woman from Dalian who worked as an accountant for a timber company near Zhang's camp. He rushed to see her to share his news, and hurriedly proposed: "Shall we marry quickly before I go?" In late November, the two traveled to Beijing to seek the approval of Zhang's uncle, and were married on December 2. Five days later, Zhang was back in Jiagedaqi alone, packing his things. The morning of December 8 was frigid and snowing heavily. He had stuffed everything he owned—mostly books and clothing, as well as a few pictures—into his wooden trunk that doubled as a desk, but it was too heavy to move. Zhang fashioned a sled and dragged his luggage through the drifts to the station platform. By the time the train rolled south to Harbin the next morning, Zhang was suffering from an intense fever, induced by the cold, exhaustion, and anxiety.

In Jiagedaqi, Zhang had been able to conjure a view of his future. He would grow into a full-fledged engineer, eventually oversee projects of his own, and, if he were successful, maybe one day head the entire Ninjiang Railway Bureau. Jiagedaqi wasn't the sexiest station in China, but it sat near the north's massive forests and oil fields and benefited from the province's prestigious heritage as part of the initial Manchurian victories of the Communist forces. It offered stability and a predictable career. As Zhang swallowed his Tibet fantasies whole, he achingly realized that the possibility for permanent denial was just as likely as it was for glorious achievement. The Tibet railway wasn't simply a construction challenge; scientists—he—had to solve a slew of so far unanswerable geologic and environmental problems and develop an entirely new way of building the train's road. Zhang, frustrated with the denials he had been handed, had hitched his future to a high-stakes project that could easily destroy his career.

UNTIL ZHU LIFTED HIS SHOVEL OF DIRT IN NANSHANKOU, ZHANG HAD been sure he had lost his gamble. Nearly three decades had elapsed, and he had accomplished nothing concrete on the plateau. His wife and son, who lived between Beijing and Lanzhou, had faltered, muttering that the hardship pay for what was basically a midlevel engineer's job was not enough compensation for the long separations. Still, Zhang stayed in Tibet, mustering a catalog of optimistic explanations for colleagues and old schoolmates when they asked about his loyal service to an obscure railway project that had never been built. He had devised structural methods for building on permafrost but never received the go-ahead to build them. The Tenth Five Year Plan presented Zhang with an unlikely chance for redemption—and at more than fifty years of age, just shy of China's mandatory retirement age, he knew it would be his last.

China as a nation had a lot riding on the project, as well. Stubborn and proud, China clings to the legacy of progress instilled by Mao Zedong. Mao's larger-than-life portrait hangs at the gates of the Imperial Palace, and a monument to the dictator stands in Tiananmen Square. Even the disenchanted Deng Xiaoping, who called for limiting the cult of the leader, still "allowed pilgrimages to Mao's crystal coffin" while pushing forward his anti-Mao opening of China's economy in the 1970s. Mao may be widely derided for bringing China to its knees, but the country is far from disavowing the founding father's philosophies wholesale. That would be akin to admitting a defeat for the state, a rejection of the nation's modern persona. Completing the impossible railway to Tibet became a similar symbol of pride, an irrationally large symbol of China's ability to persevere and succeed technologically where the world said it would not.

With the train, China was also attempting more than an engineering feat. The question of Tibet's sovereignty, and the widespread and long-standing accusations of human rights abuses against Tibetans, had for some time been a festering thorn in China's otherwise thick political skin. Hollywood, the U.S. Congress, and the United Nations were increasingly prodding if not actually threatening China about its treatment of Tibet, while India and Europe were expanding their refuge to pro-Tibetan groups, which continued to call for the end of China's rule over the region. The Dalai Lama and his supporters in Dharamsala were stepping up their political statements, not least by spurring the Karmapa to hold an international press conference, which he had done that April, about the conditions of his tenure in Tibet. With each year in exile, the calls for the Dalai Lama's return to Tibet became louder, overpowering China's quieter efforts to draw the region into a normal, provincial status. The railway would finally provide a permanent, intractable link between Tibet and China. If the tracks themselves didn't do it, the heightened economic participation and ethnic "moderation" of new settlers into Tibet would at least soften the drumbeat of critics.

Finally, the dormant but real issue of China's weak Himalayan border loomed large among Beijing's strategic thinkers. It always had. In 1904, the British Lord Curzon, the commander in the Indian colony, ordered Francis Younghusband to march a small army into Tibet. He did—slaughtering thousands of retreating Tibetans along the way and sustaining only a few dozen injuries among his own troops. When the British marched into Lhasa, it jolted the obscure Tibetan kingdom into international relevance. "The invasion focused a brilliant spotlight on the nature of Tibet's political status vis-à-vis China, India, and European powers," wrote Tibet historian Melvyn Goldstein. The event changed the paradigm of central Asia, and China has been figuring out how to cope with foreign threats on its western frontier ever since. In 1906, its troops invaded Lhasa, only to be expelled by the Tibetans five years later when the Thirteenth Dalai Lama returned from exile in India. In recent years, the relationship with an independent India has only grown more complicated. On one level, India indirectly bolsters support for Tibetan sovereignty by allowing the Fourteenth Dalai Lama to live in exile at Dharamsala. On a larger level, India, which runs second to China in terms of population and economic growth, cannot be ignored. India's status as the world's most populous democracy adds pressure to China in its machinations over trade agreements. In response to India's warmer relationship with the United States, China has been pandering for influence over Pakistan, Bangladesh, and Nepal, waging diplomatic battles over territory India has traditionally considered under its purview. China recognizes water scarcity as one of the greatest threats to its security and political stability. India's stark dependence on water from Himalayan glaciers and rivers originating in Tibet puts it at a disadvantage as long as China can consolidate its hold over the mountains and the plateau. Significantly, the actual line of control between India and China—a border that, while remote, does define the state ownership of glaciers and mountain drainages—has not been formalized in more than fifty-five years.

The long-disputed border is a nexus for many of China's flashpoint issues with India. China's relationship with India began to frazzle after the newly resident Chinese refused in 1950 to recognize the McMahon Line, the Indian-Tibetan border negotiated between the British and the Tibetan government at the Simla Conference of 1914. In the late 1950s, Indian prime minister Jawaharlal Nehru's awkward juggling act—cozying up to China while sympathizing with Tibetan human rights issues—unsettled the relationship between the two countries. When China poured troops into Tibet to quell the popular uprising in 1959, India grew justifiably anxious about the presence of foreign armies on its northern border. Two and a half more years of posturing and skirmishes led to war. On October 20, 1962, as John F. Kennedy faced off with Nikita Khrushchev over Russian missiles positioned in Cuba, Mao attacked India. Hardly anyone noticed. The conflict lasted little more than a month before India was brutally and humiliatingly defeated. According to the historian Tsering Shakya, ragged Indian prisoners of war were paraded through the streets of Lhasa as the PLA engulfed the city in celebration. The brief war was another turning point, and it set a chilly tone for the next four decades. In the 1990s, as China shifted into high-geared economic development, relations between the two countries thawed, though the border remained unresolved. With the rivalry between China and India reignited, both countries have been angling anew for a secure foothold in the Himalayas.

While the railway is China's hedge against political turmoil in its southwest, it's also a gamble on its economic growth. The country's astronomical 10 percent expansion in gross domestic product for each year of most of the last decade has been fueled by the greatest demand for resources the world has ever seen. When thugs in Romania steal electronics and strip their innards of copper to sell on the black market, they do it to satisfy China's demand. When the oil companies BP and Shell complain about rising pipeline construction costs in Russia or Alaska, it is because China's demand for iron—of which it is the world's third-largest importer—has driven up steel prices by more than double. When U.S. political leaders worry about America's waning influence in Latin America and Africa, it is because China has dedicated generous aid packages to countries whose citizens will extract their scarce commodities to be shaped by Chinese factories. And beyond this, Chinese leaders know that in order to glide into a successful and effective membership in the World Trade Organization, China needs to achieve some level of economic equality and political stability across the country—and still more resources. The resource crunch has been hard on many of the world's economies, but as much as any other country, it threatens China. In its sparsely populated west, China saw veiled promises and solutions for the quagmires brought by its development. While the eastern cities of Beijing and Shanghai are choked with people and pollution, with skyscrapers and money, the west provides the ample space and the prospect of riches to support the country's hypergrowth. It is doubtfully a purely historical irony that China's name for Tibet is Xizang, in English, "western treasure house."

But little was actually known about the resources available on the vast Tibetan Plateau at the turn of the twentieth century. An area the size of California, Montana, and Texas combined, the plateau had never been fully surveyed. A large deposit of copper had been tagged in northeast Tibet, but large-scale mining was not economical in the remote and rugged region; the truck route to Golmud, the closest interior city, was too hazardous and inefficient. Gold mining existed on a small scale—adventurous prospectors panned and dredged across Tibet. Only a few gas reserves had been staked in the far west. To many of the potential investors, Tibet's geologic bounty appeared to be a trifle compared to the cost of extracting it and transporting it thousands of miles across the wilderness.

China's central government in Beijing hoped otherwise. Unbeknownst to Zhang and the other engineers on the plateau, in 1999, the state's geologic survey secretly sent an army of a thousand scientists, divided into twenty-four research teams, on a seven-year mission to create the first detailed report on Tibet's resources. Leaking word about the exploration project would undermine Beijing's message that the primary objective of the region's development projects was improving Tibetans' welfare, and it would likely draw fire from critics who were already tracking environmental damage in one of the world's most pristine ecological environments. But perhaps more important, disclosing the survey would delay the railway project. If Jiang Zemin made resource exploration the cornerstone of the Tenth Five Year Plan, it would be strange, even by the often twisted logic of the Communist Party, not to complete the survey before beginning construction on the railway. And if the survey discovered no further resources in Tibet, there would be no choice but to jettison the entire railway project. The groundbreaking in 2001 committed China to Tibet, with only a vague guarantee of a political return on its investment. It was a classic Chinese strategy, this brisk decision whereby dozens of individual pieces were developed separately and simultaneously in the hope that they could be readily assembled later, if everything worked out.

So despite the risks and uncertainties, the vision of a great railway to Tibet was pushed through at lightning pace. From the time discussions about the train began in earnest in 2000, there was an almost irrational sense of urgency—a sense that the project had to be completed before politics or circumstance prompted a closer look at the potential for failure. The hurried project, as with so much else in China in the past ten years, would at many instances abandon caution, scientific know-how, and proper planning in favor of development spectacle. A major infrastructure project like a seven-hundred-mile mountain railway in the United States might require ten to fifteen years of planning and environmental review. Sure, China's autocratic government had the luxury of dispelling with much of the bureaucratic wrangling that can slow a Western project, but from the moment the Qinghai route for the train had been chosen in 2001, China expected it would be just seven years before high-speed trains were zipping over the mountains. Meanwhile, there were lots of reasons to wonder whether the project was even possible at all.

It was true that teams of scientists, including Zhang Luxin, had learned a great deal about permafrost and frozen soil conditions on the Tibetan Plateau. But because funding, and their studies along with it, had been interrupted by the fits and starts of China's economic reforms, their research amounted to an irregular survey of plateau geology, extrapolations from that data, and an understanding of other scientists' research on permafrost. The science was top quality but inconclusive. In his desperation to rise above the other bureaucrats in the Railway Ministry's meeting in 2000, Zhang pushed an analysis based on sporadic soil samplings and optimistic assumptions about the regularity of the permafrost over the vast plateau.

In advocating for the route over the permafrost, Zhang had no choice but to argue that it was safe to build the railroad over constantly moving ground. Under the frozen soil of the plateau, though, caverns and columns of ice could reach sixty feet deep and in places would descend beneath the train's tracks. Like a seemingly endless expanse of hoarfrost—the long, spindly crystals that grow on a snowbank after a week of sun—the mud of the plateau had been stretched into an airy mass of crystals, similar to a cotton ball pulled apart until you could see through the strands. The cavities were filled with water, which froze at the plateau's high elevation, and so ice makes up nearly as much of the earth as the soil. If the ice melts in more temperate weather, the soil will contract and settle; when it freezes again, it pushes upward, the equivalent of a miniature tectonic plate moving at geologic light speed. This would not be a grave problem where the ground remained permanently frozen, but much of the permafrost on the plateau hovered just one degree below thawing. More than 150 square miles of the proposed route were generally warmer and more delicate than that, and so each summer the glaring sun would bear down on the plateau and warm the region far beyond normal permafrost conditions, wreaking havoc on the terrain. When Zhang told the panel in Beijing that the problem of building on permafrost had been solved, he downplayed that the research, though extensive, had only sampled portions of the plateau. A more senior researcher at China's Academy of Sciences, who had spearheaded decades of work on the plateau, warned that several more years of study were needed before construction should begin. Zhang, thinking the construction process would allow for that, dismissed his criticism.

Groundbreaking was under way four short months later. That pleased the ministers, who wanted the foreign money pouring into China to be spent on dazzling infrastructure. The government did not have several years to wait. The manufacturers and hungry banks back in Beijing and Shanghai needed the injection of capital that came with such large projects. But the urgency meant the institutors of the Five Year Plan moved ahead like a pack of belligerent drunks rather than a disciplined army of engineers. At the time that Zhu Rongji presided over the Nanshankou ceremony, the precise route for the tracks had not been decided upon, the permafrost research and methods remained incomplete, and the newly created Qinghai-Tibet Railway Company, the state-run corporation set up to manage the train's construction and operation, had yet to hire a director. Still, cement was poured and dirt was shoveled, and Zhang Luxin, among the thousands of others present that day, was set forth on the final long march toward a railway to the rooftop of the world.

4

STRAY DOGS

ZHANG LUXIN AND HIS GENERATION OF SCIENTISTS AND engineers who worked on the early plans for the railway tended to think of Tibet as a peaceful, docile, if backward place that could only benefit from their mission to develop it. It was an oasis among the tumult of Mao's China. People in the east suffered horribly under those oppressive early policies of the People's Republic of China and the destitution caused by them. An assignment in the west, in Tibet, was an opportunity to escape that persecution, to go to a part of China whose beauty balanced its hardships. Their acceptance as fact of Tibet's status within China belied a naivete about the strategic importance of their efforts, but in the grip of the Cultural Revolution, it was simpler, and smarter, to stay dreamily ignorant of such things.

If the building of the railway was a dream, to be conjured by the Chinese as part of a national quest for unity and prosperity, it gestated as Tibet suffered from a relentless nightmare. The years leading to the establishment of the first railway survey camps on the plateau were among the most riotous and unstable in a thousand years of Tibetan history. They were also the years of Renzin's boyhood.

Renzin was born in Lhasa, in the fall of 1959. His father had been one of the ten thousand monks at Drepung Monastery, the sprawling fifteenth-century Buddhist complex nestled on a mountainside eight miles west of the city. It was an epicenter of spiritual study and prestigious learning; earlier in the year, twenty-five-year-old Tenzin Gyatso, the Dalai Lama, had taken his academic exams there.

By the spring, Tibet's three-year revolt had reached full boil. In the wilderness of Kham, guerrilla fighters had been engaging the People's Liberation Army. The PLA counterattacked with 150,000 troops, crushing the eastern uprising in 1958 and unleashing a rash of atrocities that the International Commission of Jurists condemned as "conduct which shocks the civilized world and does not even need to be fitted into a legal category"; John Avedon noted "crucifixion, dismemberment, vivisection . . . children were forced to shoot their parents . . . monks were compelled to publicly copulate with nuns." By February 1959, an estimated 80,000 resistance fighters were engaged and had begun to destabilize both the official Tibetan and the nascent Chinese ruling bodies in the region. Their struggles were fueled by the American CIA, which clandestinely trained Tibetan guerrillas in Guam and at camps deep inside India and supplied them with guns, and the money to buy more. The CIA had prepared an elite force consisting of a handful of Tibetan paratroopers, and dropped them from an airplane into the western wilderness one night, just before dawn. Their hope was that this small brigade would train a local army and destabilize the Chinese position. But officially, the U.S. government recognized China's suzerainty over Tibet, and though the Tibetans hoped with all their souls for a more committed U.S. intervention, it would never come. At the time, Tibet, at least superficially, still ran its own government, but the Dalai Lama and Tibet's parliament, the Kashag, were caught in an awkward dance with the Communist Party as independence-minded Tibetans grew increasingly vocal.

For the decade since China had exerted authority over Tibetan territory, the Dalai Lama—openly recognized by Beijing as the most influential figure in Tibetan politics—had attempted to negotiate a compromise with the Chinese that would preserve independence. Their negotiations, now judged as a clumsy and naive attempt at international statesmanship, was set for failure by the signing of the Seventeen-Point Agreement in 1951. At the time, the agreement garnered support among Tibet's ruling class, but it sowed doubt in the broader Tibetan community, which feared the Kashag, by Ngabo's hand, had surrendered too much to meet Chinese demands. In the following eight years, the Dalai Lama and the Kashag were positioned precariously between Beijing and the Khampa revolt. "I felt as if I were standing between two volcanoes," wrote the Dalai Lama in his memoir, *My Land and My People,* "each likely to erupt at any moment." Whether Tibet would fully embrace Chinese rule or commit to full-scale armed resistance depended on the young Tenzin Gyatso, who stood as the only person able to effectively appeal to Tibet's masses.

Rumors had been spreading all winter that the Chinese planned to kidnap Tibet's twenty-three-year-old holy leader in order to secure his influence. On the evening of March 10, 1959, Lhasa's muddied streets came alive with protest. Thousands rioted outside the Dalai Lama's summer residence at Norbulinka, and sporadic confrontations erupted between the growing mob and local Chinese police, as well as several Tibetan bureaucratic elites who had fallen from trust. For nearly a week, the Dalai Lama holed up inside Norbulinka, apparently hoping to avoid choosing between revolution, which would surely end in gory defeat, or political submission, which would surely compromise the soul of Tibet. Many Tibetans, including Renzin's young father, armed themselves with pistols and old Enfield rifles obtained through Khampa channels and the Tibetan army's caches stored in the Potala Palace. As things heated up, at least one Tibetan official was dragged from his car and beaten to death at the palace gates.

The PLA reacted little at first. Soon, however, military officials began to see the potential for the uprising to spread far beyond the Lhasa Valley. By March 17, according to the Tibetan historian Tsering Shakya, the Chinese began shelling parts of the city in a campaign of intimidation. The streets around the Potala Palace were alternately ignited and swallowed by fiery explosions and flying debris, and when two shells exploded near Norbulinka's gates, the Dalai Lama's protectors decided he was no longer safe. Disguised as a peasant, the Dalai Lama was led on horseback from the palace through the braided streams of the Kyichu River by a convoy of several dozen guides.

Already threatened by internal criticism of his ill-envisioned Great Leap Forward, Mao had little patience for instability on the frontier. Over the fifteen days it took the Dalai Lama's group to cross clandestinely through the high snowy passes of southern Tibet and the Himalayas into India, the PLA brought its hammer down on the Tibetan resistance. Loudspeakers were installed throughout Lhasa; when crowds formed, they were warned to disperse, and when they did not, the PLA descended swiftly. Norbulinka was razed by mortars even though the Dalai Lama was believed to be inside. The Potala Palace was captured, and on March 23, the five-star red flag of China was raised over the towering earth-red roof of the Potala for the first time. Ten thousand Tibetans were killed. More than four thousand were arrested, and weapons, including machine guns and mortar launches, were seized. "The streets were littered with corpses," Shakya wrote, "some of which had been there for days and were mauled by stray dogs." On March 28, Chinese premier Zhou Enlai declared the Seventeen-Point Agreement, and whatever limited political "autonomy" it had promised the Tibetan people, null as a result of the revolt. A state of martial law was imposed; it would more or less continue over the next five decades. Renzin was born a few months later.

HAVING LEFT MONASTIC LIFE, RENZIN S FATHER MARRIED, AND SOON took a second wife, Renzin's mother. The family lived on the ground floor of a traditional Tibetan building near the heart of the Barkhor, in Lhasa's Kirey district. They kept a simple home—three rooms with a dirt floor and weathered wooden windowpanes that looked out onto the roads that wound into the busy labyrinth of the Barkhor and Jokhang Temple. It was a small neighborhood, nestling a suitably small monastery and enlivened with gardens and grazing animals. Nearby there was a large pond at which their animals could drink.

The family was privileged but not rich, on par with some of the Tibetan elite and old ruling class. Throughout their living space, Renzin's father stored the vats he used in his textile-dying business: he bought rolls of fabric, woven from sheep's wool, and soaked them in drums of natural dyes carted north from Nepal and the plains of India. It was a good business—Tibetans, the few that had money, devoured the playfully colorful products of their southern neighbors, whether red and orange textiles or chewing gum. Because of this, and his father's status as a resident alien, Renzin's childhood was sheltered. Still, his mother, a full Tibetan citizen, was forced to sweep the streets, and taken for days at a time for hard labor. The PLA troops violently ransacked homes. And perhaps more than anything, he remembered not having enough food. But this was not the worst fate to befall Tibetans.

The Great Leap Forward had paralyzed most of China in the early 1960s, but in Tibet much of the annihilation that would hit other agricultural provinces had already occurred. As a result of the Democratic Reform campaign of late 1959, between a third and half of the population was imprisoned, monasteries and landowners were entirely dispossessed, all property was confiscated, and individual liberties were removed. The Great Leap years ravaged China, and they were equally catastrophic in Tibet, but it was the reforms specific to Tibet, not Mao's broader policies, that exacted the greatest toll. When China collectivized Tibet's agriculture, nomads and villagers alike were forced into communes where they would work the same land and share what remained of the harvests after half was shipped off to feed the army. Mao's game was supposed to foster a technological revolution—a strategic change that would help unite China's immense population and produce more food than they had ever known. Overnight, China would be transformed into an industrial society to rival Europe and the United States. Instead, the Chinese almost uniformly killed their fields or left bountiful crops to rot unharvested—and starved, at least in the hinterland.

In Tibet, the people paid to feed their occupiers, a different story, though equally tragic. Tibetan land is arid; the soil is thin and the ecosystem delicate. Traditionally, Tibetans farmed barley—a crop that comprised one of their primary foods, *tsampa*—which they seeded in the brief wet spring so that it would mature as the earth dried and the weather chilled. There was one crop planting a year. But the Great Leap Forward emphasized rice and, in Tibet especially, winter wheat. With the establishment of the communes, planting and tending was

centralized and formalized; alternating shifts of workers spent sixteen hours in the fields, sowing seeds close together and scheduling
three crop rotations a year instead of one. It could have stressed the
land beyond use; it did, catastrophically, in much of the rest of China,
plunging the country into famine. Instead, Tibetans harvested bumper
crops.

The army, though, took almost all of it, consuming it themselves
or shipping the grain eastward to feed the starving Han. In the Tibetan
countryside, villagers who worked the camps did not have enough to
feed themselves, and they too, though surrounded by bountiful
fields, began to starve. Prisoners—the tens of thousands near Golmud, those forced to mine borax on the plateau, and those locked in
Lhasa's own jails—were reduced to picking through sewage for undi-
gested scraps. In Lhasa's Drapchi prison, 1,400 of its 1,700 inmates
starved to death between November 1960 and June 1961. In the city,
where Renzin's family and others depended on credits that they
earned from nonagricultural communal work to "buy" rations, the
supply shelves were empty. "Tibetans had butter which they packed
in sheepskin, but there was not enough food," Renzin recalled. "So
people just ate that sheepskin, the dry leathery shell. Even I ate it."

When Renzin's neighbors ran out of money to buy food, they ate
their animals. When they ran out of animals, they climbed the rafters
for swallows. And when the swallows were gone, they chewed on boot
leather and belts, or they died. Renzin's family rationed the grain they
could buy from the Chinese—they were allowed to buy more than
the typical ration because of their alien status—and they survived.
"For a long time there were no birds in Lhasa," he said. "There were
no mice, no dogs. Nothing but people." Reprieve came through the
monthly visits of a family friend who worked in the countryside. She
would smuggle an orange underneath her clothes, sneaking it past

the PLA troops at the checkpoints. "They were very tiny but smelled so good," he said, remembering how the fruit would be torn up and shared among maybe a dozen people. "It was just one piece, but it was so delicious."

While Tibetans suffered from food shortages, bureaucrats in central China, loath to admit their failures, misrepresented the agricultural plan's achievements. Before official visits, the army was said to have planted fresh rows of healthy crops along the roadsides so that Mao's court would see only success. Harvests were exaggerated across all of China's territory, leading the cental government to believe, at least for a short time, that its policies were effective. In central China it is estimated that as many as 40 million people died. While China's exports of grains continued to increase, the country experienced the largest single famine in world history.

The rest of China emerged from the Great Leap Forward in the early 1960s in a series of quick policy reversals, but the reforms that dictated communal farming, and the shortages, persisted in Tibet. Meanwhile, Renzin's family was drawn into forced labor projects, they only slowly found more food, and conditions seemed to only get worse. PLA officers would show up at the family's door to take his mother for road construction projects and other infrastructure, including the Nga-chen power station, China's first hydropower development in Tibet. Like thousands of conscripted workers she was made to dig holes, or break rocks with sledgehammers. Sometimes Renzin, a baby, would be strapped to her back in a cotton sling while she worked. "They had a very hard life," Renzin said of his parents. "Many Tibetans had to work by force." In the evenings, political reeducation engulfed Lhasa, and the rest of Tibet, and his parents were required to attend meetings and study sessions. After a twelve-hour stint on some construction site, hundreds of people would be corralled into an auditorium and lectured for as long as eight more hours on the virtues of communism and the evils of self-interest. The routine lasted for the next twenty years—straight through the Cultural Revolution.

In those years, there was a steady flight of Tibetans across the border to Nepal and then to India; the International Campaign for Tibet puts the number of Tibetan refugees in India in 1960 at more than sixty thousand, and the Red Cross estimates another ten thousand crossed the border in search of asylum that year. But fleeing Tibet was becoming increasingly difficult, and eventually became impossible. Aside from the perils of traversing the world's greatest mountain range, usually on foot, those who were caught at the border often faced imprisonment, even execution. But those who stayed faced the wrath of the Cultural Revolution.

Though the Democratic Reforms had already eviscerated much of Tibet, the onset of the Cultural Revolution also brought a systematic erasure of all that was artistic, ethnic, and Buddhist, perhaps the most ruthless application of Mao's policies in all of China. The revolution's most ardent implementers came in waves of bureaucratic staff postings. When the Red Guards—the most zealous interpreters of Mao's edict to reboot the cultural and religious memory of society— arrived in Lhasa, they issued pamphlets that stated, among a long list, that religious festivals would be abolished; *mani* worship walls, prayer flags, and incense burners would be destroyed; no prayers would be recited; no circumambulation or prostrations or other religious rituals would be performed; monasteries and temples would be taken for public use; and monks and nuns "should be allowed to abandon their religious duties and vows."

Among Renzin's most vivid childhood memories was an afternoon walk home from his school, which was on the far side of what is now

Beijing Road, to the north of his Kirey neighborhood. In the constricted cobblestone alleyways of old Lhasa, there was scarcely room to pass, and so when Renzin and his group of young friends came upon a circle of Red Guard militia men dressed in PLA uniforms, they had little choice but to approach cautiously. As they did, a stone Buddha smashed to pieces and showered their feet. A mournful man fell to his knees, and in a doorway a woman was handing off other sacred objects—another statue, some jeweled pottery. "I tried to look these men in the face," he said. "Who are these people? I was very angry."

It was 1966—four years after the worst of the famine—when the Red Guard began its door-to-door campaign searching for Buddha statues, mandala paintings, other religious artifacts—anything that represented the old society. They would demand the men of the house carry their own belongings into the street, and then force the men to destroy them in front of the officers. The purge was meant not only to rid Tibet of its culture but to humiliate and degrade its residents. "This went on for a long time," Renzin recalled. Down the street from his house, where a Bank of China branch stands today, the army used the small pond as a dump. "Many trucks would arrive there every day. There they would smash more statues and everything from people's private houses, filling the pond. We used to go there, as kids, and hunt through it. It was not garbage, what was in there. People found corals, or valuable stones or religious crafts."

Renzin's home was spared this ruthless routing, and, a safe haven of sorts, it became the neighborhood deposit for the most prized cultural artifacts. "My father's friends would bring us their statues—Avalokiteshvara, the Buddha of compassion. We would hide them in closets. Soon we had a room full of items, because people believed they were safe in our house," he said. And beginning around that time, there was a steady flow of antiquities into Nepal and India, carried by the people walking into exile, in the hopes of saving whatever genuine objects of Tibet's religious and cultural heritage they could. Even today these statues can be found in Kathmandu.

Others had it much worse. Sonam Yeshi lived in Drongba County west of Shigatze, a few hundred miles west of Lhasa. By the time he told his story, his hair had turned whitish-gray and his broad smile revealed a toothy grin, with more than half of those teeth missing. Thirteen years old when the Dalai Lama fled Tibet, Sonam was brought to tears recalling the first decades of the occupation. In the old days, his family owned more than a hundred yaks that spread over nearly a thousand mu, the Chinese measure for land roughly equal to a quarter of an acre. His family was portrayed by the Chinese as part of a brutal ruling class that relied on teams of peasant Tibetan servants—something Sonam, though he acknowledged his wealth, said was untrue.

During the uprising in the spring of 1959, Sonam's father was in Lhasa. Whether he actively fought against the Chinese or merely joined the thousands who mobbed the city was unknown, but he was killed there that March. Sonam worked his father's land as long as he could. But then, Sonam explained, "the Chinese said we were land-lords, and we were oppressing people." His family's wealth was confiscated and redistributed to his village and to the Chinese officers who were stationed there, and his land was donated to the communes. Around his county, monasteries were burned and monks arrested or sent to the farm groups. He thought he had lost everything, but the Chinese took more. The Red Guards came, and investigated everyone's family roots. They connected his family with the man who had died in Lhasa, branded his father a counterrevolutionary, and arrested his mother and his uncle. Together with seven other people, they were tied to wooden poles at the dusty intersection of two roads at the center of their village, a place called Chuksong, and were tortured. "They were beaten to death in public," Tenzin said. "I was there. I was nineteen." Shortly afterward, another uncle fled to India and his sister was arrested by the Chinese and sent to prison. It was a wholly typical experience.

According to the U.S. State Department's 1966 Country Report, China "continued to commit widespread human rights abuses in Tibet, including instances of death and detention, torture, arbitrary arrests . . . [and] long detentions of Tibetan nationalists for peacefully expressing their religious and political views." One Communist Party cadre, asking for permission to be more lenient in his persecutions, vividly documented the treatment of Tibetans: "In the course of the struggle, extremely barbarous methods of fascism were adopted . . . Torture was used . . . scorching the body and head with fire, feeding human excreta and cattle and horse dung, muzzling the mouth with a horse bit, etc. . . . Nine people were crippled. Several had most of their hair pulled out . . . the dead included one expectant mother."

EVEN IN THESE YEARS, THE CENTRAL GOVERNMENT IN BEIJING REMAINED focused on a railway to Tibet. Nineteen sixty-six was the year that Cheng Guodong, who would become one of the leading geologic scientists on the railway project, first came to Lhasa. By his account, though, it was a different place entirely.

Part of the last class of students to graduate with a formal scientific education before the beginning of the Cultural Revolution, Cheng had graduated a year earlier from the University of Geosciences. Mao had issued a call for young educated people to move west to work in China's countryside or mountainous regions and help build a stronger national economic and social fabric for the Communist

Party. He called it the Third Front—a precursor to the twenty-first century's Go West initiative.

Cheng, a twenty-three-year-old from a suburb of Shanghai, was eager for work and romanced by the possibilities. He shipped to Lanzhou, where he joined the Institute of Desert Research, a program of the Chinese Academy of Sciences, as a junior researcher assigned to study the frozen soils and prepare a knowledge base for constructing a railway in Tibet—then a consistently stated goal but still a loosely defined project. The institute's research was unique; most Third Front settlements focused on industrialization and hard labor in collectivized factories. For the most part, intellectual pursuits— things like research—remained scorned in the rhetoric of the revolution. But early on, the government had recognized the exceptional challenges of Tibet's environment. Since it contained the headwaters of three of the country's greatest rivers, controlling, or at least understanding, the mud flows and thawing of the glaciers on the plateau was paramount. Beijing also understood, from the building of the Qinghai-Tibet Highway eleven years earlier, that the permafrost was the greatest obstacle to normalizing transportation between Tibet and the rest of China. After less than twelve months in Lanzhou, which Cheng called "just a small village on the Yellow River," he was sent to Tibet, knowing little about where he was headed.

"We learned it was an enormous region in China, a plateau, and that there are some special animals on the plateau," he said matter-of-factly. "We did learn about the history—that Tibet became a part of China in the Qing dynasty. In the Cultural Revolution there were newspapers in every province but their contents were nearly the same. You could not learn much." Cheng was stationed on the Tibetan Plateau for six months that first year. He was paid about sixty yuan per month—or a little more than seven dollars—enough to afford middle-class niceties. The posting was a privileged retreat from the hardships plaguing much of central China. "I was so lucky at that time. There were about thirty people doing this work," he said. "And we could get things we could not get in the city—like canned food. There was such a shortage, even if you had money you could not buy it." He had just a faint sense of the violence taking place in the villages and towns around him.

Later that year he made a visit to Lhasa, which he described as "pretty much like Lanzhou at the time—a poor village." Hotels were scarce, and they stayed in a simple government-run dorm. There were few streets, and those that existed were in extraordinarily rough condition, barely passable. A strong Nepali presence asserted itself; Cheng knew of a commercial area with "smuggled" goods from the south, including the thrilling sight of good-quality wool and burly mountain sweaters—items you could not get in China—and portraits of Nepal's King Birendra on the walls. "The common people, they looked very poor; their clothes were very bad," he said. "But after the change to a socialist society, well, I think the common Tibetan people were very, very happy. Before that they were just slaves. The only people who were not happy were the top class, because they had lost their social power."

THOUGH ABSENT FROM CHENG S ACCOUNT OF LHASA, ESCALATING POLITical and militia conflicts threatened to overwhelm Tibet in the 1960s. Lhasa was descending into an anarchy China could barely control. In Beijing, the Communist Party splintered over how stringently to enforce the orthodoxy of the Cultural Revolution, which in Tibet approached a state of unruly party civil war that had little to do with the Tibetans. Allegiances divided three ways: an extreme political arm

including the Red Guard; a faction maintaining a more liberal interpretation of the revolution; and the military, which seemed to keep
the coolest heads of all.

Tibetan recruits to the Party, many of whom had pledged loyalty
to Beijing and the socialist values of the Cultural Revolution, grew
drunk with their totemic position in the power struggle. They wielded
their freshly assigned authority against other Tibetans, assaulting
civilians, razing temples, and banging on doors to collect relics in a
vigilante militia. As their political gamesmanship devolved into brute
physical conflict, they started shooting, one devout communist faction against another. All farming and productive work stopped—even
the "educational" lectures came to a halt. The local government of
the Tibet Autonomous Region ceased to operate on any meaningful
level. Some of the worst atrocities occurred inside the Barkhor.

In the same alleyway as Renzin's house, a large estate, owned by
an upper-class family that he believed to be sympathetic to the Red
Guards, posted a sentry. At the roof's corners, stacks of sandbags sheltered him, though often the steel barrel of his gun poked above the
makeshift wall. Across the way, a monastery with a towering white
perimeter wall that was also fortified with sandbags had been co-opted
by a group from an opposing faction. A loudspeaker broadcast political views from the monastery onto the businesses of the Kirey. The
two sides waged a battle, and the temple compound was overtaken.
"All night you could hear explosions somewhere—big bangs, you
know," Renzin said. Fighting between the compound and the house
across the alley was common after that. On mellower days, the militia
wrapped stones into a braided woolen sling, the type herders used on
yaks, and fired the stones across the street and through the windows
of the big house. The other days, mortar fire volleyed back and forth.

One afternoon, Renzin got caught in the middle. He was walking down the slender alley, ten feet across at most, and was just a hundred yards from his own door, when a motorcycle with two men approached from the opposite direction. Alarmed by the passing bike, the sentry opened fire. Bullets ricocheted off the rounded stones of the path and sliced into the mud and mortar of the buildings' walls, spraying debris that stung Renzin's cheeks. People ran for cover. As the motorcycle skidded sideways, he was covered with darkness. An older woman had grabbed his waist like a sack of grain and smothered his view with her woolen *chuba*. She whisked him into a doorway, where they listened to the ongoing gunfight outside in safety.

A few months later, in early 1970, Renzin found himself in another sort of crossfire. Some boys from his neighborhood had scrawled a criticism of Chairman Mao in shit across the wall of a public latrine. The People's Security Bureau, or state police, were outraged, but had no idea who the culprits were, and so they began a round-up of neighborhood children. For weeks, Lhasa youth were collected, questioned in private, and required to attend daily political education lectures. Among those detained was Renzin's seven-year-old brother. Finally, police announced they had found the culprit—a young Nepali boy, one of Renzin's friends, who was just twelve. A public meeting was convened and the boy was seated on a stage before a hundred or so people for what Tibetans call a *tamzing,* or struggle session. *Tamzing* had been used to torture and publicly humiliate thousands of Tibetans since 1959, including, at one point, the Panchen Lama. Many were executed in the process. For hours the boy was verbally berated and flogged with ropes, stones, and rolled-up newspapers. None of the Tibetans believed the child was the real culprit, but someone said he was, and the Chinese demanded punishment. Because the boy was Nepali, Renzin's father grew frightened that Nepalis would serve as scapegoats if and when the conflicts between the Chinese and Tibetans worsened. "You could not prove that you did or did not do something," Renzin explained. "If somebody blamed you, then it was finished."

One night the next week Renzin and his brothers—who under normal conditions were not allowed to pass the checkpoints at the city limits—were sent to a small village in the hills above Lhasa. They remained there at a friend's farm until their father could make legal arrangements to take the children to Nepal. It took several weeks before the necessary permits were successfully filed with the Chinese police and arrangements were made for a truck to take them legally over the border. As the snow began to fall on the mountains in the late autumn, the men of Renzin's family clambered into the back of an open flatbed army truck, sitting on top of their own bags but cowering beneath a broad canvas tarp, and set out for the distant southern end of the steppe. It took the truck two weeks to trace the perilous mountain roads to Shigatze and on to the border. They passed under the cascading ice fields of Shishapangma, a towering mountain with a twenty-six-thousand-foot summit—the fourteenth highest in the world—and then down through the chasms of the Himalayas. After two weeks, tired and hungry, Renzin crossed into exile over the Friendship Bridge in the lush jungle-like Nepali border station of Kodari.

Over the next four years, much of the chaos that came before and with the Cultural Revolution subsided, but a vacuum replaced it. Nearly all of Tibet's six thousand monasteries—not just in Lhasa but in every hill station and small village from the far east to the far west—had been destroyed. The precious stones and metals from the noble Buddhas of centuries-old temples were dismantled and shipped east, for sale in Beijing, or simply chiseled and melted down. Acccording to the Tibetan government-in-exile, more than 1.2 million people died. Monks—the religious and intellectual core of Tibetan society—had all but disappeared. All religious practice, from meditation to the carrying of pictures of the Dalai Lama, was forbidden. "The effect," wrote Shakya, "was to destroy Tibet's separate identity. The Chinese now propagated a policy of total assimilation." Tibet fell under the refreshingly stable but strict control of the military, communal farming was renewed with a fresh vigor that exacerbated many of the ecological and cultural problems of the Great Leap, and Tibetans, subservient, suffered. "To all intents and purposes, Tibet had . . . ceased to have any distinctive characteristics."

DESPITE THE MAYHEM IN LHASA, BY 1975 CHENG HAD RETURNED TO THE Tibetan Plateau. In the nearly ten years since his first posting with the Chinese Academy of Sciences in Lanzhou, he had been promoted and was quickly emerging as one of the foremost researchers on frozen soils in the world. On this trip, he was leading an expedition south from Qinghai to the plains east of the Qinghai-Tibet Highway. His mission: to learn more about the permafrost and establish a viable route for a railway to Lhasa.

In a tangible way, Cheng's task was the next phase in what he liked to think of as Tibet's "liberation." But that was political talk—and he tried to avoid it. The researchers would be deep in Tibet's rural wilderness, far from Lhasa or even most of the monasteries and villages that were hobbled by the Democratic Reforms and then the haphazard implementation of Cultural Revolution edicts. "We didn't think too much about where this railway was located, or what its pretense was," Cheng said. "It was only a project—an engineering project." Twenty-four months earlier, Mao had made his high-profile promise to Nepal's king and for the first time, it seemed the train to Lhasa had serious backing. Construction crews were already starting work on the segment from Xining to Golmud.

Short and stout but with a boyish, round face and a thick mop of black hair, Cheng was an energetic young scientist. The clothes he wore were loose—faded green army fatigues that sagged around the tops of his heavy black boots and a matching oversized canvas jacket. Part professor and part expedition guide, he didn't look like a person of authority, yet he was put in command of a convoy of trucks and about twenty even younger engineers eager for their own chance to break free of the dreary labor of the Cultural Revolution.

On March 25, the trucks headed onto the plateau via the Qinghai-Tibet Highway. The freight haulers carried the research equipment and canned and packaged rations for their three-month stay. The engineers crowded into one large van, an ambulance manufactured in the 1950s with a couple of benches lining the walls. To fit the whole group, Cheng had the seats ripped out, and the men found space among odd boxes of gear and supplies on the cold corrugated metal floor. The best seats were on the wheel wells or on top of bags of rice. And one such spot, on a wooden crate full of dynamite, was claimed by a lanky new recruit from China's northeast, Zhang Luxin.

The route from Lanzhou to the Tibetan Plateau was circuitous—first heading north to Xining, then west to Golmud, then south over the Kunlun Mountain Pass. On the way they ate cold flour pancakes that had been cooked and wrapped before they left. The country was still straining to muster food supplies, and so the engineers, though government-funded, subsisted on modest rations. They had some pickled vegetables and a half-kilo-per-person allotment of pork. Occasionally, the group would stop at a military outpost and solicit water or more food. In Golmud, along the city's single dirt street, they stocked up on bags of Chinese bread. But there were no other places to stop along the way to Tibet.

Their first rest after Golmud was a truck stop named Wudaoliang—a short strip of sparse buildings huddled on a gently sloping plain a few hours past the craggy Kunlun Pass. The group had finally arrived on the plateau, and the first experience it offered them was foreboding. At a temporary military outpost, the men spilled out the back door of the old ambulance, convulsing with coldness and each suffering the throbbing oppression of altitude sickness. The air was thick with clouds, and the moisture instantly penetrated the cotton shells of their uniforms. That night, they made beds of cut grass topped with a thin carpet, but altitude sickness kept most of them from getting any rest. The next morning, the convoy inched along the road that passed for a highway—then just a thin rutted set of dirt tracks that periodically faded into unmarked fields of grass. The going was rougher than most of them had expected, and passing a few miles could take hours. The bread and pancakes were used up by day two. Even after three days at heights approaching sixteen thousand feet, the altitude did not relieve its stranglehold on their sleep patterns. Seven days into their expedition and three days after leaving Golmud's plains, just as a blistering snowstorm set in, they reached the place where they would camp, in the heart of the permafrost terrain near the village of Yanshiping. The boundless intellectuals had been whittled to stiff, hypothermic, hungry, exhausted troops in little more than a week. And now there was work to be done.

Zhang had never before set up a tent. He pulled at the broad sheets of nylon and canvas and the wind whipped it from his grasp. He clumsily chased down poles as they cartwheeled across the grassland. When the structures were finally set up the men huddled inside—ten people in a space barely twelve feet wide. They were happy for the respite from the howling wind and biting cold. Finally, sleep besieged them. "The next day we woke up with the roof blown off," Zhang said. "We were covered in snow." He tried to find motivation in these agonizing experiences—and built them up until he could feel heroic. "I was determined to become somebody. I knew that to become great, to become recognized, you have to endure this hardship."

Cheng, though, was far less histrionic, and far less affected by the brusque greeting of the wild landscape. Zhang, miserable, stumbled upon his team leader's tent that morning to find the senior engineer quietly engrossed in a book. "Despite all this hardship he was actually reading," Zhang recalled incredulously. The older man softly admonished him. "'Little Zhang,' he said to me. 'You have to remember who you are; to be a scientist, never stop studying.'"

Navigating from a crude map and the sliver of highway, Cheng's goup drifted eastward over the next few weeks—exploring for a right-of-way that would prove more passable for a train. Each day, loaded into a huge military truck, the team would strike out across the flat expanse of grassland. The truck's cab—rounded like a World War II–era Buick and with a split flat-glass windshield, sat just two or three people, so the others would climb up the three-inch treads of the tires and install themselves into the back bed for a long, open-air ride.

But the grassland was anything but flat. The grass on the plateau grows in hearty tufts and is as stiff as bamboo—the only vegetation resilient enough to grow in the punishing environment. The truck tires would roll up over them like a boulder and crash back down the other side, putting the passengers into a brief flight before a cruel landing on their hard seats. When they entered wetlands or thawing sections of permafrost, the truck could get bogged down to its axles—the five-foot-tall tires nearly submerged—forcing everyone to unload and spend hours digging the multiton vehicle back out. When they came to a river, the men would collect and pile stones to create a raised bed for the tires, and then stand in the icy current, pant legs rolled up, marking the route as the truck ground its way across the water. Cheng reported that the scientists spent as much time managing the truck's journey as they spent conducting research.

The research they did get to do consisted of digging pits in the earth to study the frozen soil layers and drilling core samples that could be hauled back to camp. There the dirt was weighed for water content and the data carefully cataloged by location, as precisely as could be identified based on the available maps and the scientists' calculations. The data were plotted onto a map—the result of which was the first-ever comprehensive recording of permafrost conditions on the Tibetan Plateau, for which Cheng would eventually earn international recognition. Later they would conduct crude pressure tests on the frozen sections to try to determine the weight-bearing capacity of the permafrost. If it could barely support their truck, could it ever support a train?

After the team had deduced the general properties of the frozen ground, its members were dispatched to explore vast areas that remained inaccessible by truck. Much like the pioneers who scoured the American West on foot in the 1860s looking for places for the Central Pacific to pass, the engineers, including Zhang, were tasked with finding the grade of least resistance over the Tibetan Plateau. Sometimes they would borrow yaks from nearby Tibetan settlements, straddling the furry beasts bareback. Other times they were forced to walk, covering tens, even hundreds, of miles over the course of a trip. Once, on a trek near the Tangu La Pass, in a roadless area the engineers labeled a "no-man's-land," Zhang was convinced he was going to die.

He had been walking for six hours. His flat-soled, Ked-like shoes, the standard issue from the Chinese military, did not provide much support for hiking on the frozen tundra. Water was seeping freely through the uncoated canvas, and his feet had grown swollen and blistered. A few yards behind him, a colleague trudged, faltering over the stiff straw. The two had stopped talking to each other hours earlier when the tattered hand-drawn map they were using began to lead to more arguments than landmarks. Besides, the tearing wind made it almost impossible to hear.

As Zhang told it, the map showed a large valley where in fact a mountain had stood. More likely, he misread the topographical elevation lines and confused the drawing of a hillside for one of a depression—a common mistake, especially for someone not well versed in the rigors of mountain travel. In any case, the pair walked confidently, perhaps eighteen miles or so, in the wrong direction. Along the way they devoured the two slivers of pork they each carried, and most of their water. After all, a hot meal would be waiting in the mess tent that should have been just over the next gradual rise. But eventually they accepted that they were desperately lost.

Zhang was just a kid—twenty-seven years old on the first real adventure of his life. His superior, Cheng, described him irreverently as "not so impressive, just an average member of the group." His hair was still jet-black and smooth, his face boyish, and with his eyeglasses, he looked bookish. He wore a wool sweater, cotton canvas jacket, and a plastic poncho. Except for the lightweight cotton rucksack containing a shovel and a hammer that was slung over his shoulder, he appeared ill-prepared for the wilderness—not hardy enough.

The two men agreed to turn back just as a storm was blowing in off the glaciered peaks at the end of the valley. Exhausted and hungry, Zhang's mind drifted. He thought of his wife, still in the north country, near Harbin. They had been married just ten months and yet he was living here, more than two thousand miles away. How had he gotten here, he wondered, almost aloud. Of course, it was because he was ambitious and still trying to prove his worth, which in those days meant giving to the larger-than-life purpose of the Party. But he also reminded himself that despite his grand ambitions, there was the ugly fact that he had very few choices. Had he known at that moment that it would be almost three more years before he would see his wife again, he may have simply succumbed to the cold and snow and the hopelessness he felt. Instead he looked forward to a return east that fall.

There were times that summer when Zhang felt empowered by this new experience, inspired to be involved in a project of such importance and magnitude. The plateau, when it was not so inhospitable, was breathtaking. Zhang described it as "blue sky, white clouds, and green grass—very idyllic." It was the first place in years where he felt free enough to read a book without disguising it within the red covers of one of Mao's policy manifestos—the only approved intellectual indulgence. At moments during the ordeal, he mused over his acquaintance with a young Tibetan man who would linger around their camp watching the curious soil tests; the man would bring dried patties of yak dung as gifts to be used for fuel and began to sell yak milk to the camp, even though the engineers would complain that it was so thick it made them sick.

On that cold, hopeless march back to the camp, Zhang ruminated on the plateau at its worst. The labor was hard and the scientists did the dirty work themselves. Food was always scarce. Once they ran out of meat and turned to an old flank of mutton coated in a loose layer of green film. "It makes me feel pain to think about the food we had," he said. "We cut away the bad part and boiled the mutton several times before we ate it. There was no taste left in it at all." As they trudged on, nearly directionless, the sour experiences flooded back to him, and one way or another he wanted off the plateau. The Qinghai-Tibet Highway was the only sign of modern civilization, if you could call it that, within five hundred miles. If they could find it, they might have a chance to survive.

Back at the camp, Cheng's group had already grown alarmed at the young scientists' disappearance and organized a search party. The winds and rain that afternoon turned ferocious, and after some time Zhang and his comrade stopped wandering and hunkered down on the open plain under their plastic coats. As rain turned to ice, and then to snow, they sat close and prayed that the couple of sweets and the bite of bread that was left would bring an end to their uncontrollable shivering. Night fell, and with frozen fingers that worked about as nimbly as bricks, Zhang tried to tear a small cardboard matchbox and the map into little pieces and light them with three soggy matchsticks. "We could not shout anymore," he said. "We had no strength." And then, as the shivering subsided and he drifted in and out of a hypothermic sleep, he saw a flashlight bouncing across the meadow in the distance. Unable to speak, he lit his final match, creating a flash of light in the still darkness that brought Cheng's party to their rescue.

When he looked back on the decades leading to the groundbreaking for the Qinghai-Tibet Railway at Nanshankou in June 2001, it was this agony that Zhang Luxin remembered. But all across China in those years, men were sent off on fantastic projects, often without logic or much support. Some were assigned to work in machine factories in desolate northwest provinces as part of the Third Front initiative; others were relegated to digging underground bunkers in preparation for an attack from Russia that never came. Projects came and went with the great visions—the Great Leap was born of like intentions. In certain ways, Zhang and his fellow engineers developed a commonality with the Tibetans: they were prisoners of the time, cogs in China's impersonal, fits-and-starts machine of development.

Two years later, one day in 1978, Cheng Guodong received news that the Tibet railway project was finished. Construction was nearly completed to Golmud, but no one had continued past it, and it appeared no one would. Mao Zedong had died, and the country was virtually bankrupt. Cheng never heard of a cancellation in concrete terms. He simply learned that he would no longer be receiving funding for the next leg of his research. For the time being, it looked as if all that Cheng's group had suffered and accomplished in those years would simply fade away. Tibetans, for their part, could only hope for as much.

PART II

GO WEST

We were over the edge, way past the old Chinese frontier, four days at least from civilization and its vast stinking cities. . . . The Kunlun Range is a guarantee that the railway will never get to Lhasa. That is probably a good thing. I thought I liked railways until I saw Tibet, and then I realized that I liked wilderness much more.

—Paul Theroux, *Riding the Iron Rooster*

If the valley is reached by a high pass, only the best friends, or worst enemies, are visitors.

—Tibetan proverb

5

MOVING HEAVEN AND EARTH

IT WAS 11:00 P.M. WHEN THE PHONE RANG IN DR. HAN MEI'S modest fourth-floor Golmud apartment. Awakened, she stumbled from her single bed, pushed aside the cotton Tibetan door curtain, and groped her way across the bare concrete floor to the handset, mounted between flecks of paint above an old Russian-made refrigerator. On the other line, apologetic, was her boss, the dean of the Golmud People's Hospital, where Han was a chief physician—and one of just two doctors who had experience with high-altitude medicine. The Ministry of Railways was in the midst of its first minor crisis on the Qinghai-Tibet Railway construction project. In June 2001, roughly three thousand workers were already stationed high on the plateau— they had been there since mere days after the project's approval in February—and they were threatening to walk off the job. Despite Zhang Luxin's promises about the livable conditions in Tibet, the first wave of immigrant labor was finding the region inhospitable, bordering on painful.

It was cold—the average temperature sat around twenty-eight degrees Fahrenheit—and often wet. Worse, however, was the mountain altitude, which was making workers sick at an alarming rate. The ministries' doctors were ill-prepared to diagnose or treat pulmonary edema, or altitude sickness. On the phone, the dean briefed Han on one particularly bad case that had set off the workers. Han's boss wanted her to take a post on the plateau, beginning as soon as she could pack her things.

Han stared out the black row of windows in her apartment—past a large poster of the Potala Palace and a photograph of her namesake flowers, pink plum blossoms on a branch—into the space where daylight would soon reveal the distant Kunlun Mountains rising above the Tsaidam plain. It was a bad time for Han to be away from home. But then again, the plateau held a certain allure, especially for her. Dr. Han had been born on the Tibetan Plateau, just a short distance from where she would be stationed. And perhaps just as important, as a native Tibetan she was accustomed to the physiological effects of altitude and therefore excellently suited to help Chinese lowland workers cope with them.

Acute mountain sickness can plague people at random at elevations over eight thousand feet. For the most part, its symptoms do not discriminate based on physical fitness or previous experience, say, climbing a peak at high elevation. When a person ascends too quickly, as he would in climbing the Tibetan Plateau by car in just a few hours, the growing lack of oxygen changes the chemical balance of the body. Shortness of breath indicates that not enough oxygen is reaching the tissues and that the amount of carbon dioxide in the blood is increasing, which then stresses the lymph nodes and leads to, among other things, the swelling called edema. You know you are suffering the effects of altitude when the frontal lobes of your brain start a coordinated drum solo with the base of your skull. Your chest can feel like it is bearing the weight of a cinder block, and no matter how quickly you suck in the air, your muscles feel fatigue and the tips of your fingers can tingle with hypoxia, or mild suffocation. When it gets worse, the nausea comes, then a twinkling of stars in your peripheral vision, followed by a string of more serious conditions. As that stress on the body reaches intolerable levels, the brain swells, liquid collects in the respiratory tract, and victims are prone to heart attacks. Once the symptoms are identified, the most effective treatment of serious cases is an immediate descent to lower altitude. On most mountain slopes, getting to lower elevations is as simple as turning around and heading downhill. On the flat expanse of the plateau, the workers were trapped. Traveling to low terrain required many hours, even days, of travel.

The lore as well as the effects of acute mountain sickness had plagued every military campaign and construction project on the Tibetan Plateau since the 1950s. The Chinese are sure that their lowland citizens are especially sensitive to the high altitudes. Increasingly that spring, the workers began to believe that humans were simply not meant to exist on the plateau, and in part, they were correct. Medical studies show that Tibetans born at such elevations have a unique genetic ability to carry more oxygen in their blood—especially in their lungs. It seems that after hundreds of years, their physiology has adapted to compensate for the low air-based oxygen supply by delivering extra oxygen through the blood's flow (a phenomenon that American doctors are studying in order to develop drugs to treat erectile dysfunction). Other research suggests that the Chinese are particularly ill-equipped to adapt to high altitude compared to most lowland people, and so may not be misguided in their anxieties. A senior Chinese military doctor who had been stationed in Lhasa since the early

1990s reported that PLA research proved that living at a high altitude had a long-term negative effect on the soldiers' life expectancy: in general, they could expect to die a year earlier for every decade their bodies coped with the effects of altitude. "In the first few years there is a very high percentage that someone who goes back will have a stroke, and some have died," he said. Ethnic Chinese women living in Lhasa had long been known to travel back to the lowlands for their pregnancies, for fear of delivering a brain-damaged baby. Some of the workers knew this, and they knew about the thousands who had died during the road-building projects of the 1950s. Those stories transformed the normal fogginess and laziness that descended on them at high altitude into terrifying concern.

Yet when the Ministry of Railways created its plan to bring tens of thousands of eastern Chinese onto the plateau for the difficult and demanding job of building the track, it did not prepare fully for the health risks to the workers. Its own medical staff—the only doctors available, besides Dr. Han, for five hundred miles—were prepared to treat only the simplest of maladies. "Most of the doctors aren't familiar with illnesses on the plateau," said Han. "They lack experience, knowledge of precautions, and exposure." Among their chief prescriptions: think happy thoughts, and that headache will float away.

On May 27, a few weeks before the ribbon-cutting ceremony, a promising twenty-six-year-old engineer named Wei Junchang complained to his superiors of extraordinary fatigue. Wei was stationed in the remote plateau stopover of Anduo, where he was leading a group of surveyors and designers for the third team of the First Railway Institute for the Ministry of Railways in mapping out the final route for the train. He told his superiors that night he didn't want to speak, let alone walk, which was necessary to do his job. Wei was a geology graduate of the prestigious Southwest Communications University, and since February, shortly after he learned that his wife was pregnant, he had been in Tibet. He was one of the first engineers to arrive after Beijing's Central Committee green-lighted the project, but until May he had worked at lower altitudes. His group had been completing a survey between the Kunlun Bridge on the northern slope of the Kunlun Pass, and Xidatan, a small strip of highway shops near Nanshankou. In the previous three months, he had worked at twelve thousand feet, at most. After a two-week vacation leave in lower-altitude Golmud, he was reassigned to work at Amdo, at nearly sixteen thousand feet.

Bed-bound, Wei became lethargic and complained of a loss of appetite—classic symptoms of altitude sickness. Yet it took three full days for his team leader to take him to a primitive first-aid center in a nearby county town for help. The doctor there, according to published accounts, had recently arrived from a small inland town and had never treated altitude sickness. He gave Wei oxygen and shot him full of antibiotics, but "didn't think it was too serious," and sent him back to camp. The following afternoon, Wei's condition suddenly deteriorated. He stopped speaking altogether and grew delirious. Only then, at the prompting of a concerned senior official for the Ministry of Railways, and four full days after Wei first fell ill, was it decided that he should be rushed to the PLA hospital in Golmud. The hospital was more than a ten-hour drive away, and getting there involved climbing over the Tangu La Pass, at seventeen thousand feet, as well as the Kunlun Pass. To make matters worse, no one with any medical experience was available to accompany Wei on the trip. He was loaded into the backseat of a Toyota Land Cruiser and set off on his journey.

By 7:30 p.m., just a few hours after the truck had left Amdo, the concerned official received a satellite telephone call from a small military camp in Yanshiping, a remote and frozen post high on the plateau just north of the Tangu La Pass, to inform him that Wei's condition had grown critical. His breathing sounded like he was blowing bubbles with a straw, and he had slipped into a coma. The driver was ordered to a small military hospital in Tuotuohe, an hour away. The doctors at the station frantically tried to help Wei, whose limbs were swollen and whose pupils were alarmingly enlarged. At 9:00 p.m. another satellite call was placed to Amdo—this time to report that the promising young engineer was dead.

Wei's death, and the apparent bungling of his treatment by railway officials and local doctors, sent a ripple of fear through the camps of already unsettled workers. A severe headache would incite panic, and the workers had little trust in their "doctors"—many of whom were complaining of exhaustion and nausea themselves. Work stalled and morale plummeted. By the second week of June, the reticent workers camped out on the high plateau, believing the harsh conditions and lack of medical expertise were endangering their lives, began refusing to work at all. The slowdown threatened crucial progress on the railway. "The leaders were extremely nervous," Han said, recounting the dean's phone call. "They needed above all else to make sure that the first period of the Tibet railway project would finish on time." The situation was all the more serious because the wave of workers who had arrived that spring was just a minuscule sampling of the large labor populations that would be needed to complete the project in the coming years. No one could change the risks presented by the environment on the plateau, but the operations had to be made safer.

THE RAILWAY S ROUTE, AT THAT TIME, REMAINED INVISIBLE SAVE FOR A few stakes flagged with fluorescent plastic tape. Besides the highway, the only other threads of infrastructure linking Golmud to Lhasa were an oil pipeline built in 1977 and a fiber-optic cable buried in 1999.

Telephone and electric wiring were sparse. Many towns along the way—those outposts that qualified for such a grand description—were still without local sources of water and relied on trucks to haul it in and deposit it in giant storage urns. With so little in place, the precise route for the train was still up for grabs. Though teams like Zhang Luxin's had worked a bit on the condition of the permafrost and proposed rough routes for the railway over the preceding decades, and though in general a link from Qinghai to Lhasa had been decided upon in February, nothing had been finalized.

In their decades on the plateau, the scientists' primary attention had stayed fixed on understanding the properties of the terrain and devising some technology that would allow the railway to be built on permafrost. They had not turned to mapping an actual design for the tracks—not only their placement but decisions about the specific materials that the construction would require. In the months between the project's green light and the groundbreaking, survey and design teams from the First Railway Institute had been literally walking the plateau, checking the hurriedly sketched plateau route as meticulously as possible in advance of the construction, slated to kick off in July. There was no time for the workers to adapt to the conditions. There was too much work to be done.

Two days after she accepted the assignment, Dr. Han arrived in the design team's plateau camp in Yanshiping, where she would live among them in a nylon tent for four months. The camp was simple: several rows of boxy green army tents surrounded by haphazardly parked freight and army trucks. There was a medical tent with supplies and an examination room, a canteen heated by an iron stove that burned dried yak dung, several meeting rooms, and monastic sleeping quarters. The camp lay on the shore of the Buqu River, a Yangtze tributary that meanders eastward until it reaches the steep gorges that drop it into Sichuan Province. To the north, the Kunlun ridge could be spotted on the skyline. Between the camp and the mountains stood a nearly overwhelming quantity of space. Han found the place exhilarating. Going about her duties, she felt inspired, by "the power of nature, the feeling of joy without realizing tiredness, the purification of soul, the consciousness of environment, and the dichotomy between human and nature."

Han is a small woman, about five feet, four inches tall with a feathery build. She likes to wear her shoulder-length hair, long ago grayed, in a ponytail that gives her a youthful look. Her features, kind and disarming, are neither distinctively ethnic Tibetan nor Chinese. She was born in a nomadic community near what would later become one of the high plateau's many truck stops, Wudaoliang, about six hours by truck from Yanshiping, in 1954. It was the same year the Qinghai-Tibet Highway construction was completed, a project that had marked the last profound change in the area and had transformed her home completely.

Originally given the Tibetan name Luoyang Zhouma, Han had been raised in the Chinese orphanage system. As she tells it, her mother had disappeared when she was still a baby, and her father died mysteriously when she was three years old. At the age of nine, she joined the many other Tibetan children in the institutional foster care system who had been separated from their parents because of poverty or, in some cases, because of political circumstances. Further, across Tibet in the early years of the occupation, John Avedon wrote, "intimidation and enforced socialization were abetted by the abduction of thousands of young children to be raised not as Tibetans in their own homes but as wards of the state in a newly-created network of minority schools." It was a primary school teacher who gave her the name Han Mei, "cold plum" in Mandarin, a term of affection for her persistence, since a Chinese snow plum blossoms in winter. "I learned to be very independent," she said. "I don't want to rely on anyone." She was first sheltered in Xining, then moved to a Chinese boarding school in a remote corner of northeastern Tibet, before attending the Qinghai ethnic group college for minorities back in Xining. Han studied Chinese language, history, and science, as well as some Tibetan. In 1971, she enrolled in the inaugural class of the Qinghai Medical College in Golmud and joined the staff at the hospital after her graduation in 1975. She did eventually find her mother, who worked as a housemaid in Lhasa, sometime around 1970. With the help of Chinese records, she also discovered she was one of nine children, and that her mother, who was extremely poor, gave up the family because she could not feed them. The closest thing Han—who had for all intents and purposes been raised Chinese—had to true roots today was this land high on the plateau.

At her station in Yanshiping, her intense enjoyment of the surroundings collided with the almost overwhelming weight of her responsibilities. She wrote daily in a detailed diary—"There were clouds in the azure sky, mantling over stretching mountains and lakes and herds of sheep on Tibetans' endless grassland"—and recorded that as many as 80 percent of the workers had symptoms of illness or stress related to the altitude, especially in their early days on the plateau, as they acclimatized. Almost all of the workers came to Han regularly for a couple of gasps off an oxygen tube—a refreshing, stimulating natural drug in the surroundings—or a dose of pills they thought would keep them safe. Even then Han had a difficult time gaining trust among her patients. "They were suspecting of my ability, considering my age and my 'emaciated' appearance," she said sarcastically, mentioning that much was made of the fact that the headlights on the camps' utility trucks met her at eye level. What helped most—and was probably the reason she had been asked to work on the plateau—was the reputation she had earned for treating a deathly ill patient in April.

Han had been sent on a short junket to watch over several visiting officials from the railways and propaganda ministries as they toured some of the railway's possible sites. The trip had been routine—rich with anticipation as their Chinese-made jeep cleared the dramatic Kunlun Mountain Pass and breached the great Tibetan Plateau. But two days later, when they first met with workers from the Railway Survey Institute on April 19, the taxing conditions of the mountain environment became clear. The first team they approached, five men in glaring orange work suits, were walking the grassland, loaded with weighty survey equipment. By their casual amble the men appeared relaxed—or perhaps it was the effect of thin air slowing their activity to a crawl. "When I got to them I saw that their faces were as purple as eggplant. They looked like soldiers in a battlefield," Han said. "They had awful scabs on their dry lips," a condition caused by the lack of oxygen and exposure to the blistering winds and intense ultraviolet rays. Later that night, the crew arrived in Nagqu, a forbidding trade and industrial village about two-thirds of the way to Lhasa and at an elevation of roughly fifteen thousand feet. That's when her own party began to get sick with discomfort and fatigue. Han's driver, Hu Jincheng, developed a nasty cough. She gave him antibiotics and sent him to bed. At about 4:00 a.m., she awoke to a loud rap on her door. The officials sharing Hu's room were frightened by his condition. Han arrived moments later to find her driver sitting upright with raspy breath and foam at his lips. Suffering from pneumonedema, a condition where fluid collects in the lungs, Hu coughed harshly. Blood sprayed from his mouth and nose. "His heart rate was 134 beats per minute, and bubbles were gurgling in his lungs," reported Han. They were hundreds of miles from lower elevations, so she was forced to resort to clinical treatment. Thinking fast, she gave the man oxygen and an IV loaded with blood-thinning agents and steroids. Luckily, it worked quickly, and Han was, for a short time, a hero.

But as a doctor stationed permanently with the design team on the plateau, her responsibilities were both clinical and more esoteric. While illness from the high altitude presented a physical threat to the workers, the Ministry of Railways also knew that any bad news in the camp posed a different sort of threat: word of a critical case of altitude sickness could scare the laborers into flight as quickly as a shotgun blast would empty a bird sanctuary. As circumstance would have it, young Wei's death in May was the first and last death reported on the railway construction project—including from high altitude, heavy machinery, car accidents, or general illness. It's a statistic that represents either the incredible success of doctors like Han and an enviable safety record or a concerted effort to keep any bad news under tight wrap. "The most important purpose," she said, "was to eliminate the survey team's trepidation. The ministry was under great pressure to complete the design within four months." When Han wasn't treating illnesses, she was engaged in a localized PR campaign, aimed at showing workers they could live normally at high altitude. She spent her first and last hours of each day jogging or doing calisthenics by the tents, and she accompanied the men on hikes and short expeditions in the afternoons when time allowed. There were also further serious emergencies. A senior engineer collapsed unconscious at a remote camp, far from the highway; an expedition truck, hours from a road, sank into the unstable permafrost, and all the scientists, stranded overnight, got frostbite. Yet these passed as bursts of drama without triggering the widespread hysteria that had followed the early altitude sicknesses. Mostly the camps settled into their routine.

On Sundays, a truck would take Han and others from the camp the fifty-five miles to Dangla village to use a telephone. She would pay an old Tibetan shopkeeper eighty jiao, roughly seven cents, to call her daughter in Golmud. Showers, other than a cold splash in the Buqu River, were a luxury reserved for R & R leaves to the lowland every few weeks. Newspapers, mostly packed with articles extolling the virtues of the "heroic railway workers" and their efforts, would periodically be brought up from the Qinghai plain. "Sincerity, kindness, and dedication: they are where the beauty of humans' hearts lie . . . We sing for every single flower, every beam of sunlight," read one, "because they gave us a beautiful environment and a beautiful life." The superfluous praise deeply touched Han, and after some time she felt an increasing sense of nationalistic purpose—likely the articles' intended effect. "Most foreigners don't even believe that it's possible to build such a railway," she wrote in her diary on June 22, as the stormy night wind whistled through tent poles outside. "But we need to earn glory for our country, as well as us workers and scientists."

Soon more workers would ascend to the plateau to dozens of camps like Han's. Construction over the scope of the railway project was scheduled to push the boundaries of Tibet's seasons—from March to December—but even the relatively warm summer could be brutal. As Han noted in her diary, a snowstorm, "a tempest," rain showers, and a scorching sun could pass through the plateau in a matter of hours. The days preceding the official groundbreaking on June 29 were among her worst. On June 24, she awoke to a blanket of snow that stranded the trucks and paralyzed the camp. On June 27, she "got up at six to find that it was snowing wildly; the world had turned white." That afternoon brought torrents of freezing rain; many got sick, and, for the third day in a row, the workers were tent-bound. The next morning, Han's fitful sleep was broken by squawking swallows that were circling inside her tent to avoid the still drumming rain. The camp's courtyard was swamped, and Han found water rushing out from a leak in her floor. She filled the hole with ashes and piled cardboard boxes on top, but they too grew soggy. Reports were coming in about a dangerous ice buildup on the no. 103 bridge of the Qinghai-Tibet Highway; flooding waters rushed around both sides, and the structure nearly washed away. The men in camp became agitated. A washed-out road meant the more senior engineers in the group would not be able to attend the opening ceremonies near Golmud the next day.

On June 29, in a turn that Han described as auspicious, the rain turned to drizzle, and finally, before dawn, stopped altogether. That morning, the distant Dangla Mountain was draped in fog, the air was crisp and still, and the sky to the east was clear as sparkling crystal. It meant that the railway would go smoothly and the project would bring great fortune. Later that evening, Han and the camp crowded around a TV strung up to a satellite dish inside one of the meeting tents for a China Television broadcast of the event. "Today is a special day," she wrote. "The construction of the Tibet railway is a dream of several generations. Today, it came true."

RAILWAY OFFICIALS ESTIMATE THAT MORE THAN A HUNDRED THOUSAND LABOR-ers migrated to Tibet to build the railway in 2001. That first year, busful after busful of men piled into various work sites sprinkled along the plateau. A typical one, plopped at a dirt turnout–cum–truck stop a short way up the Qinghai-Tibet Highway from Xidatan, was composed of rickety sheds with a rabid-looking bull mastiff outside, the glaciers of the Kunlun Mountains towering above the berating, cold wind. Smoke billowed from the thin stovepipes that jutted from the corrugated steel roofing of the shacks. The dog was chained to a steel stake, and it lunged and barked at the men as they stepped off the bus and lined up along mounds of garbage to relieve themselves. At this higher elevation, the oppressive dust clouds of the lower-elevation sandstorms mercifully thinned to a gritty haze. Mercy was hard-won on the plateau.

Beneath the snowy slopes, past their broken fields of crevasses, on the earth of the valley floor lay the unmistakable serpentine of the giant railway bed, nearly a hundred feet high in places and stretching beyond the limits of sight. It was covered in the tiny silhouettes of hundreds of men. The sheds doubled as a restaurant and rest stop for truckers, travelers, and workers waiting for rides back down the hill to their camp. A single lightbulb dangled from the ceiling, and perhaps three dozen Han Chinese—many more than had come off the bus—sipped cups of tea and huddled around a glowing stove. They looked haggard. Many wore scarves over their faces as protection against the dust, but their faces were still blistered from the sun and wind. Most wore the flat-soled shoes that sold for pennies in the markets, their toes protruding through worn holes. Their shirts were little more than cotton gauze, fine for the hot fields of Sichuan, where many had come from, but inadequate for Qinghai and the plateau.

Among the thousand workers living in Xidatan was Ren Huan Bin, a thirty-eight-year-old from southern Sichuan who seemed too wafer-thin for hard labor. Ren came to Qinghai early in 2001 because he had heard the jobs were easy to come by. Between stints of work on the railway, he earned a living cooking in a curbside restaurant in lower-altitude Golmud. Back in his home village, he and his wife owned a single mu of land, on which they grew vegetables and kept pigs; they sold the excess produce at a profit. Of the fifty or so families there, more than a third of the people traveled elsewhere for work. "It's tradition," he said, explaining that he made it home three months each year. "There are too many people for too little land."

On the railway, Ren headed a team of a dozen men charged with shaping pillars and piping, working with steel rebar and pouring concrete. Often they built prosaic foundations and drainages, but they also likely shaped the pylons to support the treacherous crossing of the river gorge. A worker with experience, like Ren, could make $250 a month, nearly twice what he earned as a cook, but on the railway he had to buy his own boots and clothing. All of the fifty or sixty men sharing his cavernous residential army tent were Chinese, and most came from Sichuan, according to Ren. Each tent was outfitted with a sandbag foundation, plywood floors, and a single toilet, and the men had to pay for lodging and mess, which usually consisted of rice, steamed buns, and potatoes.

The staff workers, as Ren called them, fared much better. Like many large construction projects in China, an immense, multilayered pyramid of subcontractors and government bureaus dispersed the $4 billion invested in the railway's construction across much of China's economy. Twenty-two different railway bureaus were in charge of constructing a designated length of the tracks. The bureaus subcontracted jobs, from road building to cement pouring, to construction firms. Those firms broke their projects into teams, which in turn hired what Ren called "headmen" to round up and manage the laborers. That army of labor reported to various levels of "staff" workers, or gang bosses. From the headmen down, each level of authority skimmed a cut of the workers' wages, so while the umbrella Qinghai-Tibet Railway Company might have been paying roughly twelve dollars a day per worker, the men in the camps pocketed four dollars, before shelling out for their room and board. Very little of the money filtered to the actual workers, and even less of it remained in Tibet. The bosses spent their weekends in Golmud, often squandering bonuses on prostitutes and lavish meals of sautéed carp and roasted mutton. You could see them on the site—pacing up and down the rail bed, doing very little manual work.

In the first eleven months, their crews had made substantial progress. According to Chinese reports, nearly sixty miles of track had been laid and work on more than forty bridges and tunnels started by the second year of construction that spring at a cost of $72 million. The construction season had originally been planned to end with the cold weather, pausing at the end of each November and picking up again in early April or May. But the same haste and sense of urgency that rushed the groundbreaking inspired the Ministry of Railways to push construction straight through that first winter. Qinghai's vice governor, Su Sen, who had worked with the Ministry of Railways to establish the project, had promised that steel rails would reach the TAR border, roughly half of the train's route from Golmud, by June 2003. The pace of building major river crossings and tunnels was completely unknown, partly because their implementation in permafrost regions was so experimental. The ministry feared that it could not afford delays in the easier areas of the plateau.

Nearly ten thousand workers remained on the plateau as a ruthless arctic chill set down in December 2001. Chinese news reports put the temperature at around fourteen degrees Fahrenheit. Aside from keeping workers warm and safe, the greatest challenge lay in pouring concrete at such low temperatures. Concrete that cures in below-freezing environments is substantially weakened, even fatally flawed. It's a polymer whose short molecular chains require heat and water in order to grow and strengthen. The engineers employed giant electric boilers to heat the water needed for mixing the cement, which should be kept at nearly seventy degrees Fahrenheit, and vast clouds of steam rose off the plateau and marked the construction camps in the barren wilderness. Once the concrete was poured, hot air cannons fanned it until it hardened, and in some cases the giant pillars of bridges were wrapped in blankets in an effort to enclose the heat churned out naturally by the cement's chemical transformation. In the tunnels, hot air and oxygen were pumped in at a furious pace.

This moving of heaven and earth was to bring great fortune, but it was still not clear to whom.

6

FREE TIBET

NEWS THAT A RAILWAY WOULD BE BUILT THROUGH Kalden's village west of Lhasa came abruptly in the spring of 2002. He can't remember exactly when, only how, and that before then his life had been satisfactory. Though Kalden and his siblings spent most of their time in backbreaking work—like nine out of ten Tibetans, they lived modestly off the land and their animals—he was comfortable in his routine, and the work and the family's needs always equaled out. The previous fall's barley had been harvested without a hitch, as had their crops of wheat, potatoes, and peas. And there was extra money that year. Kalden's older brother Gyatso had found work on construction sites near Lhasa, and the previous fall a Hui butcher had come to the village and bought two of Kalden's father's yaks and three sheep, for around four thousand yuan, or five hundred dollars, a bounty the family planned to spend on clothes and sugar in the Barkhor in Lhasa.

Of the hundred or so households in the village, Kalden's was far from the richest, but their new home with glass windows exhibited their relative success and security. The surveyors who had strolled through the fields during the harvest had been all but forgotten. Then one day, anxious rumors started trickling from doorway to doorway. "The villagers were all talking," Kalden said, drawing his recollections from a faraway emotional compartment. Foreigners often misunderstand Tibetans as having unvaryingly optimistic and lighthearted dispositions, but often that façade is more a survival technique. He had averted his own attention from the things over which he was powerless, focusing instead on those in which he could find hope. In a sense, this was "mindfulness," a step on the Buddhist eightfold path to enlightenment, which puts the mind in control of emotion. But it was also a sort of escapism. Kalden didn't like being pushed back into this moment, and he spoke softly as he repeated the village's murmurs: "They are going to build a railway; they are going to build a railway."

Soon, the village head called a meeting in the historical central administration building, or Chang headquarters. The Chang station was the village's most stately structure—a sturdy square box built not of the typical mud and mortar but of hand-hewed stone. Before the Cultural Revolution, the offices had been a master's estate, but it had been abandoned and then reclaimed for public use. At the meeting, the headman, a wealthy Tibetan allied with the Communist Party, revealed that the tracks would cut directly through the center of their town.

Kalden's estate—his father's thirty-two mu and the home they had built six years earlier—lay on the southern rim of the broad shelf that sat above the river. From his home, Kalden could see the entire village, stretching up to the Qinghai-Tibet Highway and Chang station on the far side of town. Immediately outside his family's walls, a dirt road, a concave dry runnel of worn land wide enough for a tractor that had settled where it bore the most traffic, divided their land from several ragged alleys of homes, lined like miniature city blocks and each with a modest six-foot mud and straw wall to keep the livestock and dogs in. Plastered along the walls, in patties marked indelibly with the imprint of the splayed hand that stuck them there, yak dung hung to dry in the hot sun. Near the north end of the village was a tea stall and a shop, where prepackaged bowls of instant noodles and bottles of Chinese rum were sold and, at night, people liked to huddle around the stove to gossip. The rail bed, the headman explained, would cross the river just west of Kalden's property, about where the surveyors had ambled down from the road bed the previous fall, and run between his father's house and the station.

The villagers fell into a torrent of worries: fear that an influx of Chinese residents would come with the train, stealing jobs like Gyatso's, just plain stealing, and bringing troublesome gangs with them from the cities. "So many poor people are coming, there are more muggings," they said to each other. It was a safe way to speak in opposition to the project; by discussing democratic social ills rather than ethnic or political contrasts, they could not be accused of fomenting Tibetan resistance against Beijing. Kalden openly worried about the crowding and the crime too. They wondered how they could compete if even more Chinese workers poured into Lhasa and started to fill up the land between it and them. Already the government had sketched plans to annex parts of Tolung-Dechen County into the city municipality. Most people in the village had little education. Kalden had dropped out of school in the seventh grade, while Gyatso had completed all eight years of secondary school to become the best-educated member of their family. They could both speak Tibetan and a smidgen of Chinese. Neither could read or write very well. When Gyatso, or on occasion Kalden, looked for work in Lhasa, he was up against Chinese and "city Tibetans" who were skilled, which meant they could drive cars, operate machinery, or speak enough Mandarin to be told what to do and be reprimanded if they did it wrong. So while the villagers enjoyed some of the amenities the Chinese had brought with them over the years, particularly electricity, there was an intuitive fear that accelerating development would marginalize them more than it would help.

Already the next town closer to Lhasa had a new road and its old buildings had been torn down and replaced with neat rows of cinderblock homes trimmed with a token Tibetan motif, painted in burnt sienna, on the roof. The tea stalls at the heart of Tibetan social life had been replaced with modern-style shop stalls, much like the self-storage depots found in American suburbs, except here each stall's garage door opened to display identical plastic and tin Chinese goods. Kalden's father did not think these things were needed and complained that their construction was bringing more Chinese workers and supporting new Chinese business ventures from rock quarries to television companies. Kalden's ideas were shaped by his father's. And now his village would be asked to rebuild too.

A month or so later, the villagers' fears were assuaged by word of the lavish resettlement subsidies the Chinese planned to offer in return for their town. Homes disturbed by the construction, their headman said, would be moved farther north. Kalden's father was told that those in the train's path would be given 120,000 yuan, or $15,000, to relocate. This was a great—even unbelievable—sum by any Tibetan's standard, and while no one relished the thought of their ruined and scattered homes, the fees were astoundingly fair. Not that the people in Kalden's village had much of a choice, but the Chinese had made it a hard proposition to resist. As Kalden pictured it then, the southern half of town would be moved out of the train's way and shifted to a hillside pleasantly perched above the fray of the highway. Nothing else would change.

IN THE SPRING OF 2002, HOWEVER, EVERYTHING IN LHASA WAS CHANGING. The policies designed to implement China's Go West campaign were evolving from sketches to real undertakings aimed at transforming Tibet into a civilized postindustrial society on par with Beijing, Shanghai, or the manufacturing center Shenzhen. The vision called for much more than a railway. It demanded the breakneck urbanization of not only Lhasa but the smallest villages in the most rural regions—an absurdly ambitious goal given the relatively sparse population of the region. In its Ninth Five Year Plan for the TAR, in 1996, the central government called for the creation of more than seventy new towns and several large cities by 2020. These goals, vaguely defined decades earlier when Mao declared Tibet should be home to a populaton of at least 10 million, were now being pushed with China's fresh audacity.

The most immediate step in jump-starting Tibet's transformation involved purging any antiquated infrastructure, a process that had begun in Lhasa shortly after the winter's thaw in 2002. Wandering west on Beijing Road toward the towering Potala, the city was in turmoil. The growing pains of development had left the neighborhoods between the Barkhor and Potala Square looking as if they had been bombed. Only one street corner retained the characteristic Tibetan architecture splashed throughout the tourist brochures—articulated masonry with a slight pyramid shape with whitewashed walls that gleamed in the sun.

Within throwing distance lay entire city blocks of rubble. A small alleyway, confined by a surviving set of gangly walls, led into what had been a central courtyard, the traditional core of Lhasa's residential buildings. An elderly woman, her daughter, and her infant granddaughter sat there, outdoors, shading their bowl of noodles from the omnipresent dust of demolition. Beside them a giant blue plastic tarp fluttered, replacing one of the missing walls. Each woman wore the seemingly ubiquitous gauze filter over her mouth. Behind them, dust clouds towered over a wasteland, where men, atop fifteen-foot-high piles of white rocky rubble, wielded their sledgehammers in long swinging arcs to land at their feet, shattering whatever remnant walls were still standing. The younger woman explained that the police announced the demolitions to residents only when it was time for them to leave. She and her mother expected their notice at any moment. They did not have a place to go next.

The campaign to tear down substantial parts of Lhasa—much like the comparable demolitions of quaint hutong neighborhoods taking place that year in Beijing—had swiftly reached full, unabashed force in May 2002. To leave a neighborhood for twenty-four hours meant returning to find it had changed shape, another building gone, new scaffolding erected in its place. A slowly rising tide, the Chinese shops and arcades that had hunkered down in the west end of Lhasa were inching past the Potala Palace toward the most distinctive, the most sacred, and the most Tibetan neighborhood in the valley, the Barkhor. On the south side of the Barkhor, older buildings along the Kyichu River were being razed for new construction at a harried pace. The historical sanctum appeared under assault.

Strangely, visitors to Lhasa at the time preferred to look the other way. In fact, to be a tourist in Lhasa in 2002 was to be in a sort of willful state of denial, and there were plenty of old-world Tibetan sites— the incense-steeped temples and saffron-robed monks—remaining to indulge that tendency. The Lonely Planet guide to Tibet offered scarcely more than a few dozen words on any part of the city outside the Barkhor area, as if it didn't exist. Foreigners would wander in endless circles about the Barkhor, visiting the Jokhang Temple and nearby Ramoche Temple, photographing the colorfully dressed Tibetan pilgrims who had made their way to Lhasa from the country-side, and then sampling a flavorful Indian masala or Nepali dal baat at one of the cafés set up to appeal to Westerners' tastes. When they'd had enough of the Barkhor, they might take a taxi to the Potala or to the great nearby monasteries, Drepung and Sera, or arrange for a jeep tour outside of the city altogether. It was illegal for foreigners to take public transit to most places outside Lhasa, but since Beijing had identified tourism as one of the region's "pillar industries," there was no lack for guides and agencies. Passing each other in the narrow alleys, travelers would avert their eyes, engaged in an unspoken competition to uncover the rawest nook, pretending they weren't rubbing shoulders in order to preserve their private Francis Younghusband fantasies. Each could be the first Westerner to find the real Lhasa among the rubble. More often, though, they complained about the imperfect city they found there. To some, Lhasa had been reduced to a travelers' disappointing waypoint, to Everest or Nepal or Tibet's less touched west. A Western expatriate, Matthew, would occasionally shake Westerners out of their myopia, challenging them to look clear-eyed at an endangered Tibet. "The fascination of Tibet is somehow that it is a time lock, that it has survived various changes, and people want to somehow grab that," he explained. "Most visitors are going to Tibet for something exotic—there is this idea of seeing how much can we capture of what *was* there while ignoring what *is* there."

But while many Westerners in Tibet peered narrowly back into the past, the Chinese gazed farther and farther into the future. At the heart of the hastening changes in Lhasa's alleys was China's great modern dilemma: how could its poorest provinces be transformed from liabilities to assets?

THROUGHOUT THE LATTER HALF OF THE TWENTIETH CENTURY, TIBET HAD remained an expensive but largely paralyzed appendage to China's great government bureaucracy. Politically it remained burdensome, while its economic offerings—vast lands, suspected resources, habitable space, and manpower—had not contributed meaningfully to China's global emergence. Beijing needed to establish conditions that would beckon and foster the development of industry, the settlement of skilled Chinese workers, and the attention of foreign investors: faster roads, better bridges, exportable products, and a local gross domestic product that balanced in the black. China called its plans for Tibet a process of building "national unity." The phrase implied that the development in the TAR should become indistinguishable from that in the east. And on the face of it, that seemed to mean that the people would become indistinguishable as well.

In Beijing, the chief economist at the government-run China Tibetology Center, Luo Rong Zandui, was charged with managing the cultural evolution of the TAR. The center's grand office, a white building on the Fourth Ring road, stood a short walk from the sparkling Olympic village, with its striking steel nestlike obelisk and translucent water cube. Like China's view of Tibetan culture, the building's design dispensed with the traditional architectural style, simply maintaining the trimming accents in the halfhearted burnt sienna painted along the roof line.

Inside the center's fourth-floor plush oak-paneled conference room, Luo, an ethnic Tibetan and twenty-year veteran of the center, explained the government's fresh push for Tibet's development after 2001. "Tibet's importance is fourfold," he said, unsurprisingly sounding much like the propaganda issued by the center's publishing house. "Beijing's main interest is, I really believe, to empower and enrich all Tibetan people so that they would feel they are part of China and they would like to, you know, build it." Luo spoke in nuanced terms, wavering between sympathy and the official outlines of the government's Tenth Five Year Plan. Tibet, in the popular view among eastern Chinese, remained more or less uncivilized—from the unsophisticated buildings in Lhasa to Tibetans' relaxed work ethic and anemic productivity. China was there to fix it.

Fundamentally, Luo combined a missionary's sense of righteousness and a Reaganesque philosophy of trickle-down progress. "The goal is to modernize Tibet's industry," he said. "We try to promote more urbanization to promote industry. It is the same strategy the government adopted in the inland areas: develop the township, the urban area first, and gradually the benefits will enlarge to the rural areas around it. That is the blueprint." How could Tibet *not* want and benefit from the changes China envisioned for it, he mused—rhetorically.

Yet larger questions of security and stability, not just welfare, loomed, even in Luo's practiced talking points. "Among all the autonomous regions in China, the TAR is the only region where the ethnic population is not just the majority but the overwhelming majority," he explained. "So development is vital to the central government politically." The twangs of fear stood out among his lines. In prioritizing the elements spurring China's strategy for Tibet's development, he ranked "a stabilized frontier" well ahead of everything else.

Weighing on Luo's mind as he spoke of stability was the Tibetan uprising that rocked Lhasa on March 5, 1989, and the lasting distrust that it had sowed among contemporary Chinese officials, not least

Hu Jintao. After Mao Zedong's death and the trial of the zealous Communist Gang of Four for their roles in instigating the Cultural Revolution, Deng Xiaoping launched his initial economic reforms, and they were softer on Tibet. Deng's policy, "one country, two systems," meant to address China's relationship with Hong Kong and Taiwan, implied a tolerance for ethnic regions, and perhaps Tibet, to evolve culturally without the baggage of central China's restrictions. And the tone of his rule, at the start, was apologetic. Deng installed his long-time loyalist and fellow reformer Hu Yaobang as the head of the party, and Hu made the rehabilitation of Tibet, which was crippled by abject poverty, a priority. For a short time, Hu virtually took over the governing of the TAR. He implemented a series of conciliatory policies, and under his purview the tenth Panchen Lama, Tibet's second most holy figure, who had been denounced, publicly tortured, and then jailed for fourteen years, was released from prison. In 1980, Hu appointed Yin Fatang, the old Deng follower who had pushed relentlessly for the railway, as the TAR's party secretary and denounced China's past decades of policies in Tibet as a failure. Tibetans responded with skepticism but were pleased.

For four years, Beijing ushered Tibet toward a greater degree of autonomy that allowed a religious renaissance not imagined since the Dalai Lama's flight into exile in 1959. Taxes on Tibetans were suspended, and, as the final pieces of the commune system and the remnants of the Great Leap Forward were dismantled, the land was returned to private ownership. The changes had an immediate, positive effect on Tibetans' welfare. At the heart of these policies was the understanding that Tibetans stood a better chance of being wooed into the Communist fold through economic progress and development than through brute force. But by the mid-1980s, perhaps feeling secure in its political efforts, Beijing shifted its reform policies away from progress for Tibetans and toward an aggressive economic modernization defined on a national rather than a local scale. More Han Chinese and their businesses would venture to Tibet in order to boost the economy of greater China.

In those reform years, however, the Tibetans had fortified their cultural identity. The result was a heightened sense of indignation toward the Chinese and an emboldened willingness to speak out. In September 1987, monks, enraged by China's vitriolic response to efforts by the Dalai Lama to raise international awareness about conditions in Tibet, protested outside the Jokhang Temple. At least a dozen were arrested, and a riot of solidarity subsequently erupted. Tibetans stormed and burned the Barkhor's police station. Stationed on the rooftops, Chinese police fired into the crowds, killing ten people and wounding dozens. Unrest and tension continued for a year and a half. Meanwhile, outside Tibet, the Dalai Lama continued to spearhead a vocal campaign, targeted at Western governments, to acknowledge the cause of Tibetan rights, if not independence, a pursuit that would win him the 1989 Nobel Peace Prize.

Beijing, once again, was pressed to restore order on China's raucous frontier, and it named the young governor of Guizhou Province and a party leadership hopeful, Hu Jintao, as party secretary of the TAR. With the successorship of Jiang Zemin in his sights, Hu had little room for failure. The day after his assignment, police cracked down on another protest in the Barkhor, this time shooting at point-blank range individuals who were waving the flag of Tibet. A month later, Hu traveled to Shigatze to meet with the Panchen Lama, but he met with resistance. The Panchen Lama seized the opportunity to boldly criticize China's rule over Tibet, a shrill and rare wakeup call to leaders in Beijing. Just five days later, the otherwise healthy Panchen Lama was found dead of an apparent heart attack inside his Tashi

Lhunpo Monastery, a sequence of events that has convinced many Tibetans that Hu played a role in the death. As the Washington, D.C.–based International Campaign for Tibet put it, the Panchen Lama's death "created a vaccum in Tibetan leadership in Tibet that has yet to be filled." Anger swelled. Tibetans quickly recognized that without a Tibetan advocate in the Panchen Lama, the era of liberal reform was at a close. When Chinese officials announced less than a week later that the selection of his reincarnate would be approved by the state council, emotions were further enflamed. China's denial of the right of Tibetans to choose the Eleventh Panchen Lama was seen not only as a spurn to a sacred religious process but as a repudiation of all political autonomy. In the weeks that followed, small-scale protests occurred almost daily in Lhasa.

On March 5, 1989, as the anniversary of the Tibetans' 1959 uprising approached, a small group of nuns and monks walked the Barkhor holding a hand-drawn Tibetan flag. According to an eyewitness account, they chanted: "Tibet is independent. This is a peaceful demonstration. Please do not use violence." As the protest grew larger, order broke down and Chinese soldiers fired pistols into the crowd. A few hours later, soldiers marched down Beijing Dong Road, showering the crowd and bystanders with machine-gun fire. Three days of riots followed. As Tibetans destroyed Chinese buildings, cars, and other property, the Barkhor's alleyways were consumed in fiery maelstroms. Between 150 and 750 people died before 2,000 Chinese troops descended on the Barkhor, and Hu, caught on his heels, imposed strict martial laws.

Though the uprising in Lhasa was foremost about the situation in Tibet, it coincided with a growing restlessness with Deng's increasingly conservative policies and a deepening gulf between China's rich and poor. A series of protests took place that sprang across the country, climaxing on June 4 in Beijing's Tiananmen Square. Initially, students gathered to register outrage at the lack of a state ceremony to recognize the death of the dedicated liberalizer Hu Yaobang; but the square was soon crowded with democratic activists, and the Chinese government's response stood as its most notoriously violent crackdown since Mao's death. It was also a watershed moment in Deng's governance, extracting political progress from the regime's economic plan.

In Tibet, especially, China's confidence had been rattled to the bone. Conservative parties in Beijing—the same Mao loyalists who were outraged when Hu Yaobang denounced their previous Tibet crackdowns as a failure—blamed the long leash afforded by the liberal policies of the 1980s as the catalyst for Tibetans' resistance. Hu Jintao's disciplinarian bar was set high. Video surveillance cameras were installed throughout the Barkhor, and a heightened state of security enveloped Lhasa. The expansion and activities of the monasteries were severely limited. In the early 1990s, stasis mostly reigned, punctuated by occasional minor protests that were met with small-scale crackdowns to remind Tibetans that political speech would not be tolerated. Hu's policy came to be known as "rule with both hands": the state of control would be strictly maintained, through force, so that the goals of economic development and industrialization could be pursued with vigor.

Religion was at the crosshairs of China's control strategy. Hu Jintao considered the rise of religion in Tibet as mutually exclusive with the goals of the "four modernizations" that defined China's economic policy; religion, as he and many of the other conservatives saw it, cultivated nationalism. Tibetans should be forming a commodity-based market, not praying to golden Buddhas or, for that matter, the Dalai Lama, whose extensive testimonies abroad riled Beijing. The antidote, expressed through a spate of policies in the early 1990s, was privatization and population assimilation that encouraged Han migration. Deng's "Spring Tide" campaign to "deepen" and "speed up" economic reform washed across China, and Tibet was classified as a "special economic zone."

Hu was tasked with spurring outside investment and fostering a free market. Among the first steps, the few policies that had benefited Tibetans were reversed. *Hukou*, a residence registration system, was immediately reformed to allow Han migrants to circulate into and around Tibet without restriction. Border checkpoints were eliminated. Business regulations were relaxed, and migrants and officials were offered guaranteed housing, higher wages, tax breaks, and other preferential treatment—such as assured health care and education, which did not exist for indigenous people. According to Human Rights Watch, a 1992 survey showed that just 20 percent of all businesses in Tibet were Tibetan owned.

These economic policies were accompanied by further cultural repression. In 1995, the young reincarnate Panchen Lama, who had been designated earlier that year by the Dalai Lama himself, was taken into Chinese custody—according to the Office of Tibet, kidnapped, according to the Chinese, placed in seclusion for his safety and a sheltered education. Next, the government began a period of intense repression of religious practice in the monasteries. In what it called "reeducation," monks were told to study pro-Chinese texts and then interrogated exhaustively about their loyalties, sometimes in isolation, for several days on end. The government demanded that monks disavow the Dalai Lama and pledge their allegiance to the Communist Party. Those who refused were imprisoned. Some committed suicide. As a result, the monastic system, which had begun to rehabilitate in the 1980s, was further routed and Tibetans were again forced to submit to the Chinese.

It can be argued that these darker moments in China's rule of Tibet since the Cultural Revolution have not been the result of its ambitions as much as its paranoia, and that to a degree it has always been that way. As Francis Younghusband had said, after massacring hundreds of people in the brutal British invasion of Lhasa in 1904, "all this trouble had arisen through the Tibetans being so inaccessible and keeping themselves so much apart; and now I meant to close in with them, to break through their seclusion." Had the British not exhibited such a long-standing interest in Tibet, it is possible that China's 1950 invasion would never have happened. With the empire shifting on the other side of the Himalayas, Mao feared that white colonialists would try to find a new foothold in Tibet. The Cold War did not improve China's mind-set. Meddling in Tibet by the American CIA after World War II, while noncommittal, galvanized concerns that the globally advancing Russian Soviets in the north wanted the high ground of Tibet for themselves. Much later, the Dalai Lama's speeches before the U.S. Congress, and the shrill voices of the American and European activists lined up behind him, were taken as a slap in the face. China suspected that the unrest in the late 1980s was coordinated by the Tibet government-in-exile in Dharamsala. When the Dalai Lama was awarded the Nobel Peace Prize in 1989, it was taken as an open threat—an unwelcome incursion of Western influence in internal political matters. With every Hollywood movie or student picket, Beijing's bureaucrats have been trained to see a crowbar thrust by the outside world into the healing fractures of its distant province. That perception has entrenched China in its tradition of repressive policies and crackdowns in Tibet.

Part of the problem is that China has hitched its definition of national strength to the degree of political stability in places like Tibet. A 1998 report by the RAND Center for Asia-Pacific Policy stated that "the essence of the leaders' nationalistic—some would say patriotic—appeal at home is that they are restoring China's greatness. And in the minds of most Chinese, the moments of greatness coincide with the moments of maximum unity, strength and national territorial integrity. The great leaders in Chinese history are those who brought all the rightful parts of the domain back into the fold. The despised rulers are those who contributed to China's fragmentation and penetration by foreign powers." The tough talk may ultimately hamstring Beijing when it comes to devising the smartest policy for development in Tibet. The report continues: "This rhetorical nationalism is a two-edged sword. The use of nationalistic appeals appears to rally the populace behind the leaders. But it makes the leaders captives of the sentiments they have cultivated, probably reduces their own flexibility on these issues, and surely alienates the objects of their wrath." By defining the Dalai Lama and other pro-Tibetan parties as "splittist," China has created an environment in which the state is politically weak if it is ever seen to kowtow to those interests, even when moderation is wisest. Its policy in Tibet is characterized largely by its own unease.

Pragmatists argue that the lasting conflict with the Dalai Lama and Dharamsala is outmoded. The Tibetan government-in-exile now more or less accepts the idea of Chinese suzerainty, and many Tibetans turn east for economic assistance. "The Tibet problem, we could solve it in five minutes and the world would do nothing but rain down compliments on China for doing so," said the China scholar Orville Schell, referring to an alternative approach that would allow unfettered religious freedom and practice, the return of the Dalai Lama to the Potala Palace, guarantees of human rights, and more economic development. "It's a win-win-win scenario, but China can't hear that. Because they are painted into their own corner after all these years by their own propaganda, their own policies, their own fear." The

Chinese, for their part, choose instead to grapple with the challenge of making the best use of this vast territory while preserving Tibetan "autonomy," that is, the appearance of it to outside watchers.

PERHAPS THE GREATEST ALARM SOUNDED AROUND BUILDING THE RAIL-way to Lhasa is the threat that ethnic Tibetans will be relegated to a state of irrelevance, through a drip, drip, drip process of cultural dilution. Kalden's concerns that the Han Chinese would take all the jobs, and Kalden's father's disgust with the plastic goods on sale in the cookie-cutter shops, were a ground-level manifestation of this fear. Whether such integration is a form of planned cultural genocide, as the Dalai Lama has asserted in several speeches, or simply reflects a necessary movement of goods and people from China's supersaturated east to its less populated areas, remains to be seen.

It would prove to be a difficult balancing act for Beijing, regardless. In 2000, China laid out controversial plans for a sparsely populated, ethnically Tibetan part of neighboring Qinghai Province: the resettlement of sixty thousand destitute Han Chinese farmers to an empty, fertile valley where they could find a fresh start with the available resources. To support the poverty reduction project, China solicited $40 million in funding from the World Bank, and at first the bank agreed—a recognition on some level that it made economic sense. The international Tibetan community, claiming areas of Qinghai as part of a greater cultural Tibet, cried foul and protested the bank's involvement on the grounds that it was abetting a policy to wipe out Tibetans and other minorities in China's west. Bank members and shareholders began to rebuke the bank's involvement, leading eventually to the withdrawal of support for the project. The controversy provoked a more lasting effect on the bank's other projects in western China, as well.

The bank had loaned astronomical sums to aid Chinese development, including more than $300 million for nine projects to expand China's railway system. After being criticized for the Qinghai controversy, the bank instituted a new level of caution around matters of ethnic resettlement, choosing to be far more conservative in its political exposure when it came to China. According to Lou Thompson, a former chief railway adviser at the bank who led many past funding projects, the Tibet railway became untouchable. "The obvious motivation of this project is political," he said. "China wants to continue to strengthen its claim over Tibet, and it wants to make sure it can defend it if it has to."

In a comprehensive and independent 2002 report on the broader Tibetan region—hailed by former U.S. ambassador to the United Nations Richard Holbrooke, among others—the Alliance for Research in Tibet notes that "China's presence and behavior in Tibetan areas can be distilled to three fundamentals: Control, Exploitation, and Assimilation." The two-thousand-page document attributes the rise in economic development to increasing migration and says the majority held by Tibetans in these prefectures could soon be erased. "If autonomy is to be based on ethnicity, the dilution of these populations represents a critical threat." For instance, in ethnically Tibetan Xiahe, Labrang Monastery once housed more than four thousand monks, and the village that surrounded it was almost exclusively Tibetan and Hui Muslim. Today, though the monastery is growing in its continuing recovery from the Cultural Revolution, the town has become discernibly Chinese, in both character and demographics. In 2002, an airport was built on the Sangke grasslands, and a concrete hotel complex, for visiting officials and workers, marked the edge of the wilderness. Lower down in the valley, the meandering road to Xiahe was replaced with a freeway. The river ran brown with sediment from the many projects upstream. The Alliance for Research concludes: "Current policy has switched from forced transfer to creation of incentives which render population shifts into Tibet a certainty. While the latter might be considered 'market-driven,' effects on Tibetans remain deliberate."

IN AUGUST 1999, DAJA MESTON, AN AMERICAN RESEARCHER FROM BOSTON, went to Qinghai with an Australian colleague and a Tibetan translator to investigate and document the effects of the proposed Qinghai resettlement project. The trio entered China on tourist visas in the hopes of garnering independent interviews with local residents and a true perspective on what the resettlement project would mean for the region. Poking around in a small village a few hours away from Golmud, near a farm that operates with prison labor, Meston's group was arrested.

By his account, told to me in a New York coffee shop and later published in his own book, Meston was separated from his companions, accused of being an international spy, and subjected to a makeshift kangaroo court in a run-down building deep in the Qinghai desert. There, formally dressed military guards coerced a confession from him and filmed mock proceedings on a set made to look like a real Chinese court. "They were building a case," Meston told me. "They would show the world a film about espionage in China." His interrogations, as U.S. State Department spokesman James Foley would later gingerly describe it, repeating Meston's claims, consisted of "intense psychological pressure." Meston says he was kept awake for days, dehydrated, and berated with frequent lectures and accusations. Believing his life was imminently threatened, he opened the third-floor window of his makeshift cell and jumped out, fracturing both his feet, his spine, and numerous other bones in the fall. His case drew international media attention and escalated into a diplomatic confrontation, a development that Meston believes saved his life.

For all the aspects of China's economy and government that have slowly liberalized over the past decade, the free flow of information and discourse has not been among them. Press freedoms are virtually nonexistent, and the government maintains a multifaceted stranglehold on research and reporting and even plain old conversations. Its own press is state-owned and closely monitored. International radio, such as Radio Free Asia and Voice of America, are jammed in much of Tibet, and Web sites from the International Campaign for Tibet to CNN are regularly blocked. The organization Reporters Without Borders ranks China the seventh most restrictive working environment for journalists in the world, right behind North Korea, Burma, and Turkmenistan. Its 2007 study noted that more journalists—thirty, including a *New York Times* correspondent—were jailed in China than in any other country. Fifty-two bloggers were arrested in a widespread crackdown on online chats. "The authorities, directed by President Hu Jintao, have been bringing the media to heel in the name of a 'harmonious society,'" the organization's report stated. "The press is being forced into self-censorship, the Internet is filtered and foreign media very closely watched." That said, press freedoms are considered even more restricted in China's west than in the east of Beijing and Shanghai. Journalists are universally prohibited from working independently in or anywhere near Tibet; despite pledges made to the International Olympic Committee; those caught have been punished or swiftly deported.

In July 2001, Jean-Marie Jolidon, a journalist working for the Swiss press who had previously reported on Tibet, was arrested in Beijing's airport along with his wife and his ten-year-old child. They were held, interrogated at length, and deported. In 2006, at least twenty-five foreign journalists were arrested, assaulted, or threatened. Inside Tibet, those Tibetans who help inquisitive foreigners, as tourist guides or drivers or simply friendly monks, have been imprisoned, have lost their business licenses, and have been tortured. A driver who was paid by an American reporter on a clandestine project not only lost his license—a hard-won and expensive economic tool in Tibet—and was imprisoned for a short time as a traitor, but his entire family lost their jobs and spiraled into financial desperation. To get a free view of Tibetan life, many journalists are forced to sneak into the country, under the pretense of being a curious backpacker on a tourist visa. That's how I entered Tibet.

The morning in May 2002 after I first arrived in Golmud, the end of the line and the beginning of the construction, I reported, as required, to a small, scowling woman inside the China Information and Tourism Services office, conveniently located just down the hall from my room in the only hotel permitted to put up foreigners. She went by the name of Sherry, apparently for the benefit of untrained ears, and spoke broken English. Sherry explained the rules for foreigners: For $250 in cash, she would assign me to a group of tourists and provide me with the papers to cross the checkpoints into the TAR. There I would be met by a government guide and have just four days to sightsee in Lhasa before my permits would expire. (In order to remain there longer, I would forfeit my return ticket and stay in the TAR illegally.) But there was a catch: I was the only foreigner in town, so I had to wait in Golmud until three more people showed up—enough to form a legal "tour." On the second day, two British travelers showed up. We shared a meal and some stories, but that night, impatient, they tried to sneak across the TAR checkpoint in the trunk of a taxicab and were arrested.

On day three, I was alone again.

That's when Sherry emerged as my unofficial tour guide. I wanted to interview her, but, erring on the side of paranoia that China has made a regional tic, I settled instead on cordial conversations that only indirectly considered the impact of the new railway. In the long hours when her office closed for lunch, we walked the streets of Golmud. She showed me a zoo, but there were no animals, and a garden full of greenhouses where nothing seemed to be growing but the boredom of the men who raked and shoveled mounds of dirt and broken concrete. She told me stories of her childhood. The winters had been palpably colder then, and people were curious about the change. The town used to be small. Now it held about five thousand people and seemed planned for a million. Wide paved streets spread out irrationally on a grid populated by intermittent hotels—for the Chinese workers, not the foreigners—lit up by the neon outlines of palm trees, Las Vegas style, a half a mile of emptiness stretching between each storefront. All of the pavement, the street grid, the hotels were just a few years old. Golmud was booming, as railway workers, administrators, and entrepreneurs flooded Qinghai. There was a sense, she said, that this place would become important.

Sherry told me her husband, who worked as a teacher in a nearby grade school, had asked if I would visit an English class. I suggested that she could return the favor by issuing my permit in exchange for answering the machine-gun questions of thirty or so students in crisp blue uniforms.

"Do you know Shaquille O'Neal?"

"Not personally," I responded, trying to explain that I did know who he was.

"Are all Americans tall like him?"

"Of course not," I said, my six-two frame provoking looks of disbelief.

"Do American children study Chinese in school?" I didn't have a satisfying answer for that one.

That afternoon I boarded a bus for Lhasa, a party of one. As I stepped on the bus, the driver dropped an arm across my path. He shouted something, but I did not understand, and one of the Tibetan men spoke enough English to help translate. My ticket was the wrong one, the driver said. He wanted another thirty dollars to let me ride. We argued there for a few minutes. The normal bus fare for Tibetans was about six dollars, and I had paid enough. Eventually, perhaps seeing that I was too stubborn to pay his bribe, he relented.

The bus crossed through Wudaoliang, an ugly strip of restaurants and prostitute shops along the garbage-strewn road, and continued on, across the Yangtze River headwaters at Tuotuohe. The cabin was unheated, and I cocooned myself in a down sleeping bag and rubbed at the thickening layer of frost on the window with the ball of my fist, trying to see outside. Sometime in the sleepless night, as the bus crossed the high pass at Tangu La, the pinnacle of the road and the railway route at nearly seventeen thousand feet, it began to snow heavily. Several hours later, the bus pulled into a truck stop in the high small town of Amdo, in the TAR, overlooking a flat green valley so expansive the sheer space was breathtaking. For the first time I felt I was in the "true" Tibet.

TIBET, IN THE EYES OF THE WEST, IS LIKE EDEN. WE TEND TO THINK OF reverent monks teaching peaceful meditation under the glistening peaks of the Himalayas—a magical land more congruous with the fantasies of J. R. R. Tolkien than with any actual reference most foreigners have. That dozens of books have been written about the mysteries and exotics of Tibet surely helps. It's easy to forget the travail of living in an undeveloped, isolated, subsistence economy, under harsh conditions, while much of the rest of the globe strides forward with the evolutions brought by globalization. It's hard to ignore the passionate refrain of exiles and activists who portray an unwaveringly righteous narrative of the torture and genocide of the Tibetan people, or seem to claim the decimation should be all the more offensive because of the pure and peaceful nature of the people against whom it is perpetrated.

And partly, the story appeals to the West because it is what it prefers to believe. Tibetan Buddhists represent piety that is universally appealing and a contentedness that Westerners can only dream of in their chaotic and capitalistic existences. Tibetan landscape represents unadulterated paleolithic wilderness—the kind of resources pillaged for the world's development in so many other areas. As Orville Schell put it in a conversation, "We still yearn to find some place that is from before our modern, harried experience, but there is almost no place like that anymore. It's a very powerful and seductive idea, more now than ever because of the way the world has been homogenized." An unspoken argument against the railway project, against the entire Go West campaign, seems to be, *things in Tibet should remain exactly the way they were before 1950—if not for Tibetans' benefit, then for our own.*

Yet, despite the history and precedent of China's past attempts to control Tibetans, and even despite the dust of demolition blanketed over Lhasa, the Chinese argument that economic development would benefit Tibetans living in Tibet might have merit. Along the Qinghai-Tibet Highway, nomadic camps were clustered in the fields of rolling pastureland, a fertile green and yellow in the daylight but an unforgiving, frozen wilderness at night, even in May. Tibet, though habitable by nomads and their animals, was still nearly as wild as it had been centuries before this frost-heaved ribbon of pavement was laid down. At the highway's truck stops, poor, hardened people begged for food, rides, and money. Their lives had little to do with the political standoff between Beijing and Dharamsala. In fact, it often seemed in Tibet that the government-in-exile, which faithfully campaigns for Tibetan's human rights and religious freedoms, was too divorced from its people's contemporary needs to offer anything resembling democratic representation. Exiled Tibetan officials usually have not personally experienced Tibet in decades; they based their rally cries on charged rhetoric that is in some ways as manipulative as China's own. And while their campaigns did little to make a dent in the day-to-day travails of Tibetans, they reliably riled China, often resulting in repression inside the TAR. Poor rural Tibetans were caught voiceless in the middle. At least the principal of economic reform stood to offer them a chance.

But if social equality was truly China's highest political objective in Tibet, as Luo Rong Zandui and the Go West initiative assert, then the $4 billion budget of the railway—an amount roughly equal to twice the TAR's total gross domestic product in 2001—seemed a perverse way to achieve it. The TAR's health-care system was in shambles, the budget for education was half the national average, its illiteracy rate was twice that of neighboring Qinghai, and there were just one-fifth the number of vocational schools per capita than in hinterland Chinese provinces.

In the brusque roadside center of Nagqu, another lonely truck stop offering noodles and a toilet, a bullhorn PA system thundered with propaganda—about valuing the Communist system and being loyal to China. A man on the bus from Golmud reported that political party views were often repeated ad nauseam in small towns across Tibet. For forty-five minutes, a convoy of Chinese military vehicles made its way through town—covered lorries with dozens of soldiers seated on benches in the back, flatbed big-rigs with huge industrial hardware cloaked under tarps, a short series of big armored trucks that looked like potato bugs on wheels. The idyllic stillness and beauty of the landscape was persistently, possibly permanently, broken by this physical and psychological invasion.

At 15,400 feet, near the county town of Damxung, the bus stopped on a windswept and blunt pass, about a hundred miles from Lhasa. Prayer flags flew from a large rock cairn at the summit, and Tibetan pilgrims disembarked from the bed of a Chinese lorry to walk the short distance around the stupa, a mound of inscribed stones, in meditation. Snow began to fall again, and an old man wrapped tight in a red robe against the slashing wind pulled me aside. His face, hashed by deep leathery creases, betrayed his age and decades of exposure to Tibet's elements. The man pulled a small pendant from inside his shirt—a circular silver frame with a black-and-white photograph of the Dalai Lama behind a cracked glass lens. Pictures like this one are strictly forbidden in Tibet, even today. His carrying one, a common practice, was both a sign of Tibetans' unwavering devotion to their long-absent leader and a form of tacit resistance against China. The old man was asking me if I had brought him any more.

Behind him a panoramic billboard advertisement portrayed Tibet's wild environment in oversaturated color and a complex of modern Shanghai-like sky-rises adjacent to the iconic Potala Palace. Bridging the scenes was a train—a sleek high-speed bullet locomotive more akin to Tokyo than Golmud—that streaked across the expanse. Such signs, many of them with propaganda aimed at inciting workers with a sense of patriotism and purpose, are posted at army and construction camps all along the route to Lhasa. But here, the contrast and irony were especially profound. Would a high-speed rail running eight trains a day on an elevated platform through these fields enliven Tibet or bleed it further? It seemed then that the geographic barrier of the mountains was like a dam about to collapse.

When Austine Waddell, a researcher who accompanied Younghusband in 1904, reached the city's gates, he wrote that "the vast panorama of the holy city in its beautiful mountain setting burst upon our view, and we gazed with awe upon temples and palaces of the long-sealed Forbidden City, the shrines of the mystery which had so long haunted our dreams, and which lay revealed before our eyes at last." When I arrived in Lhasa in 2002, the bus parked in a suburban area of tile and cinder-block buildings. Taxicabs and their drivers circled like hungry ravens, and a Chinese man shouted instructions. Across the street, the well-lit entrance to a Chinese business hotel—replete with fanciful green and white neon flowers and fireworks—heralded arrival in a business town that could not be too far away from being the next Lanzhou or Xi'an.

You still had to be an adventurer to get to Tibet in 2002—if not a conqueror of armies, then a conqueror of borders, of permits and mountains. There were still barriers enough, but those barriers were falling.

═ 7 ═

UNDER A HAN SUN

PASANG ALWAYS ARRANGED TO MEET AT NIGHT, AND before he sat down he walked to the windows and closed the blinds. Over time he had learned to be cautious when talking to foreigners. As one of the most experienced guides in Lhasa, Pasang, a lighthearted man in his midforties with an oxlike build from his years leading expeditions through the Himalayas, was constantly in demand among foreign tourists and geographic expeditions. His understanding of Tibetan history was comprehensive, as was his knowledge of the local ecology and geography. Most important for a guide, he knew the places outside of the tourist fray, where clients would fawn over their glimpse of the still-hidden, magical Tibet.

Several years ago, however, he started having problems. The Chinese, he said, did not want Tibetans to work as guides any longer, in part because their perspectives on the ravaged landscape and struggling monasteries tended to leave tourists—even Chinese tourists—critical of the government's policies. But it was nearly impossible to visit a monastery in Tibet that had not been at least partially destroyed, its assets ransacked and stolen, and tourists would ask about its history; they wanted to know how old the temple's glorious, shimmering Buddha was, and "we cannot explain that these are new statues," he said. If he landed a job with a large group of ten Americans, the Chinese government would often place a "minder" along for the ride, to judge his tour. "They are constructing a revisionist history and do not want to tell tourists that the monasteries were rebuilt. As more and more people come here, their goal is to say that they did not destroy too much, that they left these great things." Pasang had twice gone to prison, for several months at a time, for violating this code. It used to be his greatest occupational hazard. But lately he had come against still more threatening obstacles. Tourism had been steadily increasing in Tibet, but a new wave of ethnically oriented business regulations and economic reforms was keeping Pasang out of the game.

On February 28, 2001, Chinese president Jiang Zemin had signed into law an amendment to the bulwark 1984 Regional National Autonomy Law, a long-standing code, first established in the calm 1980s, that defined Tibet's right to govern its own internal economic and cultural matters in its own interest and outlined the government structure provided to do so.

It was a lofty constitutional parameter that, though never implemented the way the Tibetans had hoped, had at least served the critical function of reinstating Tibet as a minority region, distinct from China, and thus deserving a separate set of rules. The 2001 amendment subverted the language of self-governance altogether by directing the central government on specific channels for controlling and developing the "autonomous regions" in coordination with the national plan. Though the "Spring Tide" had set the trend in motion, this law formally defined the priorities of Tibet's development as political and economic goals of the Communist Party, not those of Tibetans themselves.

For the preceding twenty years, Tibetans had to varying degrees been shielded by the informal "special consideration" afforded them under the Regional National Autonomy Law and a general transit and work permit policy that made it difficult for outsiders, including Han Chinese, to migrate to the TAR. Some of those policies were reversed in 1992, but many more had persisted. In addition to receiving tax breaks, Tibetan families had been excepted from China's one-child policy; Tibetan farmers were allowed to keep more animals than the quotas imposed on eastern Chinese. The Tibetan language had also been allowed to continue as the mainstay language of the TAR.

In the wake of Jiang's new amendment, laws were passed requiring that the examinations for guides' licenses, business licenses, and drivers' licenses be taken annually and be taken in Chinese—a sweeping change that affected the ability of any non-Chinese-speaking person to find work in the tourism, construction, and transport industries—the components of the local economy that Beijing had identified as Tibet's pillars. The change, coupled with the laws encouraging migration in 1992, gave the Han a devastating advantage. That spring, after studying Mandarin dutifully, Pasang took the licensing exam in a government office in Lhasa—and failed. He had little choice but to start working illegally. But how long, he wondered, would it be before he was arrested again?

The newly articulated requirements sent a subtle but clear message that when it came to competing with Chinese entrepreneurs, Tibetans had no special status, even in their homeland. The changes fueled the sorts of rumors that had upset the elders in Kalden's village as they heard the plan for the construction of the railway. And they affected much of Tibet's urban working class, including Renzin, who soon received an unwelcome visit at his business on the Barkhor. For the past twelve years, his store had been called Chomolongma, the Tibetan name for Mount Everest and to him a significant symbol of the border he had crossed when returning to Tibet from exile in Nepal. That homecoming had occurred in 1979, when Renzin, a rambunctious twenty-year-old decked out in bell-bottom jeans and hippyish long hair—a style he picked up from the European and American gypsies who regularly passed through Kathmandu—decided to return to his roots and live with his father. Lhasa then was on the cusp of the reform period, and he was buoyed by the optimistic years that followed, but the change was still awkward. He was torn between the nation of his passport and this place he called home. It took more than a decade before Renzin finally found the resources and the personal commitment to open his shop on the Barkhor. By then, of course, the violence of the late 1980s had proven that nothing was to be taken for granted in Tibet. Still, he had, perhaps naively, persevered with his belief that with economic evolution would come further liberalization. That is, until the day three suited Chinese officials walked into his store and bluntly announced that the name of his business would have to change. A larger shop was being opened across the square, and its owner, a Han businessman from Chengdu, wanted to use the Everest namesake for his own.

At first, Renzin pleaded with the officials. He told them how long he had been working in Lhasa, about his dedication to making his capitalist venture successful. He told them he held a Nepali passport and that his store reflected the kind of foreign entrepreneurial investment China wanted in its development plans for Tibet. He offered to share the name. But the men's message was plain: Renzin had two days to take down his Chomolongma signs. If he did not, his license would be revoked and his store would be forcibly closed. Renzin, as a Nepali citizen, could lose the visa that allowed him to live in Tibet, though he had been born in Lhasa.

Cheng Guodong, a senior scientist posted at the Chinese Academy of Sciences' research center in Lanzhou, rides a yak during an early permafrost research expedition across the Tibetan Plateau during the late 1960s.

Chinese engineers dig a truck out of the plateau mud sometime in the 1970s. In 1978, the first major attempt to build a railway to Tibet would be halted.

Railway engineer Zhang Luxin of China's Ministry of Railway's First Railway Institute. Zhang had invested more than thirty years developing plans for the route south from Qinghai to Lhasa.

The shopping stalls in Lhasa's Barkhor offered goods for Tibetan nomads and Buddhist pilgrims as well as, in 2000, half a million tourists each year. Shopkeeper Renzin Tashi depends on such travelers for his livelihood.

A Tibetan pilgrim prostrating before the Jokhang Temple in the Barkhor.

Monks perform a masked dance at the annual spring festival at Tsurphu Monastery in the Dowo Lung Valley.

Kalden on his family home site, in Tolung-Dechen County, after earth-working crews had cleared his village to make way for the train line.

A typical religious shrine inside a Tibetan home, with illegal pictures of the Dalai Lama and the Panchen Lama. In 1966, during the height of the Cultural Revolution, such displays, as well as statues of the Buddha and mandala religious paintings, were destroyed by the Red Guard. They remain illegal today.

A chief physician at the Golmud People's Hospital, Dr. Han Mei, inside her tent on the Tibetan Plateau in 2001. Han was one of just two doctors in Golmud with experience in high-altitude illnesses, and, for a time, the only one working on the plateau. *(Courtesy of Han Mei)*

Nomadic herders in a valley near Xiahe, an ethnically Tibetan area in Gansu Province, outside the Tibet Autonomous Region (TAR). As many as a million Tibetans have been removed from rural lands since the late 1990s and resettled as part of Beijing's Comfortable Housing Program.

Traditional Tibetan buildings being demolished in central Lhasa in May 2002.

The massive earth-moving and railway construction project along the Golmud River in 2002. Construction began at the northern, Qinghai, end of the line since moving heavy equipment and material over the 16,900-foot-high Tangu La Pass of the Kunlun Mountains was deemed impossible without a train for transport.

Zhao Shiyun (left), the young bridge engineer brought in to oversee construction for the Qinghai-Tibet Railway Company, with plateau engineer Zhang Luxin. (*Courtesy of Zhao Shiyun*)

Cheng Guodong, a senior permafrost scientist with China's CAREERI research center.

Early in the process, Zhao directed work to begin on the railway's seven tunnels, including one to navigate the twisting Tolung Valley west of Lhasa. Construction jobs were almost universally granted to Han migrants like these from Sichuan, Yunnan, and other eastern provinces, in part because few Tibetans could understand orders given in Mandarin.

To cross the high Tibetan Plateau's unstable permafrost region (above), where ground temperatures are just barely below freezing, the Chinese engineers attempted to predict and account for global warming trends. The model they chose may have underestimated the thawing on the tundra, putting the railway in jeopardy.

Zhao Shiyun beside a train and the innovative thermosyphon cooling sticks that were embedded along the railway route in order to pull down the temperature of the warming earth. (Courtesy of Zhao Shiyun)

Yang Fen Ming, a migrant from Sichuan, bought drills and opened a business to punch holes for the thermosyphons along the railway line. He soon learned that several dozen other entrepreneurs were competing for the same work.

When construction over the unstable permafrost remained a major obstacle, Zhao sought to speed the process and lay track from the south. But the monster PG30 machine (above) that constructed the railway was twice the size and weight of a locomotive. To get it to Nagqu, the Qinghai-Tibet Highway had to be reinforced to handle the load.

Zhao also pushed to construct bridges, such as this pylon and rail mound near the Kunlun Pass, in order to keep the ground frozen while still meeting the government's deadline for opening the railway.

A home, in Damxung County, adjacent to the elevated railway tracks. Kalden's village in Tolung-Dechen County, to the south, would fight to be resettled after Chinese bureaucrats ruled that only those houses immediately in the train's path would be moved at the government's expense.

Two Tibetan women follow the railway tracks, the sturdiest and easiest path across the rural marshlands in Damxung County.

Two Tibetan Buddhist nuns, one holding a Pepsi bottle and the other a digital camera, seated in front of the Potala Palace. Before the Dalai Lama fled Tibet and entered exile in 1959, the Potala was his official residence. It is now a museum geared to supporting one of China's official pillars of economic growth for Tibet: tourism.

Billboards advertising the new "bullet-style" train to Tibet were mounted near the construction site of the Lhasa terminal station, about five miles from downtown.

Downtown Golmud in 2002 (top) and in 2005 (bottom). Once a dusty way post at the head of the Qinghai-Tibet Highway, Golmud itself has been remodeled with accents of the sleak, gleaming architecture of Shanghai.

With echoes of the red roof and whitewashed walls of the Potala Palace, the Lhasa railway station was constructed to handle not only the expected influx of new residents and visitors but also future traffic along a planned extension to mineral-rich Shigatze, west from Lhasa along the Yarlung Tsangpo River, and several other railway extensions.

The three arches of the bridge over the Kyichu River into Lhasa resemble *katags*, the traditional Tibetan scarves presented to guests and religious authorities.

The T27, as the train from Beijing was named, on the Qinghai-Tibet Railway, approaching the Kunlun Mountain pass in southern Qinghai, on the way to the border of the TAR. At nearly seventeen thousand feet, the railway, which opened on July 1, 2006, is heralded as the highest in the world; each car is outfitted with oxygen breathing tubes for passengers.

The Wang family, a Han father and son who emigrated to Lhasa from Sichuan, inside their clothing store in a sprawling marketplace on Lhasa's Han-dominated Dream Island. Most of the goods for sale were shipped in from the manufacturing megalopolises of Chengdu and eastern China.

Li Duo Long, familiarly known as "the Major," a People's Liberation Army officer posted to Lhasa.

A store on Lhasa's Barkhor that sells hip-hop fashions, which appeal to young Tibetans and the increasing number of middle-class migrants and Chinese tourists.

The N'eu village resettlement, one of several compounds that were built to house Tibetans relocated from nomadic villages along the railway line. Often, the cost of an apartment exceeded the government's relocation payment.

The luxury Brahmaputra Grand Hotel, one of more than six hundred hotels catering to the 4 million tourists who visited Lhasa in 2007. Opened by a Chengdu businessman, the hotel is staffed almost entirely by ethnic Chinese.

Lhasa, with the Potala Palace and the new construction under way on the shores of the Kyichu River, in 2006. Economic growth in the Tibet Autonomous Region reached 15 percent in 2006, much of it stemming from subsidies and the large-scale development of resettlement housing, shopping strips, hotels, and mining.

The defeat struck at the base of Renzin's outlook on life. But unlike many other Tibetans who were suffering under the new policies, he could choose to leave. He had forced himself to believe that as long as he adhered to the rules—refrained from political or religious talk and largely kept to himself—he would be allowed to play on a level field. Now, that all seemed to change. He mulled whether he could continue to live and prosper in Lhasa.

As the field tilted, it became increasingly clear that even the most benign or seemingly arbitrary policies could be linked to efforts to bolster the Chinese sector of the economy.

Outside of Lhasa, when Kalden's village was told to rebuild their homes, they were instructed to use granite quarried from local Chinese-owned businesses, a government subsidy aimed at building up the region's new stone industry. When villagers didn't have the money, they were pressured to borrow from China's Herculean state-run banks, oversized financial institutions that were poised to splash onto the global market with some of the largest and most profitable stock offerings in global history. Fueled by such subsidized or forced growth, a new class of rich, Audi-driving Han Chinese had sprouted up in Lhasa.

The Go West initiative had never been clearly defined, leaving its day-to-day policy makers free to use and abuse its larger principles in pursuit of local, even private, objectives. The campaign "can hardly be described as a policy in the narrow sense of a properly delineated action plan . . . envisaging a complete and consistent set of goals and measures," wrote Heike Holbig, a research fellow at the Institute of Asian Affairs in Hamburg, in 2002. "Rather, it appears as a highly diffuse decision-making process shaped by dynamic interactions between numerous actors at central, provincial and local levels over almost two decades, causing priorities to shift and policy goals and instruments to proliferate . . . an alluring playground for the projection of bureau-cratic power over other departments."

In instances like Kalden's resettlement, the new developments were linked to the building of the railway, but sometimes the reasons for a sweeping project, like the widespread replacement of residential neigh-borhoods in Lhasa, were left unarticulated but for the assumption that in China, newer was better. Tibet needed wholesale modernization—the kind of effort that would bring sanitized bathrooms, internal plumbing, and electricity—but the clumsy implementation of China's plan was also bringing less welcome changes. In the case of Renzin's confrontation, the abuses of power were manifestations not of the law but of emboldened local officials taking advantage of the fuzzy dictum of "Go West." The enforcement of Mandarin as the official business language of the TAR was billed as a stride toward "unity," but in an area already suffering the worst educational levels in China, it was prone to have the opposite impact and sharply affected the indigenous people.

Viewed alone in 2002, Renzin's or Pasang's situation could be dis-missed as an unfortunate, isolated circumstance. Virtually no one ever heard them complain, largely because they both knew their safest way forward was to keep their mouths shut and adapt. Kalden's village in southeast Lhasa had heard little about the trend toward demolishing towns in the railway's path in the northwest. Because of the severe limitations on the free flow of information in China, the Tibetans did not immediately connect the dots. Premier Zhu Rongji's claims that prosperity would result in the "strengthening of national unity, safeguarding of social stability, and consolidation of border defense" were, in the view of Western observers, "barely coded phrases for being concerned about issues surrounding the non-Han Chinese." The ethnic preferences underlying Beijing's development goals were betrayed by the chosen title of a guiding paper, published in June 2000 in the prominent party policy journal *Qiushi,* which named its report "Large-scale Development of Western China and China's Nationality Problems."

As the development edicts diffused into Tibet in ever larger numbers and were incongruously implemented, however, each incremental shift in law or physical infrastructure unfurled into a systematic reinvention of China, under modern Han rule, so that within a year of the railway's groundbreaking, the TAR was under siege by the capitalist "army" of a globalized China. It just didn't know it yet.

WHAT BEGAN TO TIP THE BALANCE WAS CHINA'S ASSAULT ON THE LIVES OF rural Tibetans. More than 90 percent of Tibetans live outside of townships, many as nomads on the plateau and grasslands. Some farm; others wander seasonally with great herds of yaks and sheep, from which they harvest meat and dairy to sell at markets in the winter.

While a Westerner, or for that matter an eastern Han Chinese, would not describe a nomad family head as wealthy, the nomads, depending on the number of livestock in their herd, can be well off relative to most Tibetans.

In the small trading town of Damxung, about a hundred miles from Lhasa, a nomadic man on a shopping spree displayed the fat of his land. He wore a large hooded leather coat, lined luxuriously with animal fur, and rode a muscle motorcycle with gleaming chrome pipes and colorful leather tassles hanging from the ends of its handles. Hooked under his arm was a new DVD player, Chinese-made, that he would connect to his television, inside his herder's tent, and power off a solar panel he had bought two seasons earlier. For six months of the year, he roamed more than two hundred miles, packing his tent and supplies on the backs of his animals and covering much of the grasslands on his own feet. Then he returned to his seasonal base, sold his goods to truckers headed for the Barkhor in Lhasa, and spent his profits.

As China began to draw up plans for dividing the TAR's landscape into new townships, it enacted a series of restrictive laws on nomadic and subsistence people across the country's Tibetan regions. In many places, open expanses of land were fenced, and each family was allocated a specific area on which they were allowed to graze their animals. Often, families were required to purchase the fencing, imported by truck from Golmud and eastern Chinese factories, and build the Beijing-imposed barns and hay sheds themselves. Then came limits on how many livestock a family could own—in many cases five animals per household member, a small fraction of the number kept by many nomadic families. Beijing evidently viewed the unrestricted use of this massive land as grossly inefficient. Instead, it envisioned industriously productive cattle farms, like those of northern Texas. The early experimentation with rangeland development encapsulated the Chinese perspective, according to the U.S.-based researcher Emily Yeh, "a pervasive discourse that conceptualizes the Tibetan Plateau as degraded by the 'irrational' herding practices of pastoralists, including their religion-based refusal to increase livestock off-take or kill rodents."

The restrictions were first rolled out in rural parts of Tibetan-populated Qinghai and Sichuan provinces. Yeh documented the intense pressure this put on nomadic people—many of whom received land plots without access to drinking water, or areas too small for their robust herds. In one case, in Gansu Province, not far from Labrang Monastery and the grasslands of Xiahe, a small-scale war erupted. Factions totaling as many as two thousand Tibetan fighters smuggled automatic weapons into the province to fight one another for the land they once shared, and in the two years or so before 1999 nearly thirty people were killed. Now, with seeming disregard for such consequences, the fencing and herding policies were swiftly being implemented on a widespread scale across all Tibetan autonomous areas.

Around 2001, the government pursued a new policy: emptying the rural land entirely of its inhabitants. A 2007 report on the resulting resettlement program published by New York–based Human Rights Watch was scathing in its assessment of the cultural impact. "Resettled herders and dispossessed farmers are encouraged to take up more 'modern' livelihoods and integrate with the new economy. People are being resettled in uniform, shoddily built new towns and villages. Deprived of their conventional livelihood, the affected populations are unable to participate in urban, commercial economies and are thus facing a bleak future," the report stated, noting that up to a million rural Tibetans had been moved. "It is also conceivable that ethno-political motives are at work: that these policies are in part designed to further an integrationist agenda aimed at weakening Tibetan cultural distinctiveness and further extending Chinese control over Tibetan lives."

AS ONE TENTACLE OF BEIJING'S CONTROL WORKED AT TIBET'S ECONOMY, another began to wrap more tightly around the region's monasteries. China's leaders could not afford any potential for instability as the railroad project began to get under way. "Rule with two fists" had always been, and clearly still was, Hu Jintao's way.

It used to be that Chinese police cracked down on a monastery for its political stance or for its support of the Dalai Lama, but after years of painstakingly rebuilding and strengthening their cultural practice, monasteries that steered clear of controversy were being targeted on size alone. Beijing began to see monastic revitalization—a process that increasingly drew Chinese Buddhist practitioners as well as financial donors—as a threat. Monks and nuns were once again routinely expelled from the monasteries, and strict quotas were implemented to keep the communities small.

One of the most prominent and disruptive expulsions took place at Larung Gar, a Tibetan teaching center in western Sichuan Province. Larung Gar, which isn't a monastery and thus never fell under the formal supervision of Chinese authorities, had quickly become one of the most vibrant places in China for the study of Tibetan Buddhism. It was also relatively new—founded in 1980 by the charismatic and revered lama Khempo Jigme Phuntsok—giving it special status as a litmus test on Tibet's vitality. By the middle of 2001, Phuntsok's community had attracted almost nine thousand residents, and Larung Gar, once a group of cottages in the mountains five hundred miles from the nearest metropolis, had blossomed into a town of its own. Phuntsok had been meticulously careful not to engage in discussions about the Dalai Lama or to suggest any political undertones in founding the Larung Gar Institute.

In an odd way, by attracting thousands of Tibetans from the surrounding rural areas to one concentrated place, Larung Gar had become the sort of urban center that the government's resettlement policy encouraged. Yet, when the purpose fell clearly outside of Beijing's interests, urbanization was dissuaded. In addition, roughly a thousand Han Chinese had joined the institute's devoted community, perhaps raising the specter of the Falun Gong movement's success in opposing the government at the grassroots level. "There are more and more Chinese people who have a greater interest not only in spirituality, but in Tibetan Buddhism in particular . . . and want to learn more about why Tibetan people are so devoted," Xiao Qiang, the founder of the nonprofit Human Rights in China, told the International Campaign for Tibet. "Now there is an extra layer of implications that Tibetan Buddhism is maybe going to have an impact on Chinese society, and in that case, what does it mean to the state?"

In early 2000, with the monastery's following continuing to grow, the central government demanded that Phuntsok expel all but fourteen hundred residents, including every Han participant. Phuntsok refused, believing strongly in the importance of religious education and feeling confident he had avoided politicization. In June, fifty trucks and jeeps arrived, backed by thousands of security officials who camped on the outskirts to secure a perimeter, according to the organization Friends of Tibet. The trucks had shuttled hundreds of migrant laborers from the lowlands near Chengdu, a twenty-four-hour drive. While police evicted as many as eight thousand residents, the laborers—for thirty-two dollars in wages—took to the streets with sledgehammers on orders to dismantle the town. Three thousand homes were quickly demolished, their walls reduced to dust while residents' belongings remained inside. Where homes had nudged up to the mountains, nothing but a scar of brown debris was left.

Chinese security forces were placed in residence at Larung Gar, and a checkpoint at the mouth of the valley started to review resident IDs and prohibit visitors from lingering for more than two hours. Beginning almost immediately after the scourge, Tibetans began stealing back into the remote valley. From time to time, Chinese officials, spotting construction, took to the hills and tore down the new homes. When Phuntsok, at age seventy, died under house arrest in

2004, an estimated fifty thousand followers streamed on foot over the backcountry mountain ridges to gather in his honor at Larung Gar, despite Chinese officials' efforts to keep a lid on the mourning.

GANDEN MONASTERY SITS AT THE TOP OF A CRESCENT-SHAPED MOUN-tain, a small city reduced to mostly shrub-infested ruins tucked into the steep curling hillside at about fourteen thousand feet and an hour and a half outside of Lhasa. The main seat of the Gelugpa order of Tibetan Buddhism, Ganden, constructed in 1417, was for a time one of the largest monasteries in the world. But while parts of it have been restored, it has not returned to its former glory.

After the Cultural Revolution, a grouping of dormitories and study rooms and the two main temples were rebuilt. The rooms are dark, with strong shafts of light piercing from small windows near the top of the monastery's cavernous ceilings. Long murals and hanging cloth *thankas* grace the faded walls, each meticulously painted canvas telling a different story from the Buddha's life. The monastery is the starting point of a classic pilgrim trek that crosses two mountain passes before descending to the legendary Samye Monastery, the first built in Tibet, about fifty-five miles away. In 2002, however, the area was strictly controlled and lay in one of the large portions of south-ern Tibet considered sensitive by the Chinese military. Traveling the pilgrim path illegally offered an opportunity to get away from the gerrymandered Tibet put forth by Chinese law and travel off-grid into untouched Tibetan nomadic lands. Near the monastery's door, a young monk was sitting on one of the room's long padded benches reading a rectangular block-printed sheaf of paper—his prayers. In horrible English, he explained to me that he was a student of Tibetan medicine. He took my hands together between his when we met, and something about this interaction put me into a sublime ease. His eyes closed, and his grip tightened on my wrists, the tips of his fingers pressing firmly between my ligaments and into my radial artery. In Tibetan medicine, the pulse is the most important of three diagnostic branches, which also include the phlegm (or fluids) and the wind (or breath). Though unexplainable, Tibetans' abilities to read the relative strength of a body's organs have been confirmed by Western doctors, who testify that Tibetan diagnosis rivals modern medical practice. The Chinese place great value on it as well; Lhasa's Mendzekhang, the central medical college, has been expanded under China's rule. Moments earlier, the monk had correctly ascertained that a woman touring the monastery was four weeks' pregnant. Now his fingers searched my own heartbeat, scanning my kidneys, my stomach, and my lungs. Then just as quickly he let go, opened his eyes, and smiled with a big thumbs-up. Apparently all systems were go.

The path toward Samye followed a high ridge south above a gaping valley for several hours and then stumbled down into the valley at the tiny village of Hepou, a gathering of wooden and mud shacks along the rocky gray line of a seasonal river. Above Hepou, the route climbed to the towering pass at Thukpa La, at seventeen thousand feet. In the village, a row of Tibetan men sat perched on an old stone wall like birds on a wire, smoking cigarettes and laughing. A mountain-hewn thirty-year-old, with wiry black hair tied brashly in the back with a band of bloodred silk, set to lashing bags to the side of his horse. Dorjee was an informal guide—a local farmer eager to make extra money by helping the occasional illegal traveler, despite the risks. While he prepared the packs, Dorjee's wife served boiled potatoes and salty butter tea, refilling the cups to the brim each time I took a sip, dashing my hopes that the polite deed of drinking it would end as quickly as I could gulp to the bottom.

After four hours' march, crisscrossing paths worn into the grassy plateau by grazing yaks, a nomad camp, called Yama Do, appeared below the first summit. The roofs of Hepou were a tiny set of dots at the bottom of the valley. Dorjee dismounted, started chain-smoking, and pitched camp. In this scarcely traveled area, nomads still find the sight of Westerners surprising, and they huddled around to watch the assembly of a phosphorescent, featherweight, high-tech tent with microscopic intensity and curiosity.

The nomads' quarters by comparison were twenty feet long by twelve feet wide, with two whittled tree branches holding a half-inch-thick wool weave, weighing at least two hundred pounds, in the air. Life among these nomads, beyond the fencing laws that plague those farther north, cannot have changed much over the centuries. One boy practiced his shot by wrapping rocks in the woven cuplike end of a long woolen whip the herders use to fire stones at the yaks. He would wind the four-foot-long rope into the air, swinging it like a lasso until it whistled, and then fling the stone out of its harness with exacting precision and enough speed to penetrate the steel door of a truck. Next to him, his younger brothers sat on the barren ground and raked at a large caterpillar with a rock, yelping when its green innards spilled onto the ground. The men, including the head of the camp, who wore a dirt-stained Yankees cap, just sat around and smoked and talked.

Inside the nomad's tent, smoke filled what little space was left among the bundles of rolled-up bed mats and stacked gear and provisions. Twelve or so people slept inside, around an iron stove, where a woman and her elderly mother plumbed butter in a cylindrical wooden urn for tea and cooked. It was strangely similar to the tent Zhang described from his time in the northeast. The nomads would continue this way until the December snows made life in the high country impossible, and then, like the nomads above Damxung, they would retreat to Hepou or other villages of the Lhasa Valley.

The next morning, Dorjee turned back to Hepou at the summit of the first col, and I dropped down an icy ridge to another wild valley. Several more nomadic camps were visible in the distance, a day's walk in any roadless direction. A day's walk later, the route reached a second, still higher, pass that was even wilder, corralled by foreboding storm clouds and capped by a stupa with Tibetan prayers carved into it. Streams of sun-bleached prayer flags fluttered in the wind, and the ground was blanketed in snow, making footing treacherous. Intimately close, like gods peering down into their pet aquarium called Earth, were larger, icier, rock-strewn peaks.

At that second pass, the elevation and temperatures approached those in which the Chinese engineers laying the plans for the railway—and the nomads—lived for months on end. How could they work? Who could use this barren and beautiful land better than the nomads, and what life would men like Dorjee find behind fences or transplanted into the bustling chaos of Lhasa? Roping these people into this new society seemed a lot like domesticating a wild tiger and then declawing it.

As quickly as sixteen thousand feet turned to fifteen thousand, the barren rock and grassy tufts turned to budding junipers and flowering roses. Temperatures soared from a biting twenty to a balmy eighty degrees Fahrenheit as the trail uncurled into the valley. Soon the glacial gurgling that was audible beneath the scree was joined by a light stream, and then another, until the confluence built into the roar of a rapid, sparkling river. This trail has been walked by pilgrims and herders for hundreds of years, but it remained empty and so raw and natural that you had to wonder if civilization had ever graced it at all.

A day later, the road reached the ancient circular wall and open gate of Samye Monastery, a prophetic, eighth-century retreat in a flat valley filled with orchards and fifty-foot-tall sand dunes. At that time, barring a circuitous rural road that wandered for miles, Samye remained separated from Tibet's modernization by the infinitely braided waters and sandbars of the Yarlung Tsangpo River. Inside the walls, an arresting four-story temple with a vibrantly restored golden roof commanded the center of a quarter-mile-wide complex meant to symbolize the universe—an architectural mandala. Like cosmological entities, about thirty peripheral buildings orbit the main temple in seemingly random placement—just a fraction of the 108 structures that originally stood there. Exploring the grounds warranted caution, as two tourists without permits had been arrested there a day earlier.

In the main hall, called the Utse, several hundred resident monks were gathered, chanting in a deeply resonant chorus of prayer punctuated by long *aum*-like blasts from sixteen-foot-long copper trumpets called *rag-dun*. The monks faced the Jowo Khang, a smaller inner sanctum accessed through three doors "of liberation"—those of emptiness, sign-lessness, and want-lessness. Through them, at the center of the temple, stood a thirteen-foot-tall statue of Sakyamuni, or Buddha. The place, its rich sounds, deep colors, and dark spaces, imbued a heady sense of profound peacefulness.

But a few miles away, the river barge was closing, and to make it back to Lhasa without camping another night, I had to go now.

Normally, people headed from Samye to Lhasa would hitch a ride in a tractor's flatbed trailer to a ferry launch several miles down a thin dirt track, from which a barge could be taken for the long trip across the shallow river. The barge takes up to two hours to meticulously weave in and out of a maze of constantly shifting sandbars and the rapid current to the far bank, where a white cube-shaped shack housed

Chinese police checking for permits. To avoid it, I waited until dusk when the boat captain was hitching his barge to a tree and offered a hefty bribe to make one last trip across the land upstream of the checkpoint.

Having arrived at the far shore, I scurried like a refugee up a broken dirt bank to the highway and flagged the first set of headlights that came storming my way. A large red semi, loaded with freight, ground to a halt, and its driver, a young Chinese man from Sichuan, kindly waved me up the short ladder and into his cab. Four hours later, well after midnight, he stopped in front of the locked gate of my hotel in Lhasa.

8

THE GAMBLER

ACROSS THE TIBETAN PLATEAU THAT SPRING, FROM GOL-
mud to Lhasa, the footprint of the Qinghai-Tibet Railway was defined.
Bridges were spanning the Kunluns' northern foothills, and many
waterways and canyons were covered in gaping concrete structures.
Near Lhasa, workers were drilling a tunnel, the longest of the route,
through the mountains of the Yangpachen Gorge. Other tunnels—
the highest in the world at a place called Fenghuoshan, and another
near the craggy Kunlun Mountain Pass—were under way. But the
construction zones lay strewn across the landscape like isolated jig-
saw puzzle sections assembling on a broad banquet table, the vast spaces
between the bridges and tunnels remaining largely unmarked. A profound sense of disconnect settled over the plateau, and it wasn't just
among the Tibetans, who lacked the aerial view to see the whole project come together; it was felt inside the railway company itself.

Twenty-two railway bureaus each worked under different authorities and, much like the various administrations deciding for themselves
how to implement the generalities of the Go West initiative, each had

been left to start the project by deciding for itself how to interpret and carry out the railway plan. Three entirely separate scientific and architectural bodies advised them: the CAREERI group; the First Design Institute; and the First Railway Institute, where Zhang Luxin worked. The Qinghai-Tibet Railway Company, the semicommercial state-owned entity that would run the railway, had only just been formed and had not filled its position of chief engineer, or director. No cogent plan had been drawn up for the rail link as a whole. To make matters worse, there were no engineering standards or specifications for building this high-altitude, low-temperature railway. Train lines had been constructed on permafrost, but a project like this—of such length and at more than fifteen thousand feet—had never been attempted.

Yet the government pushed for construction to begin, so each railway bureau worked on its own self-defined guidelines, paid different wages, and hired laborers with varying degrees of experience and training, all from different parts of the country. Amazingly the Qinghai-Tibet Railway had made it to this point without coordination, consistency, or holistic planning. To some extent, the strategy made sense to a central government hell-bent on finishing the railway in time for the country's coming-out party in the summer of 2008. The locations of the major river crossings and mountain tunnels were obvious, and those heavy infrastructure construction sites would take the most time, materials, and labor to build. So why not start them immediately, while the scientists took another year or two to work out kinks in the permafrost plan and management got its drawings in order? The approach indoctrinated a blind faith that the permafrost problem could be conquered and that it could be done on schedule, as soon as a schedule was devised. Zhang Luxin had boldly declared the permafrost issue "solved," but his statement had been born more of desire than of fact. Others weren't so sure. "It needed more work," said the scientist Cheng Guodong of the CAREERI engineering institute. "There should still be more research to study the permafrost problems, a test section built. Then come up with a good design, and then start construction. This should be the rule. It should have taken two or three years. Instead construction began right away."

Of course, China's engineers were among the best in the world when it came to big tunnels, bridges, and railways. They had cut their teeth on old projects like the Kunming Railway, which wound through impossibly steep gorges in southern Sichuan Province, built over forty thousand miles of tracks across China, and had provided the manpower for the construction of the United States' own transcontinental railroad more then a century earlier. As Henry Posner, head of the Pittsburgh-based Railway Development Corporation, which had run the world's highest operating railway, in Peru, put it, "The Chinese are the best railway builders in the world. If anybody can make a line like this happen, they can." Fueled by a brash but justified sense of confidence, they knew that momentum was the key to seeing the project through. They were comfortable, in a sense, with winging it.

In May, the Qinghai-Tibet Railway Company finally hired a general director to oversee the construction effort. Its first director had quit after just months on the job, unable to handle the high-altitude conditions. Order was needed on the frenzied projects that were already so well under way, and it was time to establish standards and make other key decisions—like how the tracks would cross the world's most treacherous and highest frozen wetland. Oddly, though, the man chosen for the post had never managed a railway before and knew virtually nothing of permafrost.

ZHAO SHIYUN WAS A RISING YOUNG STRUCTURAL ENGINEER FROM HUBEI City. He may have been ignorant of the conditions in Tibet, but he was considered intellectually capable and a quick study—the kind of man who would work hard to achieve success without getting in the way of the larger politics, power machinations, and egos of China's railway ministry. When he took the job, he got a lot more than he bargained for.

When I first met Zhao—three years after he was hired—he had refused my request to come to his office at the Ministry of Railways, choosing instead a claustrophobic oak-paneled private dining cube in a bustling seafood restaurant in west Beijing. Officially, the ministry never cooperated with my reporting, though Zhao was happy to discuss the railway. A part of him wanted recognition for his effort, but he felt obliged to talk in seclusion, where he would not be seen. Zhao was reduced to meeting like a spy to discuss what, for him, stood as the greatest engineering project in the world.

Zhao looked young, at least a decade younger than his forty-odd years. He wore a button-down shirt, untucked, and a black lambskin jacket. His hair was stringy and disheveled, partially obscuring his face. His eyes looked swollen and red—like the man had a penchant for late-night karaoke binges or had been working too hard to earn much sleep. He smoked cheap Chinese cigarettes without pause, switching seamlessly to a fresh one as each burned down to an ashy stump between his molasses-stained fingers. It was a habit he'd picked up as a kid, working deep in the coal mines in Hubei Province, twenty-five years earlier.

The directorship of the QTR project was Zhao's big break—a monumentally flattering appointment for an engineer of his age and experience. Zhao was from the other side of the great intellectual chasm that had split Chinese society during the Cultural Revolution. The senior generation—men like Zhang Luxin and Cheng Guodong—had slipped into and out of university just before Mao's moratorium on higher learning. They passed the hardest years of the Revolution in secure government jobs in the railway. Zhao was younger and could remember watching his father interrogated by the Red Guard in the street, his arm twisted slowly back to his shoulder blade until the bone finally snapped. His father was locked in a prison, and Zhao and his three younger brothers would find him there on Sundays, sitting in the corner of a windowless cell with a weighty steel ring hanging around his neck. They brought him food, because the prison had nothing to serve. By 1975, his family had been without income for several years, and Zhao found a job pickaxing coal at the head of the deepest tunnels, for eight dollars a month. Once, there was an explosion in the next tunnel over, and eight of his crew died.

In 1977, the government unexpectedly announced entrance exams for college. Powerful families might have received automatic entrance, but Zhao had to earn his admission. Physically drained from his days digging, he would study into the dark hours of the night. Often, he would chew on hot peppers or rub tiger balm into his forehead, stimulating a burning that made tears well but kept him awake. When the universities opened again that December, Zhao was among the first class admitted.

The years that followed his graduation, he said, were "the golden age for ambitious young people." Because of the decade-long talent drought that lay between him and his senior colleagues on the railway, there was a desperate need inside the ministry to find young, qualified engineers and promote them quickly, before the older generation retired. Zhao got his first job at the Zhu Zho Bridge manufacturing plant in Hunan Province, where he learned about the integrity of concrete. "We were very far behind in terms of the new materials and new structures," he said. "There was a vacuum in terms of technology." And so when the codes needed to be rewritten for large-span engineering projects in the mid-1980s, it fell to young Zhao to do it. His confidence quickly outpaced his experience. "In three years I thought I had mastered the technology of bridge making, and I longed for bigger opportunities," he told me.

He got them, consistently. In 1985, Zhao was sent to Fuyang City to work with the Fourth Railway Institute on a 250-foot span across the Ying Hu River, at the time one of the most advanced engineering projects of its kind in China. He hopped up the leadership posts. In the mid-1990s, he was promoted to be general manager of a massive project, the Wuhu Bridge over the Yangtze River in Anhui Province, a long-span enterprise that required structural artistry in steel and concrete. He was often sought out for his expertise in concrete bridge structures. Yet Zhao was not a railway man; he built bridges, not tracks. In 2002, he stepped off the train in Golmud to a crowd of new employees who were instantly dumbfounded by the thirty-nine-year-old man who had been named their boss. He also stepped into a job that may well have been beyond him.

Zhao had never been to Tibet. He hadn't even traveled in western China. He had not managed a project worth even half the $3.1 billion budgeted for the railway, or one with the army of people streaming into Tibet to construct it. He had never worked or managed workers at high altitude, and he had little experience in the freezing conditions presented by the plateau. It was a project with unprecedented geographic range, a thicket of national political issues, and an impossible timeline. And for the paramount unresolved issue—the permafrost—he was a blind man thrust into a four-lane crosswalk, relying on the elder engineers (the Cheng Guodongs and Zhang Luxins) to be his eyes and ears and brain. It was a position that seemed on the face to demand some humility, and, indeed, Zhao found a little. "I felt like I was standing on the shoulders of a giant," he said with some deference for Zhang Luxin, a man roughly the age of his own father, and the knowledge those like him brought to the plateau project.

Nonetheless, Zhao charged into his role with a New China confidence the older generation found nettling. Many of them had far more experience and much more at stake in building a railway to Tibet than he did. Like Zhang Luxin, they tied their very identities to the project. It didn't take long for the immensity of Zhao's task to rear on its monstrous legs.

CHENG GUODONG WORKS IN A LARGE SQUARE OFFICE ON THE SECOND floor of the CAREERI building in the heart of the sprawling China Academy of Sciences campus in downtown Lanzhou. This is ground zero for permafrost research in China and an important center worldwide. Behind his formal, veneered desk, a dark bookcase crammed with scientific papers and binders runs along the wall. On the opposite wall, above a fluffy black leather couch, hangs an arresting twelve-foot-wide map of the world's permafrost regions, from a viewpoint hovering above the North Pole.

The map looks a lot like a target. In the center, a white expanse marks the frozen water caps of the pole. As it moves to the map's edges, the white is supplanted by a broad band of green that shades predictably cold places like Alaska, northern Canada, Greenland, Siberia— the regions of cold permafrost. As you move farther south from the pole, the colors shift from green to red, showing the critical areas of permafrost closest to thawing. These are the places where the earth is perpetually near the thaw point, where the ground perennially melts and freezes. After a point, there is almost no permafrost at all, only the thin black contours of unfrozen continents, until the map uncovers the one notable exception: in the heart of central Asia, a blood-hued blob large enough to be the twentieth largest country in the world. This 540,000-square-mile red mass represents the permafrost of the Tibetan Plateau, the largest frozen soil region outside of the Arctic. Typically, subarctic permafrost can be found in alpine regions, near the summits of the Andes or the Alps, where patches of earth remain shoved up in the clouds and snow. But in Tibet the permafrost extends across a large, relatively flat mass of land.

Roughly one-fifth of the earth's surface is frozen, defined technically as land where temperatures are below freezing more than half of the time and the soil has been solid for more than two years. Generally speaking, much of the frozen ground has been that way for a long time. In Prudhoe Bay, Alaska, for example, scientists estimate the permafrost took more than half a million years to solidify and is almost a mile deep. But as the earth has warmed, a global melt has begun. In the nearby Yukon, the longitudinal line of thawing has moved north about sixty miles in the last hundred years. In more temperate regions, a thin layer of permafrost thaws and freezes with each turn of the seasons, while the underlying foundation stays solid as rock.

From his years of research on the plateau, Cheng has collected a file of photographs of Tibet's permafrost, and he flips through them like a family album as he explains the physical dynamics of the unusual region. It is easy to see how wily this land can be. In one, Cheng stands dwarfed next to a frost mound, an earthen dome roughly sixty feet tall that has surged upward like an ocean swell under the contortions of the freeze-thaw cycles. Another shows a collapsed highway bridge on the plateau—a two-lane sheet of concrete that was anchored to two steep banks until one of them gave the bridge the slip and shuffled completely out of reach. Images of the Qinghai-Tibet Highway black-top show stark fissures that seem to be the work of an earthquake, and crumpled ribbons where once flat pavement has been reduced to a bucking bronco of a dirt track. These are textbook examples of permafrost at work.

As the earth expands and the cavities fill with water and freeze, ice can make up nearly as much of the earth as does soil. When the ice melts and the water and soil refreeze, repeatedly, they expand, turning into miniature tectonic plates that push up past the surface. In a typical year, the ground can move up, then down again, more than twelve inches. Sometimes it can shift ten feet.

In the most dramatic image in his files, Cheng points to a huge cross section of earth, streaked with white like a marbled section of granite, where the cavities in the soil froze into windows of ice. Cheng calls them wedges. In rare places, the ice wedges run as deep as sixty feet, meaning that if they were to melt at once, that's how far the soil could collapse before it rested again on solid ground. "It wreaks a lot of havoc," said Doug Goering, the associate dean of the mechanical engineering department at the University of Alaska at Fairbanks and a foremost expert on permafrost. "You may have fifteen yards of clear ice beneath a warm roadway." He continued, "Over the years, that ice melts and the water runs off and the ground settles, and whatever is built on that eventually fails—that's what they are contending with." It is more common for the ice bubbles to be twelve or fifteen inches thick—a less dramatic collapse, but more than enough to derail a train. Several of the railway tunnels drilled through Tibet's mountains cut through these sorts of underground ice cubes. In most places, though, the soil is mixed, much like the slushy trenches of a muddy parking lot that become hard as rock in an overnight freeze. Imagine then, if they melted, just how soft they could be.

Railroads and oil pipelines have been built on permafrost since the early 1900s, in Russia, Alaska, and northern Canada. When the Alaska railway was built in the 1920s, little was known about frozen soil dynamics. The earth was solid as a concrete foundation and seemed all but perfect for building; the road's designers used the best technology available. Today, the Alaska Railroad Company boasts one of the highest rates of regular maintenance and reconstruction costs anywhere in the world, spending at least $28 million a year, a quarter of its operating revenues, rebuilding sections of track damaged by the heaving land. Despite a consistently cold temperature—between minus-three and minus-fourteen degrees Fahrenheit—it has gotten worse every year, as the climate has warmed.

In Tibet, the geography is significantly more fragile than in much of Alaska or Siberia. Nearly 350 miles of railway lie on ground just one degree from the thaw point; more than 170 miles are substantially warmer and more delicate than that, existing just a fraction of a degree below freezing. Each summer, the glaring sun bears down on the plateau and warms the region far beyond arctic norms. The cycles have left much of the plateau inconsistent—frozen in one place and soft in another—and, to the chagrin of researchers at CAREERI, constantly changing.

Cheng's efforts, going back to early expeditions with a young Zhang Luxin in tow, largely concentrated on mapping exactly where the permafrost still exists, how deep it lies beneath a melting crust, and how dramatic an effect its transformations can have on anything mankind tries to put on top of it. Along the way, Cheng had emerged as one of the world's foremost experts, spearheading a research envoy to Saskatchewan in 1975, when China's borders were mostly in lock-down. "It was very difficult at that time to go abroad—understand that," he said, reminiscing about the unusual trip that was his first airline flight ever. "We were not allowed to walk in a city freely. We had to do activities together, always with at least two people." As Cheng was one of the first Chinese scientists to travel abroad in those years, his work earned publication in numerous research journals. But for all his achievements, he still found the plateau conditions confounding and the prospect of building on it menacing.

The problem with building on permafrost is not just that it is frag-ile or threatened by global warming or entirely unpredictable. Any unnatural disturbance of the soil's surface would have the effect of drawing environmental heat and warming the soil below it. A dark surface of pavement acts as a giant solar panel, absorbing radiation and holding it against the underlying soil like a heat pack on a strained muscle. Even bulldozed dirt holds the sun's energy, while simultane-ously damping the ventilation and reflective properties that sparse plant cover provide. "When you build a railroad over it, you disturb the thermal balance and it starts to thaw in places it's never thawed before," explained Tom Brooks, chief engineer for the Alaska Railroad. "Permafrost is a good foundation as long as you keep it frozen." If the permafrost is within the range of thawing—as so much of the Tibetan Plateau is—the construction itself can make it melt, turning an other-wise solid surface into terrestrial Jell-O.

Understandably, then, much of Cheng's work soon focused not only on understanding the permafrost itself but on finding ways to bal-ance the impact of construction. "We realized we have to lower the temperature of the embankment, not just maintain it," said Cheng. "We realized cooling was our only choice." Cheng knew for twenty-five years that building a train across Tibet would fail unless his teams could somehow advance cooling technology. What he didn't know was exactly how to do it.

In the early 1970s, a team of researchers trekking across the Tien Shan Mountains of Kazakhstan had discovered one helpful clue. They came across an old grave—a pile of rocks four or five feet high and eight feet long on an otherwise open and green grassy slope. The temperatures were warm, at least by alpine standards, and hovered above freezing. But underneath the pile of rocks, the ground was frozen solid.

It was more than shade that was at work. The pile of rocks had preserved little channels of space that allowed air to flow freely through it like a filter. The grave was naturally facilitating the process of convection: since warm air rises and the space between the rocks gave it a place to go, the structure was essentially wicking latent heat out of the ground and vacuuming it up to the surface. The process, like sweat on skin, had the effect of cooling the ground enough to freeze it. Cheng and other researchers quickly recognized the discovery's implications: if structural design could result in the active cooling of soil, it could counteract the warming effects of construction and possibly even stem the effects of climate warming.

From that point on, Cheng, Zhang Luxin, and other engineers focused their attention on ways to proactively keep the ground cool and preserve the stability provided by the permafrost. From an environmental perspective, it was an arrogant undertaking, thinking that a couple of nifty tools could reverse nature's course and essentially refrigerate the underlying soil. But in tests it seemed to work. "This was the breakthrough," Zhang Luxin said.

In 1973, Cheng's group built a mile-long test section of railway bed high on the plateau. It had no beginning or end or railcars, but it did mock the shape and size of a high-altitude railway and allowed the scientists to try a variety of methods they thought might keep the ground cold. The scientists built a handful of passive cooling instruments along the trial rail mound, trying to mimic the findings in Kazakhstan and take advantage of natural convection cycles to draw heat out of the ground. The simplest, but least proven, was a stone embankment modeled on the gravesite inspiration—a layer of loosely piled chunks of granite, about the size of baseballs, that allows enough space between the rocks for air to circulate freely. The method was straightforward, but the results varied, depending on the size of the rocks used and the surrounding environmental conditions. It was too experimental. Where this method did not work, the engineers tried burying ventilation pipes in the ground. In some cases, the pipes, laid horizontally like stream drains underneath the road or rail bed, simply allowed the cold winter air to circulate underneath. They even tried to mitigate the sun's powerful stare with a series of corrugated metal shades set up like low-lying roofing eaves along the tracks.

Such methods were applicable to all sorts of projects. Scientists from Alaska and Canada to Russia—where there was increasing exploration for mineral and oil riches under the frozen north—were simultaneously attempting to employ these solutions. Stone embankments were built alongside highways outside of Anchorage, and a variety of cooling methods were installed along the Trans-Alaska oil pipeline. In 1974, the Russians set to work building the Baikal-Amur Mainline Railway, an ambitious project to establish a strategic alternative to the Trans-Siberian line in the Far East. The railway, which would ultimately take seventeen years to complete, also lay across permafrost terrain and put into practice many of the methods the Chinese were developing in Tibet. Cheng and his team watched the Russian project closely, extracting practical refinements from their northern neighbors' experience. In a photograph from Siberia, concrete pylons—a lot like the ones that had already been poured across parts of Tibet—had lightning-bolt fissures racing down their sides from the erratic movement of the permafrost underneath. The Russian project became a model of what the Chinese hoped to avoid. "The damage ratio there is about thirty percent," Cheng said. "Meaning three of each ten miles of railway has to be rebuilt every few years."

The Chinese scientists realized many of the cooling methods that had been exploited in Siberia would not be enough in Tibet, where much more of the permafrost is especially fragile. Researchers began testing still more active ways to cool the soil, this time using an array of fans and chemicals to build what the scientists call thermosyphons, or cooling sticks. A stick consists of a vertical pipe, about thirty-five feet deep and eight inches in diameter, with ten quarts of ammonia poured into the bottom. The thermosyphons look like shiny new stovepipes jutting out of the ground, each with a stacked array of disks at the top to dissipate the heat. Inside, the ammonia chemically boils at the low temperature, drawing heat from the surrounding earth and giving off a vapor that draws the heat from the bottom of the tube and flushes it out the top. The underlying earth is left cooler in the process. Versions of cooling sticks had been used on the Trans-Alaska pipeline in the 1960s and have been somewhat successful.

In Tibet their application would border on the extreme. Early plans called for two pipes to be buried every four meters, about thirteen feet, and be used in just a few, select areas—already far more frequently than their application in Alaska. As the project progressed, however, the scientists had not found another option, and they began to think the permafrost wouldn't sustain a railroad unless they could use the more extreme, and, at about one thousand dollars each, more expensive, thermosyphon method as a cure-all for the troubling terrain. The widespread use of cooling sticks in a consistently vulnerable environment was highly experimental. "The thermosyphons are pretty well known," said Goering. "But the trouble is that you have to combine them with a heck of a lot of design. I might know this cooling stick works, but the question is how many of them do I need, and where do I place them? And then, depending on how that is done, you may still have problems."

If Cheng had been allowed to adequately test the methods along the full length of the route before construction began in 2001, he would have begun to answer these questions. He had asked for the time, but instead the Qinghai-Tibet Railway Company launched headlong into building. The pace of construction required that cooling sticks, stone embankments, and every other solution in the engineers' toolbox be applied by trial and error, with little room for the latter. Making sense of the sordid details was the heavy burden that fell in Zhao Shiyun's lap.

ONE OF THE FIRST THINGS ZHAO SHIYUN DID THE WEEK HE SETTLED INTO his new job was to take a trip to the plateau. It was like crossing the Mississippi for the first time and then immediately climbing the flanks of Mount McKinley. Zhao blinked his eyes in the wild high-altitude sun and stared out over the vast flatness of the high grasslands as he passed the portal at Kunlun Mountain Pass, then Wudaoliang, and pushed on to the construction site at the Fenghuoshan tunnel—a rise of more than nine thousand feet in the space of forty-eight hours. There, his first impression of the new job set into his skull with all the violence of a jackhammer taken to concrete. "I had a terrible headache," he recalled, his hand gently cradling the back of his neck as he talked. "I could never forget it." He pulled the door handle, stood up out of his jeep, and threw up.

A ceremony had been prepared, and Tibetan dancers, decked foot to forehead in colorful silk and woolen clothing, sang and danced in a circle before Zhao and the 150 or so workers who had come out of the tunnel for the break. Zhao watched but could scarcely think as the pressure in his frontal lobes attacked him. Later, when he walked into the tunnel—a hole of about a hundred feet—he had expected some relief from the glaring brightness but was smothered by the distinct lack of oxygen inside. He saw a worker with a tank on his back and a breathing mask over his mouth. The impressions—the cold, the headache, the darkness, the crowd, the bright clothing—swirled and blurred. His body felt weak, a lifeless tube of rubber. "All I could think was that it is so difficult for anyone to work in conditions like this," Zhao said. His first thoughts weren't about the railway at all. "I was filled with personal doubt. How could I go on with this project?"

Though he acclimated to the altitude after just a few weeks, it took the better part of a year for Zhao to acclimate to his job. For six months he managed little and made few decisions, instead poring over plans and documents and the scientists' permafrost writings in his office in the Qinghai-Tibet Railway Company's staid headquarters in Golmud. When he wasn't at his desk, he was on the plateau, driving tirelessly back and forth between Golmud and Lhasa, sleeping in labor camps, trying to familiarize himself with the mountains and the routes and the permafrost terrain. He got to know the small villages. He walked some of the barren hills of the Tangu La Pass, where the train might deviate from the highway by almost forty miles, the place the scientists and the workers alike called a no-man's-land. He visited the tunnel projects where the route had to break through rocky ridgelines or higher peaks. He practiced total submersion, like an actor hired to take on a new role.

One day in July 2002, as he crisscrossed the land, Zhao stopped his jeep near a flat field somewhere between the small towns of Wudao-liang and Erdaogou, one of the desolate, high-altitude expanses where the ground is temperamentally frozen and the horizon is more than a day's travel away. Zhao walked out across the sandy grassland, the thin layer of living summer soil on top of a bed of icy earth. A few hundred yards out, the rail line would pass through—at least that was the way it was drawn on a map; there was nothing there yet. One moment the earth was sturdy, and the next he was sinking. A wet, muddy soup enveloped his boots and tugged at his ankles as he struggled to step forward. A step later he was up to his knees, and the sand was rising, along with his heart rate. Men at the road, where he had left his car, shouted at Zhao to lie down, and he did, spreading his body weight out over a greater area. Slowly, he rolled his way through the muck back to the car. Now he understood what melting permafrost might do to a train. It haunted him.

As he visited these places on the plateau and met with the scientists from the various agencies and teams, the entire project seemed a phantom. "All the data that those scientists provided were from certain sites, but I needed the whole picture," he explained. "I am looking at these problems from a more comprehensive way, as an engineer, and that is something no one has done before and no one else is capable of doing." When he asked for maps, he got separate drawings—one that showed the Lhasa area only, and another that had elevation contours but no information on permafrost. After four decades of study and countless proposals, a comprehensive map of the region should have been created, but somehow it had not.

Zhao put together a detailed set of satellite images of the plateau—photographs where he could clearly make out the white caps of mountains and the silvery snakes of rivers—and strung them together into a very long panorama, with all the pertinent details overlaid on it. "For the first time I had a systematic thinking," he said. The four-foot-tall map ran the full length of a long wall in the Golmud offices, and for a month after it was posted Zhao meditated on it, studying every detail.

What he learned from it made him nervous; petrified, in fact, that even after so many years of study there was too little plan and knowledge on which to move forward. He found a plateau project riddled with problems. Things like the quicksand incident, or leaky tunnel walls, or where a culvert had been designed to let water flow through but instead froze solid and made a dam that turned a half-mile stretch of the sensitive permafrost into a small lake.

On top of it all, the entirely unpredictable risk of a major earthquake always loomed. The Tibetan Plateau, though flat and docile-looking, makes up most of the largest continental collision zone on the planet. As India continues to forcefully crash into Siberian Asia, Tibet gets shorter, on the north-south dimension, by roughly two inches each year. The Himalayas, the world's tallest and most severe mountain range, are the crumple zone, and they absorb a portion of the continents' kinetic energy. But the balance gets pent up on the plateau, where it builds until earthquakes, which are common, release it. In 1997, a magnitude 7.6 rocked the northern plateau. Then, on November 14, 2001, the 991-mile-long Kunlun fault sustained a whopper—a magnitude 8.1 earthquake that ripped down from the range's high peaks and lasted for two minutes, rupturing a 174-mile-long crack in the earth that split the Qinghai-Tibet Highway and toppled a monument at the Kunlun Mountain Pass. That quake, said to be the largest in a hundred years, had brought construction of the railway to a temporary halt. Another one could happen at any time.

In December, the railways vice minister, Sun Yongfu, announced that the Qinghai-Tibet Railway construction would enter its most active period. The following spring would require the largest single-year investment in the project—almost $675 million—and see the laying of track over a full 118 miles on the highest part of the plateau. Not only would this double the track-laying pace of 2002, but it was slated to take place on the most sensitive habitat and fragile permafrost of the plateau. If the permafrost problems had indeed been solved, this would put those solutions to the test. But Zhao was quickly losing confidence that the permafrost scientists had done enough specific research to map a railway. "The earlier design engineers were so eager for the government to approve this project, so they said we could solve all the problems," Zhao quipped. "In fact there were many problems we hadn't found solutions for at this time."

No one in China surpassed Cheng Guodong or Zhang Luxin—who both served in a sort of advisory role to Zhou—when it came to understanding the physical properties of permafrost, but they simply didn't have all the information Zhao felt was necessary to begin construction. "Their study has mainly provided a theoretical framework to the permafrost problem," Zhao said. "They studied the characteristics of the different types of permafrost according to the ice content, and they divided the plateau according to different ground temperatures. But those only capture the basic phenomenon of the permafrost. For the engineers to build a railway, those data are far from enough." So while Zhao claimed the utmost respect for Zhang Luxin and the CAREERI team, he was frustrated. "They have only done partial experiments in limited areas—very small scale," he said with a heavy dose of conceit. "Based on their study they had proposed many measures—the stone cover, proper width and height for the embankments—and those proposals offer very valuable concepts. But I emphasize *concept.* Before the railway was started there was very limited funding for the permafrost research, and many of the researchers had to borrow a lot of experience from other countries." Chalk it up to the typical tension between scientists and engineers, or that Zhao was the guy who claimed to have mastered bridge building after only three years in the profession. But after just a few months in Tibet, Zhao believed he had learned enough to identify the scientists' shortcomings and began to chart a radically revised path forward. He had to. The pressure was mounting.

The first thing he did after the winter thaw in 2003 was order a systematic survey of the permafrost conditions all along the railway route. Previous studies had focused on the hot spots or the high zones, but no one had consistently measured the ground underneath every mile of the planned route. Zhao was particularly worried about the zone between Wudaoliang and Erdaogou, the high plateau flatlands that had almost swallowed him in quicksand the previous summer.

That stretch was an area Cheng Guodong had long before flagged as the most critical warm-permafrost part of the plateau. Zhao thought the permafrost there might be too fragile to build on no matter what precautions were taken to cool the soil underneath. But the CAREERI group had already seen the railway project abandoned once because of its price tag. Now it worked within a tight budget, and, in an effort to keep costs down, had settled on a recommendation to build across the region using the stone embankments and thermosyphons alone. In the few places where those methods couldn't possibly work, they would run a bridge over the soft ground and leapfrog the most dangerous sections. But they intended that technique to be used sparingly. Their 2001 designs called for less than forty miles of bridges along the route.

Zhao, having nearly drowned in dirt that should have been frozen, thought the plan was far from a sure thing. He called Zhang

Luxin to his office. "They did a more thorough geological investigation and found the permafrost was more complicated than we had thought," Zhang said, though still taking umbrage at the suggestion his research was faulty. Together, they searched the new data and considered possible scenarios: worst case, the tracks were deluged and needed to be completely reconstructed after just a few years; best case, the connecting bridges held out for a while but eventually succumbed to the stress of their inevitable shifts and dropped off their supports, just like in the photos from the railway in Siberia. If the permafrost was estimated to be just a fraction of a degree below freezing, and the cooling sticks had the ability to lower temperatures by just one to two degrees, then at most Zhao could count on only a single degree of room for error—too close, he felt, for comfort.

In March, when Vice Minister Sun again visited Golmud, Zhao and Zhang Luxin proposed their solution. Zhao had prepared a detailed presentation in the Golmud offices, and on the first of their two days of meetings, Zhao gave Sun a microlevel tour of the project through the long panoramic satellite map and a giant scale model. He outlined the early plans and explained gently to Sun that he thought those plans would have to change. "I can see you are really into this business," Zhao remembered Sun telling him before they retired for the evening. "Please work hard. Do a good job."

Having tactfully opened the door for his proposals, Zhao began the next morning's meetings with the big news: Where the permafrost posed its most lethal threat, Zhao wanted to keep the railway from touching the ground surface at all. He would revert to his primary area of expertise and proposed building long bridges to elevate the railway—over 65 additional miles for a total of nearly 105 bridged miles in all, a seventh of the entire route. The bridges would run like endless viaducts across flat ground and look a lot like the Disney monorail running across the surface of the moon. Where there were no bridges, Zhao would add another sixty miles of crushed stone embankment and countless more thousands of thermosyphons, and undertake a widespread regrading of the rail bed to make it wider than originally planned.

The proposals, he said, would boost the project cost by more than 50 percent, to nearly $4.5 billion. Some experts expected the real cost would be substantially higher. American engineers put the cost of railway building in the United States at $400 per foot, and bridge building at roughly $60 million a mile. Surely, with cheap labor and materials, China's costs would be substantially less, but at half the North American cost, Zhao's additions alone would run more than $2 billion. "I can tell you, if we divide it to find the average cost per kilometer, then the Tibet railway is not the most expensive railway in China," he promised when asked about the discrepancy. But that wasn't saying much. China had recently made plans to build a $20 billion, 186-mile-per-hour bullet train between Beijing and Shanghai.

The Qinghai-Tibet Railway, though, would proceed at almost any cost, and Vice Minister Sun provided no resistance that day in Golmud. A few weeks later, state news reports quoted him explaining the following in Beijing: "Due to the complexity of the situation on the frozen belt, track-laying has been hindered . . . This year marks a crucial period in the railway's construction." To make up for lost time, Sun pushed still harder for 2003 to be a banner building year. Zhao's plan was rubber-stamped. It was time to take those disparate puzzle pieces and put them together.

PART III

TREASURE HOUSE

Mineral resources, waters, forests, mountains, grassland, unreclaimed land, beaches and other natural resources are owned by the state, that is, by the whole people.
 —Constitution of the People's Republic of China, Article 9

Rigya Lungya Domba is a popular saying, a forceful reminder that it is our duty to protect the earth, waters, and skies as a solemn vow. Tibetans take this vow seriously and it governs their entire way of life. It is a vow that, to date, China . . . has clearly failed to understand.
 —Central Tibetan Administration, 2007

9

THE RACE TO REACH LHASA

FROM THE MOMENT ZHAO MADE HIS PRICEY PROPOSALS, his plan leaped from paper into execution with the inertia of a great locomotive barreling down a mountainside. Right or wrong, there was no more time for measurements or debates. Beijing wanted the construction on track, seemingly no matter what.

Tracks were laid up the mountains from Golmud, and the first locomotive powered itself through the finished Kunlun Mountain tunnel that April 2003. It began ferrying its own supplies up onto the plateau, building on itself like a tree trunk that sucks nutrients up its own roots to grow. Prefabricated sections of track that looked like ladders—seventy-five feet of steel rails already attached to concrete cross-ties—were stacked on freight cars, dragged to the plateau from Golmud, and then installed by a praying mantis–like locomotive that reached the section of track out in front on a giant boom and dropped it into place. The Chinese-built erector machine, called the PG30, could lay its own rails and roll over them at a pace of almost two miles a day. A similar but even larger contraption could lay entire sections of prefabricated bridges as long as the pylons were already in place. By May, the railway had reached as far as Wudaoliang and a plateau altitude of more than fifteen thousand feet.

The concrete for Zhao's endless bridges, which would cross the treacherous permafrost at the headwaters of the Yangtze River, had begun being poured while the words of his proposal still hung in the air. The support towers were drilled deep into the ground to a level of solid frozen earth that wouldn't be melting anytime soon no matter what happened on the surface—ice as good as bedrock. Soon, the track machines, just fifty miles or so north, would catch up, and as fast as the cement could dry, the prefabricated bridges would be bolted on top of the support towers and the whole machinistic endeavor would push farther south, toward Lhasa.

Along the rest of the route, other pieces were beginning to take shape. The demand for labor had reached fever pitch, and to keep the workers healthy, more than 480 medical staff had been hired and 137 medical stations built. Engineers, racing ahead of construction to polish their surveys and data, had settled on a high point for the route and more or less finalized the design. Tracks would deviate from the Qinghai-Tibet Highway by some thirty miles to the west and instead cross the alpine ridge of Tangu La, at just over seventeen thousand feet, at a broad bulge in the ridge deep in the wilderness. New roads had to be built to get the workers there, and once the platform and small station were built there—though it would be virtually useless— Tangu La would become the highest train stop in the world.

On July 1, railway officials chose the site for the terminal station— an idyllic farming village called N'eu that lay on the gurgling south shore of the Kyichu River about nine miles from downtown Lhasa and within clear site of both the sprawling Drepung Monastery and the crowning Potala Palace. By the middle of the month, bulldozers had turned the earthen walls of more than a hundred homes into a level, graded site, and the $35 million building project—one of the most expensive buildings ever constructed in Tibet—got under way.

That fall, workers near Lhasa reached another milestone. The steep rocky cliffs and raging whitewater of the Yangpachen Gorge, fifty miles north, had presented a low-altitude but gnarled obstacle for the train that designers circumvented by boring straight through two miles of mountainside. It would be the longest tunnel on the railway route, and one of the most dangerous. Despite Zhang Luxin's assurances that tunnel-boring technology had improved since the disastrous escapades of the past decades, the insolent wilderness of the plateau had proven too remote and difficult to transport the large German drilling machines that he had planned to use in place of human labor. So thousands of workers continued to hand-drill holes in bedrock and ice much as they had in the 1950s near Xining, pack them with explosives, and then retreat to the thin mountain air until the blast dust settled. They wore oxygen masks and carried heavy tanks on their backs—not enough, apparently, to keep them safe.

From time to time, Tibetans in nearby villages would see railway officials burying dead workers on the hillsides outside the tunnel—a scenario Zhao Shiyun first denied, insisting on the government line that the railway project had not resulted in a single worker's death. When pressed, though, Zhao explained the burials at Yangpachen as the result of a tragic food-poisoning accident. In any case, the tunnel work had begun shortly after the groundbreaking in 2001, and on September 9, 2003, workers finally struck through and found daylight on the other end.

Zhao, it seemed, had worked magic. In a little more than a year on the job, he had proposed bold solutions to the most vexing problems, jump-started construction in the permafrost regions, and overseen marked progress on other visible components—the long tunnels and the Lhasa station. But rather than calm his anxious superiors, the news seemed to only further intensify Beijing's metabolism for progress in Tibet.

In the winter, boosted with confidence at seeing actual trains rise from Golmud up onto the Qinghai portion of the plateau, Bejing accelerated the pace of the project to near warp speed, and Zhao received the news that he was to finish the construction of the Qinghai-Tibet Railway in less than twenty months. Beijing expected trains to be running the full route to Lhasa starting in early 2006—twelve months ahead of the Ministry of Railways' hyperoptimistic, original deadline and several years ahead of the timeline international experts had realistically put on the project.

To meet the new schedule, China would have to quickly procure 110,000 tons of steel at a time when international markets were taut with heavy demand. Western companies working on the line, like Canada's Nortel, which was building the communications network, felt they were under siege by the change in plans. Bombardier, another Canadian company whose Chinese subsidiary was contracted to build hundreds of the train's passenger cars, was forced to refit its entire Qingdao factory to focus solely on the Tibet project. "In China things are happening in different ways than we are used to," said Amir Levin, general manager of the Bombardier plant. The acceleration was dizzying and put him off balance. "We discussed this train for more than a year with the plan to be online in 2007. One day I get a call, and they say, 'We changed the plan. Can you be ready a year in advance?'"

But the toughest challenge of all was the most straightforward, and it rested on Zhao's shoulders: if all the supplies were in place, could tracks be laid on the ground fast enough? It was a replay of the transcontinental railroad's race across America, except this time there was no race to beat a competitor, just the arbitrary time pressure applied by the central government. The problem from Zhao's practical standpoint was that the track building, still 550 miles from Lhasa, relied on the extraordinarily large erector machinery that itself had to be transported by rail. The tracks could only progress as fast as the single budding line heading south, over the complex permafrost, could grow.

Somehow, that needed to change. Zhao needed to find a way to start railway construction inside Tibet, on the other side of the treacherous and slow-progressing permafrost regions. If he could get things moving there, then tracks could simultaneously progress from both the south and north, closing the distance between Lhasa and Golmud. He chose the small town of Amdo, the first major settlement south of the TAR border, as the site of a makeshift rail yard and production station for prefabricated materials. But he still had the problem of moving the monumentally large machinery needed for installation into Tibet. A single locomotive weighs nearly 140 tons and is longer and wider than a tractor trailer truck. The PG30 and the similar bridge-building erector were nearly twice that size and weight. If they couldn't be rolled into place on train tracks, they would have to be taken apart and transported by truck on the delicate ribbon of the Qinghai-Tibet Highway. And the highway, dilapidated and collapsing in places from the permafrost upheavals and harsh weather, could never support the load.

In a frantic rush, Zhao turned his attention from the railway construction to the section of the highway between the end of the existing tracks, in Wudaoliang, and Amdo, putting hundreds of laborers to work rebuilding it. The road was regraded, widened, and reinforced to handle the massive burden of the oversized loads. New bridges were built. Expensive thermosyphons and other cooling devices that had been developed for the rail line were hurriedly installed along the roadway in the hopes they would prevent the highway from self-destructing before it had served its purpose.

By late spring 2004, convoys of slow-moving diesel tractor rigs burdened with impossibly long flatbed trailers were loaded with the trains and ground their way toward Amdo. A typical semitruck and trailer in the United States can run sixty feet long and carry forty tons; these trucks were twice the length and bore three times the weight. The road softened under the weight of the trucks' wheels, wearing deep ruts into the pavement. But it held, and by the summer of 2004, the Qinghai-Tibet Railway was rushing to completion from three points on the plateau instead of one.

WITH THE FURIOUS PACE OF CONSTRUCTION, PROSPERITY WAS EXPECTED to rain down on western China—at least that was the way it was supposed to work. In the construction phase, there would be work for all who wanted it. Once the railway was up and running, a new age of economic ascension would dawn on the TAR. And no doubt, even by 2004, the project had transformed Golmud and southern Qinghai from a desert outpost to the land of opportunity, and the increased economic activity began trickling even to Tibet. More and more migrants flooded the region in search of jobs, and any Chinese man who wanted to find work could find it on the railway. Others made easy money, driving taxis or cooking in restaurants, if not in Golmud, which had ballooned, then in Wudaoliang and Lhasa. But for some of the Chinese migrants swept up in the project, the early days heralded disappointment as often as newfound riches.

Yang Feng Ming, a wiry thirty-year-old, had thought he could cash in on the train project. He had come from Sichuan a few years earlier and had worked on the railway since its start. In 2001, he had joined an explosives team in the tunnel at Fenghuoshan, and in 2002, he graded and laid steel reinforcements at the proposed high point of the line, at Tangu La Pass. But by 2003, he was sitting in a dirty auto shop in Golmud, surrounded by fan belts and broken carburetors, dead broke. He had spent entire summers without bathing and paralyzed by fears of being crushed by collapsing rock inside the railway tunnels. His determined jaw made clear that he was the type of guy who would keep trying to make something of nothing.

The time pressures placed on Zhao Shiyun had become the talk of the town, and everyone was buzzing about the impossible construction project across the permafrost. The thermosyphons that were being used in mass numbers along the railway route required drillers, and the multitudinous railway bureaus didn't have enough of them. Each siphon hole had to be cut deep into the rock and ice, and the work was specialized. The railway company paid six hundred yuan, or seventy-five dollars, to a headman for each hole, and the workers actually piloting the drill would receive twelve dollars of that. Why make twelve dollars when the whole shebang was there for the taking? Yang hatched an entrepreneurial plan to start his own contracting company. "So I bought the machines myself," Yang said, walking outside to pull a moldy tarp off an eighteen-foot-long rusty steel-framed drill that lay in the dirt outside his shop. "With two machines I could drill twenty holes every day—I could make fifteen hundred dollars. It would be very profitable." Yang collected money from everyone he knew and bought two drills for five thousand dollars each—an extraordinary amount of money for a Chinese laborer.

At the start of the 2004 work season, Yang landed a *contract*—a loose term, at best, in China's west—to drill on the railway line. He was assigned a thirty-five-mile-long stretch along the route, where he would punch five-inch holes fifteen feet into the ground every couple of yards. When Yang arrived on the plateau that spring, however, he learned the railway company's loyalty was to expediency more than fairness. "It wasn't just me," he recalled. "Several dozen teams were on the same stretch, and we had to compete." It devolved into a scrappy race over a pile of pennies, but even that was tougher than Yang expected. An easy drill hole could take half an hour—a quick seventy-five dollars. But if he hit rock—and he often did—he would spend an entire day churning his bit while his competitors hopped around him to other holes and he watched in despair at all his lost profits. Half of the hundred or so teams drilling cooling stick holes along the railway that year lost money, Yang reported. The experience had soured his take on Golmud, he said back in his shop, and he doubted that he would use the machines again. Instead, he would move to Lhasa, where it was easier to compete.

The Tibetans watching the bustling development taking place along the route often fared worse. Chinese media reported large influxes of investment and jobs into Tibetan communities during the construction years. A 2004 report claimed Tibetans in Nagqu County had received $2.7 million in income related to the construction and that forty thousand people there had participated in the project. If the figures were accurate, it would mean that each Tibetan had earned the equivalent of only ten days in wages over the first three years of construction, hardly an economic boon. Independent reporting showed that in fact very few Tibetans had found jobs related to the railway, and that these jobs were the lowest-paying hard labor. Tibetans—whether in the northern border towns of Nagqu and Amdo or the southern towns of Damxung and the Lhasa Valley—universally described widespread rejection of their efforts to find work. Yang hired just three or four Tibetans to work on his summer crew of seventy men. Chinese headmen complained the Tibetans, who had no experience operating machinery and couldn't understand orders in Mandarin, were unemployable. Those Tibetans who did get jobs were hired to plant grass, break rocks with hammers, or dig drainage ditches by hand. In many cases they were paid half of what the Chinese earned—less than four dollars a day—and had to cover their own living expenses.

IN THE TWO YEARS SINCE HIS VILLAGE OUTSIDE LHASA HAD LEARNED OF the plans for the train, Kalden had discovered that life with the railway would be far from easy. Almost immediately after getting the happy news that displaced families would be compensated by the government, he learned that only those people whose houses were directly in the path of the tracks would be moved, and the definition was painfully literal. Only eight of the fifty households—making up a twenty-yard-wide line from the north to the south end—qualified, and his family's was not one of them. His family, and the dozens of others outside the track's path, would receive no money at all. By the middle of 2003, the row of homes across the small alleyway from Kalden's gate had been razed, and the thirty-foot-tall trapezoidal mound of the rail bed had been constructed in their place. It was so close, he could reach out his window and touch it. Dust descended on their home night and day, for twenty-four months. It coated their meat, turned their water coppery and their windows opaque, and clung to their skin.

That fall, at the age of fifty-seven, Kalden's father died. Monks came from a monastery to perform the funeral rights, and the elder man's body was cut into small pieces on a hilltop across the river, where the vultures could come and carry it away. Soon after, as is customary, the family gathered in their small courtyard, now beside the railway, and set everything the man owned on fire: his clothing, his writings, even the few photographs that existed. All that was left of him was the home he had built together with his children. The family now needed to support themselves, and they looked, in part, to jobs on the railway to do it.

Kalden's youngest sister, Pema, had the best luck. There was a labor camp down the road hosting about seven hundred Chinese workers, and when those teams were not enough for the day's or the week's project, the foreman would come to the village headman to ask for help. Sometimes he needed three people; sometimes he needed thirty. The headman would call a village meeting and deal the jobs out like prizes. The headman's sons always had work. Every time, Kalden and his older brother Gyatso would try to find a place on the team, but in those two years, they worked only a handful of months. Eighteen-year-old Pema, perhaps because she was pretty, with long brown hair and rose-painted nails, found work most consistently—for nearly three months a year. The women, though, earned less. Pema was paid just $2.75 a day. "The jobs we did were just by hand," she said. "Mostly I would flatten the earth on the side of the hill."

Gyatso grew especially frustrated. He was motivated, and if not well educated, he was smart. He had learned enough Mandarin to speak in broken sentences. He could drive and even owned his own tractor—a simple rectangular trailer welded to an engine and two drive-wheels. The camp was a shout away, but the Chinese kept their distance. "We don't have much interaction," he said. "They don't welcome us to their tents. Probably they are afraid we would take their things. We don't care about their things." He watched the Chinese hands tightening bolts and measuring the bed widths—and getting paid fifty yuan, or six dollars a day, to do it. With a little training, he felt he could do it too.

Village life grew increasingly intolerable. Heavy diesel trucks and steamrollers pounded the earth, feet from their doorway. The house shook and the windows rattled every time the machines came through. Once, a pane shattered. How would it be when the real trains started barreling through? Besides the discomfort of living amid a work site, the village had effectively been cut in half. When traders came to buy animals, Kalden's side of town never knew they were there. If something happened—a neighbor grew sick or there was a fight—they might not know for hours. They felt amputated from their community and cheated of the promises officials had made when construction began. "It's hard to be angry," said Kalden, clearly cautious of stating anything bordering on criticism of the Chinese. "It's not going to be helpful. There is nothing we can do even if we are." But there was something they could try: if the village banded together as a single voice, they might be able to persuade the railway to give them compensation and better living conditions. One complainer would be persecuted; one hundred would be tougher to ignore. Kalden didn't want to leave his home, but he could barely live there anymore. They had to find a way out before the trains came.

THE PG30 DROPPED TIBET S FIRST SECTION OF RAILS TO THE GROUND with a thud. The sky hung unseasonably low, dark, and gray over Amdo that morning, June 22, 2004. As always, there was a ceremony. Two thousand workers were assembled and dressed in freshly laundered uniforms for the event. The seventy-five-foot section was quickly linked to another, and the Amdo station, the first stop inside the TAR after crossing the extreme heights of the Tangu La, was marked on the plateau. Fifty-four years after Mao had ordered them, train tracks had been laid in Tibet, within 255 miles of Lhasa.

Soon the line extended another eighty-five miles to Nagqu, the commercial center of the northern TAR, and one of the most resource-rich parts of Tibet. When the train got there, the local government could hardly contain itself. "It's been our long-cherished dream to have a railway in Nagqu County," a senior Chinese official remarked to the Chinese state press. He promised the railway would improve the living standards of Tibetans and promptly went on to explain that the metals found in Nagqu could be worth as much as $722 billion—or more than half the total mineral value in China. The comments began a wave of Chinese investment and exploration into the hillsides and grasslands of Nagqu.

Zhao Shiyun's jump forward had worked. Tracks progressed downhill to Lhasa at admirable speed, and the intense scrutiny he had felt over his work in the permafrost region had eased. Officials in Beijing focused instead on high-profile benchmarks closer to the railway's terminus: the Lhasa station, the Yangpachen tunnel, and the impressively long triple-arching span of the railway's final bridge over the Kyichu River into Lhasa. It allowed Zhao to return to the tedious work of the permafrost of the plateau, north of the Tangu La Pass. There, the drillers continued to race against time and bedrock, and the PG30 waited patiently for the troublesome ground to be readied for its tracks.

The work was slow-moving and delicate. Melting ice would shock work sites into jeopardy. Tunnels could collapse from a steady drip. That summer, with the thermometer inching up, a football-field-length section of the hillside, rail bed and all, slid twenty-five feet down the Buqu Valley on a mountain north of the Tangu La Pass. The collapse required a regrading and new foundation on one of the most treacherous parts of the route. "The ground here has a very high density of ice permafrost," Zhao said. "The rainfall on top of the slope caused the melting of the permafrost and has led to this slide. The earlier surveys had not found a problem with this slope." Yet it was unclear whether the warming had caused the permafrost to liquefy or if the steep slope had simply been poorly engineered. Zhao had little way to know for sure.

Chinese state media called the summer of 2004 unseasonably warm and crowed that the temperatures were advantageous to the railway construction because it extended the building season well into the winter. But the warm weather also began raising questions: Were the railway's design and Zhao Shiyun's solutions adequate? The last decade had proved the warmest on record, with all but one year in the past five posting a record. If the warming trends continued, would the railway last?

All of the permafrost engineering, and a great portion of the cost of the railway, had been based on the assumption that the rate of climate change, and thus the rate of permafrost melt on the Tibetan Plateau, was predictable. That was a controversial notion in itself. Climate change scientists who had attempted to model the progression of warming had pegged the expected shifts across a wide spectrum. To determine a prudent, long-term solution to the permafrost problem, Zhao needed to establish engineering standards for the railway based on some climate change model.

Cheng Guodong and the rest of the CAREERI group in Lanzhou had determined that the climate could warm an average of two degrees over the next fifty years. Another set of models, created by the Beijing Climate Center at the China Meteorological Society, predicted a three-degree change. Zhao could have chosen the most conservative scenario for building—a model that set the outside limit for the degree of warming scientists, inside China or out, felt was possible. But Zhao did not. Instead he chose a more optimistic model, one that differed from the expert opinions of these two prominent groups of Chinese scientists but that would provide the data on which to build the train more easily and cheaply, now. He picked a less dramatic perspective, from inside the Ministry of Railways, that allowed him to plan for the railroad's terrain to warm by just one and a half degrees. The difference between that level and two or three degrees might seem negligible until you looked again at Cheng's map of the plateau and how much of it hovered within a single degree of melting. Zhang Luxin, too, had labeled vast stretches of the plateau as "critical." The one-degree variance moved solid frozen ground into the category of slush, far from a stable foundation for a train running at seventy miles per hour.

In the years that followed, the climate picture would grow more dire. Soon after the 2004 building season, a more troubling view of the warming trends on the plateau began to emerge as new studies and data rolled in. A 2004 report on the length of the growing season by the government-run China Meteorological Society noted that the most rapid increase during the 1990s in all of China had occurred on the Tibetan Plateau. The year 1998, the report said, had been the longest season in forty years. Luo Yuong, the deputy director of China's National Climate Center in Beijing, deemed 2004 the hottest summer on the plateau in an eighteen-year upswing and said temperatures could increase by three and a half degrees by midcentury. "By 2050, safe operation of the Qinghai-Tibet Railway will be affected if temperatures keep rising steadily as observed over the past decades," he said. Each of the next three years after his statement—2005, 2006, 2007—would be hotter still.

The signs pointed to a rate of warming that outpaced Zhao's model and suggested dire consequences for the railway to Tibet. Cheng Guodong, when asked about the discrepancy, sought to avoid contradiction and insisted he respected Zhao's figures and believed there was sufficient room for error in the railway company's models. But a professor on his staff, a senior expert at the Chinese Academy of Sciences named Wu Ziwang, felt differently. In late 2005, Wu told the Xinhua News Agency he believed the thinking behind the permafrost engineering standards was hazardous. "Due to the melting permafrost, I am worried that after ten years the railroad will be unsafe," he was quoted as saying. Wu, having stirred up a storm of controversy and anger with his comments, declined to be interviewed again. His colleagues claimed Wu had been misquoted, but stopped short of saying they believed the statement was wrong.

The concept of a ten-year lifespan for the railway was alarming. Then, in 2007, more data emerged to compound the fears that the Qinghai-Tibet Railway was doomed by global warming. The United Nation's Intergovernmental Panel on Climate Change report contained some of the most detailed information on the plateau's warming ever made public. The depth of the frozen permafrost on the northern slopes of the Kunlun Mountains, it said, had decreased by seventy-five feet in the last quarter century. Permafrost islands on the plateau proper had shrunk by more than a third in the last few decades. Its most alarming statements pointed to the future: "Temperature projections represent strong warming . . . likely to be well above the global mean in Central Asia." It predicted nearly a four-degree increase in temperatures in the twenty-first century—enough to turn an estimated 60 percent of the plateau's permafrost surface to mud. The U.S. Congressional-Executive Commission on China went so far as to insinuate that fears about the rate of warming on the plateau were the driving motivation behind China's rushed construction schedule; the sooner the train was operational, the more use could be derived from it before it became defunct.

Zhao remained optimistic in the face of every statistic, even if he didn't entirely disagree that the railway was threatened by climate change. "If the rate of warming turns out to be more than [what we projected], it would be worth it to us to build another new railway," he said, claiming the most economical strategy had been to proceed as he did, then adapt to changes later. Designing for a four-degree change would have been impossibly expensive, and by the time the plateau warmed enough to disrupt operations, he argued, the technology for reengineering the railway would have improved. The railway could simply be rebuilt as often as necessary to keep it running—a tack not so different from that taken to maintain the permafrost railways in Russia and Alaska, after all.

In any case, the controversy over the threat posed by global warming never interfered with Zhao's furious pace of construction. On March 14, 2005, the third plenum of the National People's Congress—the country's most prominent legislative body—met in Beijing and railways minister Liu Zhijun made Asia-wide headlines with an unexpected announcement: "The Qinghai-Tibet Railway, the world's highest, is to complete track laying by the end of this year and start trials on July 1, 2006." But Zhao had been told that the track laying would have to be finished by October 2005—just six months away. Zhao knew that the calendar held a hidden coincidence: if the tracks could be completed in time for the fortieth anniversary of the establishment of the TAR, for which huge celebrations were planned for September 1, all the better.

The rush meant Zhao's railway bureaus would now have to work around the clock to get the job done. Hot, bright spotlights lit long strips of the plateau like professional-league football fields while the PG30 laid its gear in the middle of the night. The rhythmic chug of progress was almost audible. On the high plateau, the concrete of the long bridges cured, and rail was laid over the braided drainages of Tuotuohe, the upper Yangtze River, and the long frozen tundra, right up to Tangu La Pass. By April 3, tracks from Amdo had reached Damxung County and were nearly a hundred miles away from Lhasa. On May 13, the last concrete was poured for the sweeping Lhasa bridge, whose design was supposed to evoke the traditional shawls worn by Tibetans. By July 23, 312 miles of steel had been laid inside the TAR to within sixty miles of the Potala Palace. Tracks slithered past the spiritually revered Nyanqentanglha Mountain, the twenty-three-thousand-foot mass of snow and ice that towers above the lower Damxung Valley. The Qinghai-Tibet Railway could claim a full 90 percent of the railway was completed.

On August 27, Party Secretary and President Hu Jintao convened a closed-door politburo meeting in Beijing to talk about what to do in the Tibet Autonomous Region once the railway was done. According to Chinese state news reports and a paper published by the International Campaign for Tibet (ICT), in Washington, D.C., the talks focused on the further elimination of any sense of Tibetan separateness and full assimilation of Tibetan areas into the wider Chinese economic and cultural models. Beijing's social policies of integration and religious restraint were working and should be continued, and the economic development programs would be further accelerated. The railway construction was the final threshold to cross before unbridled commercial benefits could flow east. In four days, Lhasa would be engulfed by the largest state-coordinated ceremonial event since the Chinese had taken grip of Tibet in 1965, and the celebration would flaunt the profound economic and developmental benefits that, Beijing insisted, had rained down on Tibetans ever since.

That China claimed such progress where Tibetans felt little was a key testament to the differing views of what was happening inside

Tibet, and who was benefiting. China says that the TAR has experienced a roughly 12 percent annual growth in GDP (it would reach 15 percent by 2005), a figure that far outpaced the entire country's impressive boom. Hundreds of millions of dollars a year had been pumped into subsidizing commercial, land, and services development in the region. "Tibet has a 'leaping frog' development model," said the Tibetology Center's Luo. "The government has very good intentions. If it can succeed in reforming the traditional industry and introducing new industry, then the urbanization and resettlement is sustainable. But the problem is the local Tibetans don't have enough skills to participate in this new industry." The fix, he said, could come as a pledge in the central government's Eleventh Five Year Plan to spend $2 billion on education and vocational training in the TAR.

Yet the majority of investment dollars flooding Tibet has been spent on large build-outs of government and military bureaucracies. Analysts note that nearly half of the GDP growth could be attributed to government staff and operations expansion. Much of the rest could be pegged to construction, most of which is also for government structures. The government buildings do not include the schools, hospitals, or other social infrastructure that Tibetans need. New construction in small townships consists primarily of large government or police office buildings; new staff consists of the officials to fill the buildings. Their costs and their salaries—indeed, every yuan spent on the railway itself—are counted in Beijing's total subsidy figures when it brags about its generous spending on Tibet. The degree to which the local economy is dependent on army and official employees can be seen in any of the dozens of dry cleaning businesses in Lhasa, where the racks are universally full of pressed green Party uniforms. The day state employees receive a raise prices for everything from food to bathtubs in Lhasa bump up with it. This western development, according to the pro-Tibetan ICT, indicated "that an expansion of the control apparatus of the state is seen as an essential pre-condition to the spending and investment under the fast-track economic policies currently being pursued."

When September 1 and the fortieth anniversary celebration arrived, a monumental stage, bright red and replete with traditional Chinese architectural adornments, was constructed in the heart of the Barkhor square. Behind it, the traditional Tibetan white court-yard buildings—those still standing—quietly receded. Thousands of neatly assembled Chinese and Tibetan officials, carefully selected residents, and traditional performers filled the square. The event had been scrupulously concocted and coordinated. For weeks lead-ing up to the day, Chinese military and armed police had been increasingly present on Lhasa's streets. Monks were advised to stay home, inside the monasteries, and those Tibetans across the country-side who may have been listed for political activism or separatism in the past were told not to travel. Foreigners, with few exceptions, were not granted permission to visit Tibet, and tourist permits were nonexistent. Many of those who did attend the ceremony had no choice. Tibetan officials, and even those loosely connected by family to someone employed by the government, were instructed to attend and threatened with docked pay or worse sanctions if they did not. They were told what to wear—traditionally and culturally vibrant outfits that are not a regular part of Lhasa's urban dress but were intended to convey a thriving intercultural success story. The streets and alleyways were adorned with strings of colorful flags that from a distance looked like traditional Tibetan prayer flags, each containing scrolls of spiritual text to be sent off to the heavens by the wind, but instead were printed with a commemorative badge and Chinese propaganda.

The city was in lockdown, but on television, all of Lhasa celebrated. Outside the town limits, perhaps the only officials not present were those still busily pushing for the train line's completion. The oversized Lhasa station was taking shape on the horizon but remained enshrouded in a vast gray web of scaffolding. The construction details of the railway weren't quite finished, but they were very close. For all intents and purposes, September 1, 2005, marked the end of Lhasa's last hold on separation.

═10═

PARADISE REBUILT

BY THE FALL OF 2005, VISITING TIBET HAD BECOME ROU-tine. A 313-passenger jumbo jet—a sparkling new Airbus A340 more typically used to get from Bangkok to New York—flew daily from Chengdu to Lhasa. Running on specially built, high-altitude Rolls-Royce engines, it catered to the wave of tourists that Tibet had been hosting since the early media blitz surrounding the Olympics and the railway had hit. Out the spotless windows, the passengers could see the spindly summits of Sichuan's Qionglai Mountains stab the cloud layer. Somewhere in the distance, clawing at space, was Everest. Then the plane descended and touched down, at 11,680 feet, on a long, freshly cemented runway. Like so much of Tibet, the airport had undergone a massive renovation, in this case to allow it to accept the largest airplanes in the world. At the sparkling new glass and steel terminal, rows of Chinese fighter jets and a dozen armed helicopters were parked.

Lhasa, the top of the world, was teetering on the cusp of a transformation. Its essence remained unchanged: The bustling markets thrived. The same sweet smells of incense tangled with the sour wafts of curdling cheese and burning butter. Monks sat in clusters on the ground begging for alms, as they always did. And the pilgrims' circumambulation flowed like a strong river current whisking me from the shores and into its channels.

But the container that held this ancient place was changing shape. The downtown demolition along Beijing Road had been replaced with a new strip of shops, large grocery stores and clothing boutiques to rival London's Knightsbridge. Late into the fall, anniversary celebration flags still fluttered over the streets—as they would for many more months. The hand-hewn cobblestones of the Barkhor had all been ripped up in the winter of 2004 and, after a rainy season in which pilgrims to the Jokhang skipped across muddy morasses that bordered on small lakes, were replaced with a mall of neatly quarried granite blocks. Construction in the heart of the city was continuing but took on a fresh sense of cultural restraint after groups including UNESCO started to express concern about the systematic raking of architectural heritage. Instead of the rote assembly of generic buildings inside the Barkhor, new ones reflected a patently Tibetan style. Cinder-block walls were given a facade of inch-thick stone and a whitewash that mimicked the traditional hand-hewn masonry. The idea that Tibet's tourism value lay in part in preserving a sampling of its old-world heritage had begun to grow roots. Even the Potala Palace, which had a Ferris wheel installed in a new park behind it, was undergoing a theme-park-like restoration.

In an Internet café, Tibetan youth fought for space to play Halo— all networked together with headsets and microphones. On the Barkhor, the market was syncopated by the stinging electronic high notes of the Beverly Hills Cop theme song, "Axel F," from the cell phone of a monk, who dug into the folds of his red robes to stop the ringtone.

Along the main strip of Beijing Road, a series of folksy bars advertised live music and cappuccino—made from real coffee. One, the Music Bar, was owned by a hippyish young Chinese couple from Beijing—he, a long-haired songwriter and guitarist, and she, a painter with a taste for good marijuana. Tibet, they explained, was an idyllic escape—a place where they could slow down, burn candles, crank music, and live a more alternative life. A friend of theirs, a local DJ, had created a mash-up of Tibetan monk chants interwoven with electronica drumbeats, which he would burn for tourists. What kind of Tibet was this?

Down the street, another bar—creatively named Another Place—was tucked into one of the dark, narrow Barkhor-area alleys where Renzin had grown up and dodged bullets as a child. Its owner, a young woman from Beijing, had festooned the three rooms with halogen lighting imported from Beijing that created a dim, loungy feel. Couches and chairs circled a warm red rug. Library books, mostly in Chinese and Tibetan, some in English, filled wall-to-wall bookshelves, and a small DVD library of Western blockbusters was stacked beside a large-screen TV. Lhasa beer was available for a dollar; a bottle of Chimay or Boddington ale cost five. For the wealthiest tourists, a fifth of Hennessy brandy could be had for a hundred bucks.

A twentysomething Chinese woman from Guangzhou, Helena, had settled in at Another Place, running it for the owner by day while teaching English to Tibetan and Chinese students at Lhasa University by night. When she explained this to me, she laughed and covered her face, embarrassed by the irony because her English, though sufficient, was fragmented and basic. She had moved to Lhasa in 2002, in the early days of construction, and her blue jeans, fake gold jewelry, and flowery blouse were those of a modern Chinese woman, not an interloper hoping for Shangri La.

"Lhasa is the ideal," she said. "It is small, not crowded like the rest of China. It is sunny, the air is clean and it is beautiful." Helena is lucky, she explained, in that her parents allowed her to move when it has been customary for Chinese to stay closer to home. Modern China was becoming more mobile, and with it, Lhasa too was evolving. Chinese men, and then a Tibetan group, walked in and ordered drinks. The sound of edgy guitar filled the room, and Helena continued, lighting a cigarette. She did not want Lhasa to become just like Guangzhou, just like so many other Chinese cities, but she welcomed the modernization. She hoped she would be able to save enough money to buy one of the new condominiums being built, and sold, inexpensively along the river.

The Tibetans were far less comfortable in the new Lhasa. A woman in a rug shop on the Barkhor, after chatting with me for more than half an hour about trivial things, suddenly picked up and ran away when I asked her if she had attended the anniversary celebrations in Lhasa. At a Tibetan club for English-language practice, foreign visitors were warned at the door not to discuss anything related to religion or politics. Tibetans would even shy away from walking with a Westerner in public. The security crackdown on Lhasa before the anniversary events had sent a clear message: keep quiet and stay home. An invisible wall separated Tibetans from everyone else. They were burdened by a deep distrust and fear.

Under the weight of the railway project, I too was growing paranoid. In the United States, Tibet experts from Robert Thurman and Robert Barnett at Columbia University to Tenzin Tethong, the former head of state for the exiled Tibetan government, expressed a reticence about Westerners reporting from Tibet. Tibetans, particularly guides and "fixers," had often faced severe retribution for working with journalists. Midnight hotel raids, temporary detentions, and searches at immigration were still common. Daja Meston had been arrested for poking around a remote Qinghai housing settlement, so reporting on the largest civic infrastructure project China had undertaken in Tibet was likely to press buttons. It was essential to remain "off the grid."

I needed help, and I counted on it coming from an erudite but obscure and eclectic Westerner named Matthew. Fluent in Tibetan, he had done more firsthand research and interviewing in Tibet than most Westerners alive. He lived in Nepal—and so he was close, but ethnically and diplomatically insulated from Tibetan politics. He had been in Lhasa shortly after the 1989 uprising, again in the mid-1990s during the "reeducation" years. He could prove to be a mischievous and knowledgeable partner, buffering Tibetans from a haphazard American scribe.

For months Matthew and I had exchanged vague and noncommittal intercontinental e-mails through a litany of anonymous shell addresses like traveler@gmail.com. His paranoia outpaced my own. He had been watched by the Chinese for years, expelled from Tibet twice, never sure how welcome he would be in coming back. He insisted on a dictionary's worth of code words and opaque expressions in any letter. Pinned up against the language and political barriers of Chinese-dominated Lhasa, I needed his help more than ever. Still, I wasn't sure he would show up. Lhasa, at the time, seemed cemented into a lockdown mentality.

THE NEW BEHEMOTH OF THE EMERGING LHASA STATION WAS PLANTED just down the road and across the river from the headquarters of the Tibet Military District, a massive Southwest Command base—the military epicenter for much of the western half of China. Cordoned by guards and corralled by construction equipment, the area was far from inviting. An old path sketched the *lingkor,* or holy circumambulation route, that encompassed the historic city, darting alongside the raging torrents of the Kyichu River, its aqua eddies littered with garbage and human feces. At the west end of town, the path intersected an Erector set–like steel bridge, the kind of temporary structure armies lay across a gorge in battle, with an armed guard post at its gate. Across the bridge—which emitted a deafening rumble as heavy trucks lumbered across it—and a few miles farther west, stood the station.

Nearby, bridge workers poured concrete on a new four-lane freeway, and graders smoothed an immense flat in the direction of the station. Otherwise, the wide-open landscape looked as though it could be a hundred miles from Lhasa. Goats and yaks grazed on the fields, and several small villages dotted the funnel-shaped valley as it arched uphill. But this was changing. By the new road, huge billboards pictured sleek cars zooming around cloverleaf exit ramps and a Shanghai-style glass sky-rise with Lhasa's Potala Palace sitting austerely in the background. Poster versions of the scene were tacked to the walls of the Barkhor's streets, even in front of the Potala itself. Dozens of similar billboards trumpeting the high-speed train that would hurtle into Lhasa had stood on the plateau over the past three years. Now that those advertisements for the new China had been realized, it seemed naive to dismiss the skyscraper-and-freeway vision as fantasy.

Down the road, another guardhouse blocked the hulking construction of the eight-story-high station. The spot had not always been a part of Lhasa. In fact, until two years earlier, this complex of graders and dozers and worker camps and exit ramps had been a small village called N'eu (the Chinese called it Liuwu), at the mouth of a quiet agricultural side-shoot valley. The road was single lane and dirt. Goats and chickens straggled within the walls of about 150 homes of red earth and thatched roofs. A century ago, Lhasa had been another world away from N'eu, across the river and half a day's walk. Five years earlier, the road was drivable and the sprawl was encroaching, but still the glint of modern green glass remained on the other side of the river. Then, in the summer of 2003, a pair of suited government officials drove up in a black sedan to speak to the head of the newly minted N'eu Chang—Beijing had recently begun turning such rural villages across Tibet into official municipalities. As in Kalden's village, they issued a directive for the villagers to move. They handed the chief a piece of paper bearing the state's offer: residents would be compensated 11,000 yuan, or $1,300, per mu for vacating their homes and land and would be moved to a new town in a valley a short way from Lhasa. "We told them we will not leave," said Yeshe, a farmer whose family owned a large portion of the land around N'eu. "We have lived our entire lives here in this village." Yeshe and the group that protested the government's order got a little extra money for their trouble, but ultimately they did leave—they ultimately had no other choice.

Just a few miles away from the station, up the dusty valley, about fifteen long, barracklike cinder-block buildings had been constructed at their resettlement site. Each contained adjacent two-bedroom apartments with electricity and plumbing, but no land for animals or farming. The units weren't free; the villagers, if they wanted resettlement, had to pay 120,000 yuan for each one. Yeshe, who moved with the families of his three brothers as well as their elderly parents, needed four apartments—at a cost that dwarfed the money promised for leaving N'eu. Their compensation would take months to process, but the money to move was required right away. A year later, Yeshe still had not received a check. "They wouldn't give us the key until we paid them the money," he said. "It's like we were forced to pay for our own compensation." The new N'eu had given its body and soul for the shrouded terminal down the road.

Near the station, some mud and stone buildings appeared abandoned. This was the old N'eu. Across the road, a large worker camp was packed with dilapidated green army tents and a makeshift shantytown of plywood walls and plastic sheets. Beside them, a grouping of small buildings with straw mats for walls looked as though it would blow over with a strong gust of wind. Inside, people were laughing, smoking, clanging glasses. The first door opened onto a store, about seven feet square. On the walls were rows of brandy and Chinese-labeled liquor, enough cigarettes to smoke out Beijing, snack packets of pickled chicken feet, neatly tiered pyramids of instant noodle bowls, and piles of green rubber army-issue work shoes.

In the next room, about fifteen people huddled around a small woodstove and smoked and drank. It was dark, but a single beam of sunlight shot through a tear in the plastic, looking as solid as a pillar of marble as it caught the smoky air. The signs on the walls were all in Chinese, as were the men drinking. The owner wanted three yuan, or forty cents, for water, expensive for the plateau. An open-bed truck filled with army and police drove by.

Beyond the work camp and the guardhouses, the Lhasa station was taking its mysterious form underneath its gray web of scaffolding. The building's walls, painted red and white, sloped subtly from a wide base to a slimmer top. On its flanks, smaller buildings spread out in arms and tiers. Unmistakably, the Lhasa station had been designed as a modernized echo of the Potala Palace, Tibet's single most important and internationally recognized symbol. It was as though the Chinese were hijacking Tibet's copyright, turning the image of the Dalai Lama's residence into a badge of China's modernization and domination of the region.

A FEW MILES FARTHER NORTH FROM THE STATION, AND NINE MILES from Lhasa, a steady stream of workers marched along the roadway near the first visible steel tracks. All of them wore the ubiquitous yellow hard hats of construction; some carried shovels over their shoulders, the blades pointed like arrows toward the sky. Most wore dark overalls and those green rubber army-issue boots. They had suffered from the work. Some of the workers shoveled on the grade while heavy equipment and cranes unloaded piles of ties. Everyone stared. "*Tashe delek,*" I said—*hello* in Tibetan. No one replied. Perhaps a hundred workers to five answered to the Chinese greeting, "*ni hau,*" instead.

To the east, the enormous gray webbing of the station was still visible. The dark clouds began spitting hail, then a steady cold rain. At a tunnel entrance, the arched opening into a mountain, workers huddled around a small fire, protected from the storm. The light glinted off two steel rails that dove deep into the darkness of the half-mile-long tunnel, ending at a needle-hole of light at the other end. Most of the men were Tibetan, and one spoke the barest of English. With a dismissive expression that said it was lame work, he made a motion to describe his job: shoveling. He was paid thirty yuan, or a little less than four dollars, a day.

The hospitable mood shifted when the men suddenly realized how strange it was that I had shown up and how much trouble they could get in for letting me in. By the time the rain abruptly stopped, it had become palpably awkward. I rushed to fire off a few photographs as I heard a car honk outside. The men scattered. A silver Toyota Land Cruiser with a red emergency light on the roof had parked a hundred feet down an embankment, and two men were getting out. At the head of the tunnel, one of the workers waved me in the opposite direction. But as I hurriedly rode off, the rear tire of my bicycle hissed and went flat.

I had pushed my luck. I had calculated that I could afford to be seen once. I would be a random mystery, gone in a city of workers as quickly as my presence could arouse suspicion, and I planned on returning along the long road on the other side of the river to avoid doubling back past the military guards and shopkeepers. Nine miles out of Lhasa, on the bed of the Qinghai-Tibet Railway, I was stranded.

At the grand Lhasa railway bridge—the last major building project on the entire route—the construction had been completed days earlier, and the workers had moved on. It was sleek and large, and designed with glaring cultural significance. Its three gaping white arches emulated the draped white silk *katag,* the scarves Tibetans use to greet and honor each other and give in blessing to their monks and lamas. But the enormousness conveyed speed and modernity first and implied some sort of magic mechanism that could whisk a person out of the shambles of the old Lhasa's third-world streets.

The river at this point was at least fifteen hundred feet across and was too rough to swim. The bridge, forty feet above the water, did not have a walkway, and the ties were spaced uncomfortably far apart. Under those conditions, it would take me at least fifteen minutes to cross—during which time I would be conspicuously exposed to passing traffic while trespassing on one of the single most sensitive structures in western China. From the road behind the last bend, I heard the steady grind of an engine: a green taxicab. Its driver was commuting from his village to town. I paid double, reclined the front passenger seat, and covered my face with my hat until he had passed through the construction zone back into Lhasa.

Late that night, long after I had bolted the door in the back halls of the Banak Shol hotel, I heard a soft knock on the door. My room was littered with journalistic paraphernalia I normally kept out of sight: a laptop, flash cards, digital cameras, microphones. I threw a blanket over my gear and slipped the latch to pull the door back a cautious crack. The light from my room illuminated a stark line down a man's white face, a broad forehead pulled tight by a long gray ponytail and pale piercing eyes. He wore a dark wool cloak like a cape. He said nothing. "Matthew?" I said. The back of his hand brushed my door, and my long-awaited guide stepped inside. Later, over a pot of sweet tea, he delivered his terms for the first time. "I don't follow the rules," he said. "I don't bother with permits. I go where I want. I stay off the main roads. I carry everything I need to camp, cook, eat, and be totally self-sufficient. I live like I am Tibetan. Does this suit you?"

The next morning, we caught a public bus west out of Lhasa, itself a feat because the Chinese forbid tourists to use out-of-town public transit.

MATTHEW S LECTURES STARTED SOON AFTER THE BUS ARRIVED IN TOLUNG, a suburb on the other side of the railway bridge, on the way to walking and hitching to the town of Damxung. "In the 1950s the Chinese were trying to demonstrate that they were well intentioned, that they had come as liberators," he said, pointing out that the original Qinghai-Tibet Highway was a thin strip that ran innocuously along the contours of the mountains. "'Never take a needle and thread from the people' was a famous catchphrase; invading forces made a point of not imposing themselves." According to Matthew, the first highway had been built along the edge of the valley "to minimize land confiscation and impact on farming. The party in general was going out of its way to demonstrate goodwill." Only later, long after the political attention of the first Chinese incursion had evaporated, and those who advocated a true policy of autonomy had been replaced by Maoist factions, did the Chinese do what came naturally: build the road straight down the middle of the valley. For Matthew, to consider the impact of the railway project without this historical context was to miss the forest for the trees. "Now this, the railroad, is the last word," he stated. "It's the final expression of that contempt for compromise, for harmonizing the development with the landscape, and for giving a damn about anything here frankly."

Damxung was another uninspiring dusty strip of connected shops, self-storage units separated by the occasional pompous official building. A new municipal administrative headquarters appeared to be a pink and green glass copy of a Romanesque church, with a grand central staircase, broad pillars, and a peaked portico. The streets were filled with Chinese workers laying rebar for wide paved sidewalks, and a few blocks off the main street, the rail station was being built—also with Chinese labor. In a small courtyard shanty enclave, Matthew hunted out what seemed to remain of the original Tibetan community. Among a handful of tea shops and a few dollar stores selling plastic cups and bubble gum, dozens of idle young Tibetan men stood around outdoor pool tables. Nearby, others, visibly drunk, jiggled to Bollywood tunes inside a party tent. The ground was saturated with sewage and garbage, and few people felt like talking.

Damxung literally means "center of the marsh," a deserved name for a broad, flat valley that was pocked with boggy puddles. Even here, north and west of the town, the landscape could be brutally harsh. It was raked by an invasive wind that burrowed forcefully through the throat and nostrils and seemed to circle in little vacuous tornadoes all the way down to your belly—a sinus enema. The new Chinese agricultural programs had triggered a lace of barbed-wire fencing.

Between the muck and the wire, the valley was impassable. A Tibetan herder on horseback, a middle-aged man out of a cowboy Western, offered an ironic piece of advice: the best way to get across the Damxung Valley was to walk the railroad bed.

He had been herding his yaks on the plain since around the time the Chinese broke up the commune system, and in a sense he and the land had become one. The earth was so embedded in his leather coat, his wiry graying hair, the seams of his homemade pants—deposited there by the wind—that these things cracked when they bent. His fingers, which stuck out from fingerless gloves to wrap around his horse's leather reins, were like wood—all calloused and swollen and brown. "The Aba-hor," he began, referring to himself by the slightly derogatory term used for nomadic people. "The Chinese all look down on us. They think the Aba-hor are stupid and say that if we can't think enough to speak Chinese, then we can't work. So we don't get work. People who do speak some Chinese do get work." The nomads lived among the settlers, but the cultures remained divided. "The Chinese are renting houses in the village next door. Sometimes they steal [from the railway or the camps], and then they sell to other Chinese on the black market. But if anything goes missing, they say the Aba-hor took it."

Across the field, it was just a short, if steep, incline to the top of the rail bed. If a piece of industrial infrastructure can be beautiful, these tracks were. They snaked gracefully over the hills and off toward the horizon in technological contrast to the raw earth surrounding it. The tracks were empty save for the handful of Tibetan women who were using the rail bed to get up and down the valley. There were no workers, no machinery, no security.

As the railway crept out of Damxung and into more populated areas, it had sliced through both countryside and villages without deference for what stood in its way. Some of the villagers had insisted on staying, even as the railway construction thundered past them. They had nowhere else to go. Farther along the tracks, Pemba Norbu's whitewashed mud and log cube was awkwardly wedged between the rail bed, which towered twenty feet above it, and the highway, which constrained the land on the other side. In between, he still kept his yaks and goats and threshed piles of wheat, not unlike the way it would have been done four hundred years earlier.

Inside his home, smoke billowed from a wood-fired hotplate, trapping against the low woven-twig ceiling and coating it with a layer of thick black powdery creosote. His dirt floor was meticulously swept, and his salty Tibetan butter tea was stomach-curdling. In his fifties, Norbu had a broad nose that was weathered thick by a lifetime in the plateau sun. Only his eyes still had youth, and they shined out from under graceful, Buddha-like lids. Above him, on one wall, he had hung a glossy poster print of the Potala Palace—the kind that travel offices in Beijing used to advertise trips to the far-off province. On the other wall, a three-inch crack shot from the floor to the ceiling like a craggy oak branch. "When the train first moved across the new tracks, it was deafening; our house began to shake," he said, explaining the fissure. "We thought it would collapse. But we have nowhere else to go."

Norbu couldn't say exactly when he had built his home. He had lost track because time here didn't mean much. But he knew the creases on his face didn't run as deep and the Chinese had just released his family from the communal labor camps. That meant it was during the early 1980s. He talked about the train like something Providence had dropped on his family but he could do nothing about. Asked whether he had sought compensation or complained to the county town administration, he returned a dead-pan stare—such a confrontational gesture was beyond comprehension. What he did understand, though, was that, like it or not, his livelihood was changing. Since construction had begun, a full third of his yak herd, which represented most of his assets, had been killed—if not by construction machines on the tracks, then on the roadway after they'd been driven into it by the loud sounds of the train engines.

But what was most striking about Norbu's little acre of technological confluence was the degree to which he had been excluded from its benefits. Within months, the trains would begin to run, and passengers would gaze down on his thatch roof from behind the thick glass of an oxygen-enriched passenger cabin, sipping waitress-served tea and marveling at his way of life as if it were a museum exhibit. On the hillside above his home, a new cell phone tower, built by Nortel, was being erected—by May the entire plateau would have a stronger signal than San Francisco. Underground a fiber-optic cable and a web of power lines ran along the railway. Yet Norbu didn't have a telephone—he had never even used one. His home was without electricity or plumbing; for water, he walked half a mile to the icy river with buckets. His only experience of anything modern was a hitched ride to Lhasa on a diesel flatbed truck to sell yak butter in the markets, and it was likely to stay that way. Whatever development was happening in the Damxung Valley, it apparently wasn't meant to be used by people like Norbu.

"You have to understand, the People's Republic of China as it was drawn in 1950 was pure fantasy. It was more like a wish list," Matthew noted, pointing out that even Qinghai was only made a province in the 1920s. "It's not about eliminating their culture; it's about occupying their culture. With the Tibet Autonomous Region, China is looking down on all of India and holding hands with Pakistan." China has been transparent in its aggressive intentions in the region. Nearly 90 percent of its total arms transfers go to Pakistan, Iran, Myanmar,

Bangladesh, Thailand, and Sri Lanka—all neighbors of India. It is developing naval port access in Bangladesh, and, besides providing Pakistan with nuclear technology and supporting its weapons program, it is building a major deep-water port in Gwadar, in Pakistan's south. That port, which is directly connected to China's Xinjiang Province with a new freight-dedicated highway, is not far from the Strait of Hormuz, through which 40 percent of the world's oil passes.

All of this should have been ringing alarm bells for India, but for most of the four decades since the two countries fought over their 2,250-mile border, relations had remained cordial, if unresolved. The border is among the longest in the world between two countries and is China's only disputed boundary. China claims thirty-five thousand square miles—almost the size of the state of Maine and comprising the whole of India's Arunachal Pradesh—as its own. It might have done something about it sooner if it had the strength; another RAND defense report assembled for the U.S. Air Force identified the lack of a railway on the Tibetan Plateau as one of the major hindrances to China's ability to quickly and efficiently deploy its army into South Asia.

Sometime in late 2005, India woke up, and tensions between Delhi and Beijing reignited. In January 2006, India's Cabinet Committee on Security approved the first expansion of road building in its northern border areas in decades—with plans to bring the roads from one hundred to within twenty-five miles of the disputed line. News reports cited a growing Chinese military fortification, including the railroad and the tens of thousands of miles of roads China had built near the border in the last twenty years. Indeed, China's foreign ministry, perhaps emboldened by the new railway, infuriated India when it denied a visa to the governor of Arunachal Pradesh as part of a wider diplomatic mission of Indian officials headed to Beijing. The governor was already considered a Chinese citizen, the ministry explained, as he presided over Chinese sovereign territory. On April 12, 2007, India successfully test-fired its Agni III medium-range missile, capable of carrying a nuclear warhead to Beijing or Shanghai for the first time. Two months later, Indian defense minister A. K. Antony conspicuously announced India's plans to order 126 new fighter jets, bolstering an air force already considered superior to China's.

The escalation was integrally connected to China's long-term strategy for building muscle in the TAR. When much of China's Southwest Command moved to Lhasa, it established an uncontestable military presence there. Now at China's helm, it seems Hu Jintao wants to build up Tibet to be a military fort as much as an economic resource. A senior PLA official in Lhasa said defense accounted for more than half of the strategic purpose behind the railway. Matthew called it the last, winning, and most definitive move in a fifty-year effort by China's orthodox wing. "It's checkmate: the final solution."

Few people understood the nuanced dynamics of the plateau's politics better than Matthew. He had either witnessed or recorded firsthand accounts of much that had happened. The events of the past and the social politics of the present were forever entangled, in his view, with the issues of developing Tibet—at least so long as development projects were not aimed squarely at the welfare of the Tibetan people. That view, though justified, made it difficult to allow that the railway could herald benefits. Lawrence Brahm, an expatriate entrepreneur in China who had served as a political adviser to Zhu Rongji and who heavily invested in businesses in Lhasa, said Tibet's evolution has always been oversimplified by its detractors. "All culture is based on economics. If you can't grow rice, you don't have culture. Culture disintegrates when there is not an economic base for its sustainability—then it goes into a museum," explained Brahm, sitting in the lobby of his new boutique hotel in the heart of the Barkhor. "A young Tibetan dresses very fashionably and uses a mobile phone but that same person may go to the Barkhor and do the long-form prostration. It doesn't mean they are less Tibetan, or less Buddhist." As another longtime expatriate resident of Lhasa and a doctoral fellow in Tibetan studies at Cambridge University, Kabir Heimsath, put it: "Where else but Tibet do people argue against clean water and electricity? That educated development experts around the world want Tibet to stay the way it is, is baffling."

Yet Matthew's thinking, even the way he physically moved throughout Tibet, reflected a rebelliousness toward the Chinese that stemmed from a deep personal slight, accumulated on behalf of Tibetans over the years. When he crossed the street in Lhasa, for example, he was deliberately slow and disruptive, as if his getting in the way of the choking traffic was a subtle act of protest against Lhasa's modernization. In this way, everything he did was a form of resistance to the bureaucratic apparatus and burgeoning new economy. His views were immovably strong—almost as strong as his knowledge. Like many of the pro-Tibet Westerners protesting the railway from beyond its borders, he was too sure-footed in his universal condemnation of the railway project, but, unlike so many others, Matthew's views reflected what he heard from hundreds of Tibetans: they simply didn't want the project. It wasn't that he thought Tibet should remain the way it was a century earlier, but that all of China's policies peripheral to the railway project seemed to reinforce the travesties of the past few decades and were an inseparable burden to the politics of the train. Between the arguments, though, there was little room left to acknowledge a basic characteristic of globalization: Zhang Luxin and Helena had not come to Tibet to destroy it; they had come to build their own lives and fortunes.

In the long Gyama Valley, not far from Lhasa—home of the ancient Tri-Khang Monastery and the former residence of Songtsen Gampo, the seventh-century king who had built the first palace at the site of the Potala—the villagers were getting a newly paved road. It was a sign that in all likelihood the Chinese were exploring for mines, and there were mines in the valley—two or three large underground iron operations that appeared to have been there for many years and a few more new ones up the hill. The buildings of the old town surrounding the monastery had been reduced to rubble. Tufts of grass and saplings grew out of piles of collapsed stone or from inside the walls of a roofless compound. The monastery, Matthew explained, had contained three of the largest prayer *gompas* in Tibet, but they too had been mostly reduced to piles of rock. Still, a spirited small temple had been rebuilt, incorporating restored twelfth-century murals. The open green valley, with the remains of the monastery and villages that hung like ornaments from the steep mountainsides, was sublimely beautiful, raw, and resilient. "All I can see is a land that has been raped and pillaged and destroyed," Matthew responded.

TWO DAYS AFTER MATTHEW GUIDED ME BACK TO LHASA, ON OCTOBER 15, 2005, the city went into a deeper state of lockdown—literal rather than figurative. The steel bridge leading to the Lhasa train station was barricaded with army personnel. A few miles behind them, the scaffolding around the station had come down, and polished Land Cruisers and jet-black Volkswagen Passats made a high-speed show of shuttling government officials from their fancy hotel in the city center to the new terminal, leaving a rooster tail of dust on the narrow dirt roads. In the Barkhor, the streets, including the holy kora circuit, were completely closed to the public, and soldiers with Plexiglas riot guards and machine guns stood at the ready, looking for the subtlest sign of trouble or protest. Above the square, closed-circuit cameras whirred away, as they always did, most likely transmitting their images back to a control room in the towering police sky-rise on the east end of town. But there weren't any protests that Saturday morning. Instead, another multiethnic ceremony was staged, this time right in front of the station itself, on pavement that must have barely been dry, and was broadcast around the country. Seven hundred and ten miles of tracks had been laid connecting Lhasa to Golmud. The railway to Tibet—what the Chinese had taken to calling the "Sky Train"—had been finished.

Traditionally dressed Tibetans danced and sang folk songs in front of politicians in black suits. Premier Hu Jintao wasn't there; he sent a controversial vice premier, Huang Ju, the former mayor of Shanghai, in his place. Huang brought a letter in which Hu called the railway an "unprecedented triumph . . . on the rooftop of the world," and then spoke a few rhetorical words of his own. "The new line is a landmark in railway engineering . . . a huge step forward to develop China's western regions," he announced. Every news outlet promised windfalls for Tibetans: prices for goods and food would drop by half; wages would increase with new business. The Xinhua News Agency wrote that Lhasa "basked in glory as merrymaking crowds . . . hailed in Tibetan and Mandarin the completion of the railway."

Mostly, that was a lie. In town, talk was suppressed. Conditions were strictly controlled. That was the week I first met Renzin. He was a friend of a Tibetan exile I had met in New York, which meant I had a reference. Snitches for the Public Security Bureau—China's state police—commonly befriend travelers, so it was not safe to just sit down and interview the first Tibetan who was willing to talk. And Renzin knew better than to speak to a Westerner in public. He insisted that after the confrontation over the name of his shop, his store had been bugged. Yet he never seemed overly conspiratorial; when he talked about spying in Lhasa, he spoke evenly, as if imparting the blandest of facts. It was something a Tibetan dealt with, like the weather. One of his employees, he suspected, was baiting him because she frequently made political comments. For eighteen years he shared his building with two warm and kind Tibetan women who owned an adjacent restaurant, but they knew nothing about him and vice versa. "I try to keep to myself," he said. "It's a measure of self-preservation."

This was the climate in Lhasa—a place where seeds of division had long ago been planted and had destroyed any sense of community. Tibetans had been so conditioned to distrust that they no longer needed policing. They had been broken, in a sense, and they would police themselves. "It is not possible for us to protest or organize to change China's politics," Renzin said. He chose to talk with me mostly because of that very fact: "It is the responsibility of each of us to do what we can—to tell the story of what happens here. It is our duty."

We took frequent walks or bike rides up into the hills outside of Lhasa. These trips to the city's rural fringe were among my fondest moments there; just minutes away, we could be walking a narrow mountain ridge or sipping tea inside a farmer's modest hut. One day, out of the blue, he offered this observation: "The swallows are back," he said, sweat rolling off his chin. He was referring to his childhood memories of starving in Lhasa, hunting for anything edible in the surrounding valley that had become devoid of birds. It had taken a long time for his wounds to heal, and his statement was a way of saying that things had gotten better. From the distance of the Lhasa Valley, the old city center fell into malignant rings of modern sprawl, complete with its glassy sky-rises, around the mountains. The Potala Palace poked above the skyline.

Renzin wasn't against the train by any means; in fact he looked forward to the changes it could bring. Who could have envisioned in those rough days of eating bootlaces and being whipped onstage by police that a Tibetan businessman could buy a ticket in Lhasa and arrive on the streets of Beijing forty-eight hours later? How could anyone say this wasn't progress? And Renzin had a soft spot for the imported goods a middle-class person could afford; he wore Nikes, a black DKNY sweatshirt, and a fake Seiko watch almost every day. But he felt strongly that the larger changes occurring in Tibet weren't benefiting Tibetans and that the Chinese vision was grossly out of step with what the TAR really needed. "What is happening here is not development," he said. "It is just construction. Development would include new schools, health care, and programs to improve the standard of living."

Above all, he wanted vocational training for Tibetans, who were simply being left behind. "I'm not saying it is a conspiracy," he said, "but the Tibetans do not have the skills to compete. They do not know trades, computers, electronics, hardware. And the more the Chinese come, the more the economy increasingly becomes Chinese language based, which becomes one more reason most Tibetans are not employable—they can't speak the language of commerce."

He considered with sadness how Tibetan culture was disintegrating as a result. Names of towns and streets were revised to Mandarin. Business signs were all in Mandarin, with fine-print Tibetan as a subscript. The more Han who established businesses, the more they hired their fellow Chinese, perpetuating a trend that excluded the Tibetans. The economic progress rolled over many of the indigenous people like an unstoppable wave. They increasingly turned to crime and alcohol and idleness—all of which already seemed to be on the rise in Lhasa. Over the past few years, prostitution had ballooned in Lhasa, with literally thousands of young girls leaning out the doorways of "hair salons" all across town. Until recently, the girls had all been Chinese, catering to the officials posted there. Now Tibetan girls were prostituting too—and the trade was becoming still more prevalent. At the same time, the religious and moral architecture of society was rotting—there were few senior lamas, or traditional teachers, and enrollment in monastic society, once the cornerstone of Tibetan culture, was strictly curtailed by the government. Renzin himself only went to Tsurphu Monastery for the annual festival; when he stepped inside the temples at other small monasteries, he was reverent but unsure what to do. As Tibetans were becoming increasingly secular, they were forgetting their heritage, and with it, their Tibetan vocabulary.

"Moving forward is both inevitable, and needed—Tibetans do not want to be rid of the developments that the Chinese brought," Renzin added. "But what is most important is our identity and freedom. Tibetans want to be who they were a hundred years ago; they want a society that supports the flourishing of their religion and culture, and they want individual personal freedoms of speech, of protest, of economy, of gathering, of religious practice. China on the whole has problems on these fronts, not just Tibet." Economically, China has moved in a more liberal direction, and that has also been true for Tibet. But politically, according to Renzin, Tibet is no more free now than in the 1980s or the 1960s. His frustrations had grown so much, he said, that after decades of perseverance he increasingly contemplated packing it all up and moving to Kathmandu. He thought the move might come within the year. "Today it is very tight," he said. "It's the social reforms we want most."

On certain days, Renzin would be jovial, relaxed, open. But underneath, a fear was growing. He would hesitate, or his gaze would turn steely. On a cloudless Sunday morning that fall, we crossed the Kyichu

River to a flat mat of golf-green grass beside a rippling brook. Poplar trees offered respite from the plateau sun, and an old stone wall ran along the border of an idyllic pasture. Yet, Renzin was on edge. He did not say that anything was wrong, but he was quiet and smiled less. As we walked through the meadow, the sound of a car bludgeoning its way up the old dirt road broke the stillness. It was most likely just another rickety Ibiza hatchback, catching big rocks on its low-slung chassis, driving a little too fast. But the car, red and packed front and back with five Chinese men far too large for its compact design, took the right turn in the village, toward us. Renzin stopped, his body rigid as a flagpole. All four doors were already open as the car swerved off the dirt, slalomed through the poplars, and slid to a halt. The men got out and took a few steps in our direction.

"Do you want a beer?" one of them asked, stumbling as he walked toward us.

"No," Renzin answered flatly. After a quick pace over a rise, he sat down, visibly shaken. Someone from the Nepali consulate had recently called to tell him they had heard something about him spending a lot of time with a foreigner.

We had become friends, but I was pushing the very boundaries of his safety that so many people had warned me about. It was time— perhaps past time—for me to leave Renzin alone.

═ 11 ═

WHEN THE WANG FAMILY CAME TO TOWN

ON JULY 1, 2006, CHINESE PRESIDENT HU JINTAO STOOD ON the concrete platform at the Golmud station and delivered the Qinghai-Tibet Railway's inaugural speech before 2,600 railway workers and a national television audience. Regular programming was interrupted. "This successful practice has once more made clear to all the people of the world that the wise and hardworking Chinese people have the aspiration, confidence, and ability to make uncommon achievements and . . . to stand like a giant side by side with other advanced nations of the world," he began. "The completion of the Qinghai-Tibet Railway . . . is of very great significance to speeding up the economic and social development . . . and consolidating the motherland's frontier defense."

At his side, dozens of handpicked international journalists—those willing to accept the government's condition that every interview be precleared—dutifully wrote everything down. Those who wouldn't accept the junket's conditions, including the *New York Times'* Joseph

Kahn, were denied access, and subsequently, permission to travel in Tibet.

Zhao Shiyun heard the speech through the thick walls of a control room somewhere nearby. As chief engineer, his job wasn't to indulge in ceremony but to make damn sure, on this long-awaited day, that everything went exactly as planned. Soon, without fanfare, he would retreat back to a dull office in Beijing and await his next assignment. Similarly, Zhang Luxin raced back and forth across the plateau by jeep, inspecting stations and track junctures and signal lights. He even worried about the litter and debris lying around the freshly evacuated work sites. But when it was all said and done, he could finally retire.

Months earlier, the Dalai Lama had described the railway as an instrument of cultural genocide, and, though he acknowledged that the train alone could bring economic benefits, he condemned the larger development policies. Controversy around the railway had erupted. At Chinese consulates across Europe and the United States—and at shareholders meetings of the North American corporations that had contributed to the project—protestors marched and sat in against the train. In the days preceding the official first day of service, three protestors, from the United States, Britain, and Canada, were arrested in Beijing when they climbed onto a second-story window ledge in the city's central train station and unfurled a banner that read: "China's Tibet Railway, Designed to Destroy."

Their actions provoked a rare and angry response through China's official mouthpiece, the *People's Daily*. An editorial called the international community hypocritical and said protestors wanted Tibet "to maintain its status quo and remain a stereotyped cultural specimen for them to enjoy." The editorial continued: "Why shouldn't Tibet progress like the rest of the world? These people are opposed to any development project the Chinese government maps in Tibet, and their pretexts are always high sounding: under the excuse of protecting the Tibetans' interest, their culture and environment . . . [Yet] those people choose to shuttle around the world by air in Gucci shoes and designer outfits, preaching the 'art of happiness.'" Its end note was dismissive, if not foretelling: "Now that Beijing is only 48 hours away, the roar of the locomotives is sure to mute all the irresponsible clamors."

In Lhasa, the city's mayor, Norbu Toinzhub, sought to calm concerns more diplomatically. "The Tibetan culture will not have fundamental changes with the opening of the Qinghai-Tibet Railway," he said. "Only with constant exchanges, reforms, and development shall a culture have a stronger vitality . . . Tourists admire the Tibetan culture because it is unique. The Tibetan culture will not disappear when there is a market demand for it."

At 11:05 a.m. the first train, code-named "Qing 1," rolled out of Golmud carrying 600 passengers. Seven minutes later, its counterpart left Lhasa station, heading north. Each train consisted of a full set of eight cars, with capacity for 940 passengers, and two engines. With four passenger runs planned each day, the railway was scheduled to bring 111,000 travelers to Lhasa each month, and within a day of opening, trains departed Beijing, Lanzhou, and Chengdu headed for Tibet. On the national railway timetable, the route was assigned a curiously plain name, T27, which seemed to say that for all the hubbub it was just another line in a sprawling forty-thousand-mile network of railroad spilling over this sprawling, booming country.

But there was little else that was commonplace about the train leaving for Tibet. At its head was a special General Electric engine designed to provide extraordinary torque and power at high altitudes. Though they looked nothing like the streamlined aero cars depicted on giant billboards across the Tibetan countryside and were based on an antique-looking 1980s shell, the cars were state-of-the-art machines manufactured for China by its joint venture with the transportation giant Bombardier. Beneath their pine-green skin was a veritable fortress on wheels. The undercarriages were sheathed in metal to protect against the sandblasting effect of windblown dirt and snow; their windows, which did not open, were double paned with compression systems to keep them from cracking under the intense pressure of quick barometric changes. Each seat, bed, and table was equipped with an oxygen hose to assist passengers breathing in the thin air, and fresh oxygen was pumped into the main cabins. Its designers had originally wanted to pressurize each car, like an airplane cabin, but the concept was deemed impossible because of the dangers of rapid depressurization when the train's doors opened during frequent stops.

Most of what made the trains so advanced was invisible—like the electronics. The trains were the first in China to run all their signaling and communications on a wireless GSMR network. But instead of building one independent cell network, with corresponding systems in each car, the railway built two; should a train break down in one of the plateau's notorious storms, a rescue mechanic could be as far as a three-day drive away, and the redundancy, though astronomically expensive, substantially lessened the chances that could happen.

Thirteen hours after it left Golmud, in the middle of the night, the Qing 1 aimed its powerful headlight across the homes of Kalden's village, then the suburb of Tolung, and finally, having crossed the Kyichu River, blew its whistle as it arrived in N'eu and onto the sweeping platform of track one at the Lhasa station. From that moment, 12:31 a.m. on July 2, 2006, the city and the province succumbed to, as exiled Tibetans have put it, the "second invasion of Tibet."

BY THE END OF 2006, JUST FIVE MONTHS AFTER THE OPENING RUN, 2.5 MIL-
lion tourists had visited Tibet—more than the entire official population of the TAR according to data published by Xinhua—and of those
visitors, 1.2 million arrived on the new railway. The growth quickly
began to exceed the government's wildest expectations. Beijing began
to forecast numbers for the future: 4 million tourists in 2007; 6 million by 2010. Of these, almost all, a full 93 percent, would be Chinese.

As the train began dumping more and more people in Lhasa, the
airlines struggled to compete, lowering fares. By year's end, a million
passengers had strolled through the bright new terminal in Lhasa—
the highest number yet. Development raced to keep up. That fall, a
$10 million shopping complex opened, and by January there were
5,000 stores and 3,200 restaurants and bars, a one-fifth increase over
the year before. The hotel business also bloomed; for most of the latter half of 2006, it was nearly impossible to find a room in Lhasa. By
January, there would be 606 hotels.

Among them was a place called the Brahmaputra Grand Hotel—a
sweeping 186-room luxury complex with a gaudy gold-leafed lobby
replete with Volkswagen-sized crystal chandeliers—built in the then
rural east end of town. At its entrance, a series of eight tall palm trees
reach fifty feet toward the sky, their waxy bark leading to long verdant
branches that stayed green into the cold, dry winter because they were
made entirely of plastic. The hotel contains a museum of Tibetan antiquities of unknown provenance—one of which is valued at forty thousand dollars. Ethnic music is played live at the check-in desk, but the
hotel, where suites cost upwards of $1,100 a night, employs almost
entirely Chinese or, when it wants a more "ethnic" look, Nepali staff.
The Nepalis are more skilled in the hospitality industry, the general

manager explained to me. The hotel was opened by a Chengdu businessman, Zhang Xiaohong, a supermarket mogul who had also opened a chain of the largest grocery stores in Lhasa. "Tibet is so unique," Zhang said in an interview with Chinese television reporters. "We decided to use Tibetan culture as a unique selling point." Soon afterward, Starwood, the global hotel giant, announced plans for the construction of a five-star St. Regis hotel near the heart of the Barkhor—"where the Tibetans live," as the company's Web site put it.

By most accounts, Lhasa was overwhelmed. The streets of the Barkhor were packed with people; the restaurants were almost always full. Suddenly, there was traffic everywhere—thousands of taxicabs and new Mercedes and BMWs. By the end of 2006, there were forty-three thousand vehicles in Lhasa, or about 1.3 per household, and the local registration office was recording thirty new vehicles per day. And prices—for everything from lettuce to televisions—didn't go down, as the government had promised. Instead, the cost of living for those in Lhasa sharply increased as demand for everything skyrocketed. The train carried 1.2 million tons of cargo over the course of its first fall season, but truck drivers in Golmud said there were more trucks than ever plying the Qinghai-Tibet Highway too, despite state news reports that the train was quickly becoming the primary shipping method. Lhasa seemed to be consuming as much as China could bring to it, and it was hungry for more.

As a result, the economy, having already been exploding at 12 to 14 percent annually, turned up the volume even more—to almost 15 percent in 2006. Investment in the region for the first nine months of 2006 exceeded that of the thirty months that came before it. Tourists alone spent an estimated $24 million in Lhasa that year, a figure expected to jump to $447 million for 2007. So much of it went into more building that Tibetans started calling the tall elevator cranes that marked the edges of the city the "Tibetan Crane," the official provincial bird—a joke once used by Chinese in the interior. Along the Kyichu riverfront, the new gated complexes of condominiums that Helena coveted were sprouting up like poppies, the buildings advertised in glossy full-color spreads in the real estate sections of the airplane and railway magazines passengers read on their way in. One Tibetan man said he bought a small condo for about $50,000, and six months later it was already worth $80,000.

The boom was certainly benefiting lots of people—shop and restaurant owners and the upper echelons of Tibetans included. And it instantly turned Lhasa into one of the most seductive entrepreneurial frontiers in China. Big businesses chose the premier avenues downtown or sought large-scale industrial sites. But the economic mood of the city was best exemplified in the small shops on the peripheries, where China's hinterland poor had flooded in with hopes of remaking themselves with small import businesses.

On the south side of Dream Island, a busy, dingy market had sprung up. A carnival ground surrounded it—bumper cars and other amusement rides, even a roller rink. Street vendors sold Chinese snacks: fried potatoes, hot dogs on sticks, and lots of bent and twisted mystery meat shaped like lollipops and glazed with a sweet, dark coating. Inside a giant temporary building with a huge domed roof of corrugated plastic stretched twelve acres of endless rows of cheap Chinese goods—jackets, shoes, flashlights, pocket knives, and wristwatches— much of it with faked brand names from Europe and the United States. It looked like any market in any big city in China.

One of the shops belonged to Wang Li, a forty-nine-year-old recent immigrant from Sichuan with a marinelike buzz cut, high, pronounced cheekbones, and a jutting jaw. Wang had been desperately poor for most of his life, and this opportunity in Lhasa stood to change that. His circumstances were not uncommon. There seemed to be a roaming populace of desperate Chinese, trying to find work on the new frontier. They were mobile families—like migratory railway workers—long accustomed to finding a paycheck far from home and always willing to play a hand in a new town, with new opportunity. It meant that places like Lhasa, though they eventually did receive an influx of wealth- and investment-oriented migrants, were often first overwhelmed by a wave of China's most desperate and lost economic orphans. Some Tibetans complained that this group brought the crime that had in the last few years made Lhasa's streets less safe. Mostly, though, it meant there was always a motivated Chinese man around willing to do just about anything to earn a living. At the market, Wang played the slick trader. He dressed for the role: a faux leather jacket, a dark gray sweater, worn slacks that had been pressed so many times they were shiny, and dark dress shoes. He was talkative, smart, and laughed a lot. He would chat with fellow entrepreneurs between the staccato sales pitches for a North Face Gore-Tex parka that he flung at passersby.

Wang had been traveling since he was a teenager in the mid-1970s. He had a son and daughter, but the money he made was never enough to support them, so both he and his wife roamed in whatever direction seemed lucrative, across thousands of miles of China, looking for work. After an eleven-year stint in China's south, Wang landed in Kashgar, in Xinjiang Province, the northwestern corner of the country that is home to both the Uigur ethnic minority and the ancient Silk Road. He worked in a cement factory, and then a brick factory, for nine years. "We businessmen we're like the water lily," Wang said. "We flow with the river, wherever it goes. We don't have a home. Life is difficult this way."

For Wang Lin, the son who now helped his father run his shop, it was an awful time. He and his sister had to raise themselves from about the age of nine. She would give him half a yuan—roughly six cents—as pocket change. In six years, his parents, who sent them about twelve dollars every month, came home twice. "If they came once a year, they would never have been able to save any money," Wang Lin said.

His father, however, had learned a valuable lesson about railroads and opportunity along the way. Everyone knew how the city of Urumchi, in Xinjiang's east, had boomed since the railway reached it in 1961. It was legendary. Then, in 1999, the train network was extended to Kashgar, connecting western Xinjiang with eastern China for the first time, and Xinjiang became one of China's very first big pushes in the Go West initiative. Xinjiang boomed overnight. Its population skyrocketed, along with real estate prices. New Western-style mansions became common in suburban neighborhoods, and the ethnic portions of downtown Kashgar huddled under the looming shadow of the modern city. Like Urumchi, it has been held by the Chinese as an example of the economic reform that a railway link can bring, and by the Tibetans, because the ethnic Xinjiang minorities have been largely marginalized, as a case study in the sort of commercialization and Sinofication they hope to avoid. For Wang, it was just a missed opportunity. He was there at the wrong time.

So the news of a planned train to Lhasa struck a chord. If he could get established before the railway opened, he might have a shot at finally making some money. In early 2005, Wang moved his entire family to Lhasa, starting with his son, Wang Lin, who traveled ahead to set up the shop. "We had all heard about Lhasa," Wang Lin said, "that it was undeveloped and easy to do business." In the mall, a fledgling development at that point, they had the pick of the litter, and they leased a corner stall on the outermost ring, one of the most visible and busy parts of the complex.

Wang Lin rented a sparse concrete room near the shop for the entire family—eight people—to live in. He hung cloth curtains from the ceiling to divide the room into four spaces, providing a semblance of privacy for each couple. The bathroom was outside, down the street, in a concrete public latrine. And to cook, he arranged a two-burner electric hotplate propped off the floor on a couple of furnace bricks. There were an endless number of similar rooms, and identical family situations, around Dream Island. Several lookalike streets run the length of the island, each with ground-level shops and restaurants and upper-level rental apartments filled with new settlers, who build makeshift walls with the studiousness of bees fortifying a hive. According to Wang Lin, it was not so different from anywhere else he had moved for work, except that here, things were going well enough that he thought the family would be able to stay.

"We've made tens of thousands of Quai," Wang Lin said. "It's been successful." His customers are often Tibetans from outlying areas—pilgrims who make it to Lhasa in the wintertime or nomads who come to town in the off-season flush with cash. Unlike the Barkhor and Renzin's shop, the Dream Island mall offers a tantalizing taste of modern consumerism, and infinitely more choices among its flashy gadgets and showy clothes. As a result, it is not uncommon to see in the Tibetan countryside nomads in American baseball caps and Tommy Hilfiger jeans; it is a globalization based on trade by small people, not simply multinational corporations. But for all their trades, Wang Lin and his father have gained little understanding of Tibetan culture nor do they care much about where they live. Neither have been to the Potala Palace or the Barkhor, and the unique heritage they are surrounded by, at least when they do venture toward the older parts of town, is almost an afterthought. "We were told the Tibetans get angry easily—don't irritate them. So I was a little afraid," Wang Lin said. "Soon, I realized they are not that different from us."

Bigger businesses than the Wangs' coat shop are thriving too, often with investments that started flowing quietly into Tibet as much as two years earlier. In 2004, Carlsberg, the brewing company, bought a large stake in Lhasa Beer and has since begun expanding the brewery and marketing its name in eastern China and abroad. Amway, though it is still not permitted to run a direct-to-consumer marketing company in Tibet, set up an office in downtown, near the Barkhor, where it will reportedly wait patiently for China's regulations to change. Tibetan carpets and arts have become commodities, selling for tens of thousands of dollars in New York City shops. Tibetan medicine, including the prized caterpillar plant that the Chinese insist improves virility, is blossoming from a small local industry to one that is increasingly attracting Chinese patients and industrial investors. And in one of the biggest new ventures, Tibet Glacial Mineral Water Company has tapped into a glacial melt spring near Damxung and begun marketing crystal-clear water in bottles to the rest of China, and maybe soon, the rest of the world.

PERHAPS NO BUSINESS DEVELOPMENT IN TIBET HAS MORE GROWTH PROMise, and is more controversial, than the extraction of the land's natural resources. Many Tibetans, and many Tibet advocates, had always suspected that mineral resources were one of the greatest motivations for the railway to Lhasa. But China always repeated a solemn refrain in answer to these critics: that the $4.3 billion project was not aimed at plundering Tibet. Yet all the while, and since well before groundbreaking on the QTR, China had quietly been pursuing a plan to do just that. Near the end of 2006 and into the early months of 2007, China's Ministry of Land and Resources disclosed monumental new resource discoveries all across Tibet.

The discoveries had not popped up overnight. The findings were the culmination of a secret seven-year, $44 million survey project that had preceded the railway construction, and even the decision about the route along which to build. The one thousand geographers who had been sent to map the plateau in 1999 found what they were sent for: a literal treasure house, sixteen major new deposits of copper, iron, lead, zinc, and other minerals worth an estimated $128 billion, according to articles by the China Tibet Information Center, a government-run portal. "Lack of resources has become a bottleneck for the economy," Meng Xianlai, director of the China Geological Survey, said in those statements. The discoveries in Tibet had prompted China to reevaluate its potential domestic resources and "will alleviate the mounting resources pressure China is facing."

The new reserves make Tibet one of the richest regions in China's territory and could shift the country's reliance on imports of copper and iron altogether, immediately affecting China's ability to continue on its current economic growth trajectory and even affecting international commodity markets well beyond China. Altogether, Tibet is now said to hold as much as 40 million tons of copper—one-third of China's total—40 million tons of lead and zinc, and more than a billion tons of high-grade iron.

As it was, China had grown into the world's largest importer of iron ore—326 million tons in 2006—much of which was used to feed its insatiable steel mills and its ballooning construction and auto industries. High-grade iron prices had more than tripled in the previous two years, driving up development costs worldwide, not just in China. Among the discoveries in Tibet was China's first substantial rich-iron supply, a seam called Nyixung, which alone is expected to contain as much as 500 million tons—enough to put an expected 20 percent of Chinese iron importers out of business and, according to China

Geological Survey's deputy director general, Zhang Hongtao, it "may relieve the country's three-decade-long dependency on iron imports."

The new copper reserves are no less substantial. A 250-mile seam of the metal was found along Tibet's environmentally cherished Yarlung Tsangpo Gorge and is being developed by a Vancouver, Canada–based corporation, Continental Minerals, at a cost of nearly half a billion dollars. The mine, Xietongmen, has been developed as a model for large-scale resource extraction. First, Continental Minerals provided the foreign capital for the project. In return, the mining company's local counterparts, such as the Chinese company Jinchuan, which owns a smelting facility in nearby Gansu Province, invested heavily in Continental Minerals. At the same time, Beijing offered generous development incentives, including a multi-year tax-free start-up period, subsidized power, and heavily discounted transport on the railway. "Five years ago I would not be talking about this project," Continental's CEO Gerald Panneton told a Canadian trade magazine in 2007, explaining his gamble on Tibetan resources. "What makes this project economic . . . is that they built a railroad between Golmud and Lhasa, and it will be extended all the way toward the project. What this does . . . is give you access to all the smelters." Xietongmen is expected to process forty thousand pounds of material a month, with an annual bounty of 110 million pounds of copper, two hundred thousand ounces of gold, and 2 million ounces of silver.

Another copper mine, Yulong, in Chamdo Prefecture in the northeast, has been described as the second-largest reserve in China and is now estimated to hold as much as 18 million tons, according to Xinhua. Its development, after being stalled for many years because it was not economical, is now expected to proceed quickly. There is even talk of construction of a dedicated railway to the site, a route that would more or less follow the proposed Lanzhou-Nagqu line.

Soon, Yulong could become the largest copper mine in the country, helping to satisfy China's hypercharged metabolism for electrical wiring and generation. In all, three new Tibetan copper finds increase China's total copper reserves by a third, and once production comes online, they will decrease imports by the same amount. China, which had imported much of its copper from Chile, is now estimated to hold 5.6 percent of the world's copper and will become its seventh-largest producer.

For big companies seeking to pursue large mineral development, the railway brought a degree of feasibility to exploration on the plateau that had never existed before. Whether for gold, lithium, or copper, at least six Canadian and Australian mining companies have stakes in Chinese consortiums set up to mine on the plateau, and more are talking about joining the scramble. According to figures published by the International Campaign for Tibet, less than 1 percent of discovered mines have yet to be prospected and only 15 percent of mines under operation have begun extraction. Western Mining, one of China's largest minerals and resources conglomerates, listed publicly on the Shenzhen Stock Exchange and raised over $800 million based in large part on the potential of the company's mineral assets in Tibet. That stock has been one of the notable international Chinese stock investments of recent years, brought to market by an arm of the Switzerland's UBS bank.

Beijing's resource hopes go deeper than minerals. Petrochina, of which the British oil giant BP owns a half-billion-dollar stake, is developing oil and natural gas fields in northern Tibet and Qinghai. And Sinopec, the Chinese oil major, recently announced plans for a renewed initiative to explore the plateau, where, as the Geological Survey's hopeful Zhang Hongtao put it, there are "superlarge" crude oil and gas reserves in Tibet's far-western Chang Tang Basin, as well as oil shale deposits in areas west of the new train line. According to Sinopec documents, an estimated 65 billion barrels of oil will become accessible in Tibet, a find that, if proven, would make the region one of the next great petroleum envies in the world.

The gold rush that has brought these big industrial resource companies to Tibet has pervaded on a small scale too, luring freshly arrived entrepreneurs with grandiose visions of pay dirt. The thinking that all you needed was a few investors and a hole in the ground to strike it rich in Tibet became so pervasive that the government quickly moved in mid-2006 to ban private-entity gold mining—a bold-stroke legislation heralded as an environmental safeguard. But the law, which skeptics point out only reserves the gold mining for government-sanctioned operations anyway, did little to slow the pillaging for less precious metals and minerals.

Satellite images on Google Maps show a large increase in road construction branching off the new railway route—much of it likely to be exploration projects for hundreds of small-party mining start-ups in the Nagqu area. From almost any vantage point in the Lhasa Valley, or any of the main arteries connected to it, the scars of mining are inescapable to the eye. They start with a tiny hole, somewhere high on a ridge, and then lead into a zigzagging brown line—a rough-cut road—that works its way down to the valley floor. Soon the road, constructed in a matter of days with little if any engineering oversight, starts to "bleed" as it erodes down the mountainsides, and eventually the fragile dry desert is turned into a wash of loose rock and rubble. The result is a telltale triangle mark of erosion, like a branded sign, on hundreds of mountainsides across Tibet.

But the visible scars of erosion, or even the large open pits that will be left after the copper and iron operations kick into high gear, are just the tip of the environmental impacts that could quickly rain down on this otherwise pristine region. With oil drilling comes oil transport and, as in every region around the world where hydrocarbons are extracted, inevitably some oil spilling. Oil shale extraction is the most environmentally intrusive. Along with the plans for copper mining there is talk of building the smelting operations to process the metals, and in the meantime it will be shipped to Gansu. Copper smelting is one of the single most polluting processes in the world.

Though it is nearly impossible to get a gauge on the current state of any soil or water contamination that already exists in Tibet—the data have never been collected and would likely remain secret if it were—recent reports from researchers working within Human Rights Watch detail localized contamination in at least one small village near Lhasa. Several people reportedly died from abrupt illness in this village, and based on fears that mining waste chemicals like arsenic had been dumped in the water upstream, the villagers protested to the police, who chose not to take action against the mining group working uphill. Though the large projects are subject to some environmental review, it is a legal environment where virtually no regulations exist—or at least no practical enforcement—to prohibit dumping in the future.

DESPITE ALL THIS INVESTMENT, AND THE PROSPECT OF MUCH MORE, it remains questionable whether China's economic plan in the TAR is sustainable. Almost all of the visible changes wracking Tibet—the roads and buildings and mines and the largest employers, along with their employees—come not from a revenue-rich provincial government seeking expansion but from the deep pockets of a central government that still believes it can force an economic revolution through one of the greatest subsidization programs ever attempted. Virtually none of the economic expansion, and only a minuscule portion of the existing economy, is occurring organically. The Qinghai-Tibet Railway, for example, could end up paying more to transport copper than the developer of the Xietongmen mine, Continental Minerals. According to Andrew Fischer, a Canadian development economist, total government subsidies, based on official government data, rose to "an astonishing" 120 percent of the economy in 2004 and 2005. "In other words the government was spending more than the entire economic activity," Fischer said. The result has not been the shot of adrenaline and self-sustenance one might expect from subsidization, but has instead served to further increase the demand for more money, as well as the burden on Beijing—flipping the standard economic model upside down. "To put it simply, for every one yuan the GDP increased, government expenditure increased by 2.1 yuan the same year."

It's happening because a very large portion of the investments in Tibet—and the revenues of "Tibet-based" businesses—are funneled out of the province rather than remaining in the local economic bloodstream. Just as the twenty-two railway bureaus reaped profits that went back to corporate headquarters in Chengdu or paid wages to workers who sent them home to Hunan, much of the building in Tibet is sponsored by other provinces and business groups who skim off the revenue flow and then export their profits. That may not be accidental; the subsidies represent an injection of cash into the larger Chinese economy and, in a sense, set up Tibet as a laundering mechanism for outsiders. But it also means that very little of the community's cash flow makes it into the hands of Tibetans, whether to earn, reinvest, or spend. There is no trickle-down effect. "They have less and less opportunity to act as significant participants or beneficiaries in the rapidly growing parts of the economy," Fischer said, "even while their traditional bases in farming and herding are less and less able to sustain their livelihoods."

Overwhelmingly, the fastest-growing aspects of the Tibetan economy have been in the administrative and services sector, which excludes all industry and agriculture. Administration even dwarfs tourism. That sector contributed almost 80 percent of GDP growth in 2005, according to Fischer, and makes up roughly 65 percent of the economy. Amazingly, it doesn't include army staffing and budgets, which would undoubtedly raise those figures much higher. The next largest contributor to the TAR's economy is the construction industry, which is now as large as agriculture and much greater than industry. But, as Fischer noted, almost all of the major projects are contracted to firms outside the TAR and are subject to extraordinary graft and corruption, resulting in shoddily built "white elephant" projects that end up burdening Tibet with future costs. "Without an encouragement of local ownership, management or employment, none of the so-called pillars of the economy will be able to sustain current economic expansion. Instead of capturing wealth within the local economy, they produce a form of boomerang finance, decapitating local autonomy while boosting short-term growth rates."

Between 2002 and 2007, the size of the Tibetan economy doubled. It quadrupled in the last decade. The overall Chinese economy, universally lauded as the fastest growth the world has seen, by comparison, has tripled in the same period; Tibet's expansion has outpaced it by a third. "Basically, the government is stuck," Fischer explained. "I'm not saying it will become a boom-bust scenario, but if it is not, the government will have to keep pouring in immense amounts of subsidies to just keep the boom going."

AFTER DECADES OF PERSEVERING THROUGH GENOCIDAL THREATS, RENZIN was so fed up with the unfairness of the changes in Tibet that a permanent move to Kathmandu seemed inevitable. He was far from alone. As the migrants and tourists and entrepreneurs poured into Tibet, a steady number of Tibetans were leaving. Each year an estimated two to three thousand Tibetans find a way across the ragged Himalayan border into Nepal, and often on to Dharamsala and the Tibetan community in India. Many of them are on a pilgrimage to meet the Dalai Lama or to attend the Tibetan schools in India, and they may eventually return to Tibet. Others seek permanent political asylum, freedom, or a place where they can devote themselves to practice in a nunnery or monastery without government persecution. Several said that, after decades of hardship, it was the current development that finally forced them to leave. More and more so, according to refugees' testimony in 2005 and 2006, they are farmers and nomads who have been pushed off their land by the new agricultural policies and feel lost in the new officially sanctioned economy.

For most of the emigrants, getting across the border has not changed much over the centuries—they walk. And before the Tibetan Plateau drops some fourteen thousand feet back down to the foothills of South Asia, of course, one has to cross the great Himalayas, the tallest, most severe, jagged, and remote mountain range in the world. It is possible to take a truck, even to sneak along in the back of freight, down the Friendship Highway and through the official border checkpoint in the Nepali town of Tatopani. But most Tibetans don't have a passport or a permit, and crossing there is a lot like walking into the sheriff's office looking to swipe a wallet. Instead, they cross the mountains at their next weakest point, in Tibet's far west, near the prominent peak of the spiritually revered Mount Kailash or, most commonly, at Nangpa Pass, a high mountain col on the icy flanks of Mount Cho Oyo, which, at almost twenty-seven thousand feet, is the sixth-highest summit in the world.

The pass, at 18,750 feet, is as treacherous as any Himalayan mountaineering journey, and so the pilgrims pay guides exorbitant fees—
between $400 and $1,200—to usher them across. Often a family will
pool all its assets, or a man will spend his life savings in order to send
himself, or his son, across into Nepal, where, if they make it safely all
the way down into the Kathmandu Valley, they are welcomed at a
small compound on the outskirts of the city called the Tibetan Refugee Reception Center, processed by the United Nations High Commission on Refugees, and given transport on to India. The authorities are
a great risk on such a journey, but so is the terrain, and the prospect
of spending up to four weeks in the mountains without proper clothing, shoes, or food. It is not uncommon for a refugee to die of dehydra-
tion, exposure, or starvation on the way out of Tibet.

In 2006, an estimated 2,600 Tibetans fled to Nepal, slightly less than
normal, according to the International Campaign for Tibet, which
conducts an annual review of emigration from Tibet. It is difficult to
know exactly why the numbers had fallen—a change in circumstance
or interest. But around the time the railway was completed, the Chinese government had begun stepping up efforts to keep Tibetans
locked within the border. Beijing began to wield its influence with the
royal government in Nepal, pressing for the repatriation of any refugees caught inside Nepal, of which there are tens of thousands in residence. In January 2005, Nepalese authorities responded to Chinese
pressure and abruptly announced the revocation of permits for the
office of the local representative of the Dalai Lama and ordered the clo-
sure of the Tibetan Refugee Welfare Office—both establishments that
had been present in Kathmandu since the 1960s. Tibetans in Nepal
began to fear a policy of refoulement—the forcible return of people to
a country where they fear persecution—and indeed there were several reports of Nepalese authorities handing Tibetans back over the

border, or Chinese authorities crossing over the border in order to arrest and then extract Tibetans. And the borders themselves seemed to be getting more secure.

On September 13, 2006, a guided group of about seventy-five young Tibetans, many monks, nuns, and children, left Sakya outside of Shigatze to walk toward Nangpa Pass. They had come in trucks on a nascent Tibetan refugee underground. Many were spirited away from homes as far as Nagqu and even western Sichuan, first to Lhasa and then to monasteries for safekeeping and finally to this trailhead in south-central Tibet. Among them was Dohna, a girl who paid $515 to a guide who promised a two-day walk. She was traveling with Tenzin, the young daughter of her neighbor, but aside from the girl, she knew no one else in the group. Dohna traveled light—she had no idea until her first day's march turned to night, and then day, then night again, that it would in fact take her twenty days to the other end of her journey. "I was carrying only a little *tsampa* and I did not dare to eat too much," she said. "So we stirred a little *tsampa* with water and we drank it for food and we walked like that for fourteen days. Then we did not get any food for the next six days."

The morning of September 30, the sun rose above the snow into a deep cobalt sky. The refugees were nearing the pass. Above them, one-thousand-foot-long plumes of snow clung onto the ever steepening face of Cho Oyo, until it gave way entirely to black rock cliffs and bright patches of vertical ice that glinted in the sun as they melted. The landscape dwarfed the hikers, who trudged along, postholing in the deep drifts in a single file like tiny pebbles dropped from far above. There was a base camp nearby, and several of the Tibetans broke off to beg the foreign climbing expeditions there for food. That was the last thing Dohna remembered before terror set in.

"The guide appeared in a rush," Dohna recalled. "He said hurry up and run; soldiers are coming." The soldiers, members of a group called the People's Armed Police, were part of a paramilitary unit formed by the PLA. They gathered down the hill from Dohna, whose group had dwindled to around forty-five people, as some had apparently been arrested during the walk the previous night. Methodically and purposefully, according to witnesses who were at the mountaineering camp, four of the soldiers arranged a stance in the snow and settled the long barrels of their Chinese Type 81 assault rifles, a domestic knockoff of the AK-47 Kalashnikov that is the standard automatic weapon used by the PLA, into the snow for a clear shot.

Everyone panicked. Dohna was in the middle of the line, with Tenzin running up behind her. But running in deep snow at eighteen thousand feet is like one of those bad dreams where no matter how hard you try, everything grinds into slow motion. "I was telling her to run as fast as she could and to throw the bag from her back," Dohna said. "I could hear the zinging of bullets in my ears." Behind her a young brother from Kandze, a Tibetan prefecture in the southeast, was also trying to make it to the top of the pass. Dohna looked back to see that the Kandze man was shot—first in one leg, then the other—and as he sank to the ground, she shouted at him to run, but he waved her on. A bullet tore through her own pants too, but miraculously when she felt the hole it had left, there was no blood. It had only grazed her clothes. She gasped for breath and rushed uphill.

Ahead of her was Kelsang Namtso, a seventeen-year-old nun from a rural, forty-family village near Nagqu. Kelsang was the only daughter among a family of boys, and she dreamed of studying in one of the large nunneries in India, which was her destination. There were no nunneries at all near her home, and so for the two years since she had become a nun she had practiced in solitude. Hundreds of feet below, the soldiers continued to methodically fire off single shots, the back-coil striking them in the shoulder with each report of the weapon that echoed off distant glaciers. The bullets struck Kelsang in the chest, and she dropped forward, landing facedown, as blood spilled out into her maroon robes, and then into the soft white snow. "They are shooting them like dogs," shouted one of the mountaineers at base camp, a Romanian man, as he watched in horror. Dohna kept running, and after some time, she made it over the crest of the hill and found a hideout in the snow, where she remained for four hours. When she went back to check on Kelsang, she described her eyes as white, and her body frozen.

It is not known exactly how many people were shot or killed on Nangpa Pass on September 30. Of the group of seventy-five that started out, only forty-one made it to Nepal. The official Chinese report tallies two deaths. Initial international media reports put the number possibly as high as ten. Those who did not make it across the pass were taken back to Shigatze, where, according to the ICT and a later report in London's *Guardian,* they were tortured and interrogated. A fifteen-year-old boy, after he had been released, told the paper that police beat him with an electric cattle prod and interrogated him about the identity of the dead nun. Later, he was chained to a wall while a guard wearing a metal glove struck repeated blows to his stomach.

The railway had brought a new age for Tibet, but some things had not changed at all.

12

HU'S WEST

ON A CHARACTERISTICALLY OVERCAST BEIJING AFTERNOON in late October 2006, a few short months after the line opened for service, I took a taxi from downtown, past Zhang Luxin and Zhao Shiyun's offices at the Ministry of Railways, to the Beijing West station. There, I bought a ticket for the T27, a small pink piece of paper with some numbers that designated my berth and car, followed by the simple misspelled English word *Lasa*. Just like that, I was guaranteed painless first-class passage on the journey to the end of the earth, Younghusband's fabled Tibetan kingdom. I walked down to the platform, found my car, and, with the ease of catching an Amtrak line to Boston, boarded the Lhasa express.

Besides being brand-new, there was very little to distinguish the train to Tibet from any other train in China. The floors were carpeted in a faintly ethnic pattern that made the cars quieter and slightly more comfortable, but that didn't stop passengers from covering them within minutes with discarded peanut shells and noodle soup wrappers. The compartment doors were etched with frosted glass in the shape of a Tibetan infinity knot, a small gesture most likely implemented by the Canadians at Bombardier rather than the Qinghai-Tibet Railway Company itself. And each bed—there were four in each soft sleeper car—had its own LCD television screen and a nipple to connect each passenger to his or her personal oxygen breathing tube.

A day and a half from Beijing, the train passed through Golmud station, a few minutes before dawn, and began the final and remarkable leg of its journey. It made its switchbacks up the Kunlun Mountains, gaining around six thousand feet, then slowly, like a tired old dog almost out of breath, crested the Kunlun Pass and burst forth into the expanse of the Tibetan Plateau. The passengers—the cars were full with Chinese tourists and businessmen, some Hui salesmen, and a few Tibetans—pressed their faces against the large glass picture windows to soak in the highly anticipated scenery of this last, new section of track. Gloriously, the high peaks rimmed the horizon, a white ruffle on the edge of an elegant gown. The permafrost tundra swept away in expansive flats of flourishing green vegetation and orange, mineral-rich soil. All the while recordings blared incessantly from the train's speakers, alternating between classical Chinese elevator music and Mandarin and English propaganda. Each announcement began with the same packaged cheeriness.

"Dear passengers and friends," one began. "The Kunlun Mountains are regarded as the backbone of Asia . . . Surrounded by familiar mountains, you will feel yourself flying on top of the clouds. The ancient people shared great respect for the Kunlun Mountains . . . many stories or legends have come out of them."

Over the announcements, two young, blue jean–clad Chinese men, toting acoustic guitars, buzzed about how they wanted "to tap into the new opportunity" of Lhasa and hoped to find gigs in Tibet's growing small cities, playing in bars and saloons. A Tibetan man from near Xining was on his way to visit his son, who had moved to Lhasa to study as a monk. One young speculator, a thirty-four-year-old glass and ceramics salesman from Hubei Province, had never been to Lhasa but was convinced he had a jump start on a smart new venture. "Because the train just opened, maybe there are not so many people doing business and there will be less competition," he said, admitting he didn't have much of a plan. "Tomorrow we will arrive in Lhasa, find a hotel to sleep in, and in the morning we will just walk the streets. If we don't see many stores, we will rent a shop and ask our factories to ship our product here." And five loud and drunk Chinese men, executives for a Qinghai coal company, were enjoying an all-inclusive three-day trip to Tibet paid for by their local political official. They were entranced with a DVD of the modern Kung Fu epic *Hero* playing on a thirty-seven-inch Japanese-made plasma TV mounted in the train's dining car.

In the neighboring car, two Hui traders from Linxiu, the part of Gansu Province where much of Tibet's entrepreneurial Muslim community first emigrated from, were traveling back to their butcher shop in the Barkhor. The men, both older with long gray hair, spindly goatees, and white prayer caps, commuted to Golmud once a week and bought animals in Qinghai to sell in Tibet. Though they still preferred to import their meat on trucks—it was cheaper—the train provided a comfortable improvement over the punishing ride of the public bus. As they explained how they had come to Lhasa two years earlier, an angry conductor marched down the aisle. "You cannot talk," she said, inexplicably. My Chinese interpreter, astounded by the order, pressed for an explanation. "Foreigners may not talk to people on the train to Lhasa," she repeated. "It is not permitted."

The hours stretched. "Dear passengers," the announcement droned, "most parts of the region still remain in their natural status. You will be lucky enough to see groups of Tibetan antelopes feeding on grass and drinking in rivers. Let's enjoy the eyes' feast bestowed by nature, never to invade their colonies and let the lovely antelopes enjoy their leisure lives." A conductor shouted and pointed at a couple of small brown figures dotting a field a few hundred yards from the tracks: Tibetan antelope. The rare, elegant chiru, with its exquisite, sandy wool and spiraling dark horns, had dwindled in the late 1990s, when poachers were killing more than twenty thousand of them a year to make luxurious *shahtoosh* pelts worth ten thousand dollars in Milan or Paris. Starting in 1991, Chinese authorities attempted to protect the animals by creating a series of nature reserves and then built thirty-three tunnels for passage under the railway line that cuts through their traditional range, and the chiru population has actually experienced a comeback, according to Wildlife Conservation Society biologist George Schaller.

The endangered antelope has become one of the ecological icons of the plateau, cast as one of China's newly invented brands in the exotic far west and in the enrollment of Tibet into the national fold. It was chosen as one of the five cartoon mascots, known as the "friendlies," for the Beijing Olympic Games. At the conductor's prompt, every one of the train car's passengers jumped from their seats and leaped across the aisle for a view of the chiru, crowding against the windows of the north side of the car with a zealousness that seemed to put the train at risk of tipping over.

Such moments of excitement punctuated the trip as often as periods in one of Emerson's epic poems. The bus or truck ride over the plateau was a character-chiseling journey that meant days of freezing temperatures and coping with the microscopic wind-driven dust that worked its way into everything—a deeply tactile experience, rich for all the senses. Riding the train was more like being locked in a sterile, hermetically sealed fishbowl. Behind the plate-glass windows and their inch-thick rubber seals, in the constantly filtered and boosted air, the plateau raced by, a kaleidoscope of fantastic imagery. But like the flat-screen TVs throughout the train, the Tibetan Plateau could be easily tuned in to, and just as easily tuned out.

"Dear passengers . . . on the plateau the temperature often drops to twenty degrees below zero at night, so it is easy to catch cold while going to the toilet. To solve the problem, the railway company installed toilets with electrical heaters inside. Due to these effective measures, the health of constructors of the Qinghai-Tibet Railway could be well ensured."

The announcements lectured on permafrost construction techniques, Tibetan Buddhism, environmental sustainability, and cultural integration. Scientifically, they were informative; culturally, they simply chimed platitudes and, at times, blatant misinformation about the history of China's relationship with Tibet. Of course, there was no mention of the train derailment earlier in the autumn near the Kunlun Pass, or of the freight train collision that first summer near Damxung that killed a handful of railway engineers, or of the young Chinese businessman who died of altitude sickness on a passenger run just a few weeks earlier. Nor did the scientific lectures mention the cracks that had already begun to appear along the railway bed that summer, a tell-tale sign of the slumping soil caused by permafrost warming. The train raced past the station at Tangu La, a barren platform of concrete, a sign in three languages, and a single terminal building that stood in the wilderness disconnected from any hint of civilization that might use it.

Then it descended into Amdo prefecture, and Nagqu, and the places where nomads still roamed the grasslands as far as the horizon.

The Chinese government estimates that by the year 2020, more than eighty-five thousand hotel rooms will be needed—not in Lhasa, but here, along the plateau wilderness itself. It is calling for the wholesale tourist development of the plateau but claims that development will happen sustainably: "The tourism industry will not encourage the building of high towers and star-rated hotels," said one Chinese article on the campaign, "but focus more on family hotels." Separately, plans are in the works to launch a luxury train—one that will charge tourists a thousand dollars a night and give them private four-hundred-square-foot apartments complete with private dining lounges and hot tubs. According to the chief executive of the Shanghai-based TZG Partners, a young American Stanford University graduate named Josh Brookhart, a series of high-end resorts are also on the drawing board for several of the remote stations along the plateau route. "People think it can be something that can destroy the place, or it can be the exact opposite," Brookhart noted of his $130 million investment. "It's very hard to make an argument that it is for the good of the people to be cut off from the world. If you look at how Tibet will be with us or without us, clearly we think it will be better with us."

What had once been a trophy journey, where the wonders of Tibetan civilization and culture and history were a reward for the persistence and discomfort required to get there, was now routine. A journey to Tibet had become comparable to a journey to any other stop on the main Chinese line. And people like Renzin, Kalden, and Pemba Norbu were now bystanders to a land hijacked for a gamut of political and economic motives.

As I jotted thoughts into a small black notebook, another official approached.

"What are you writing about?" he asked.

"It is just my travel journal," I explained, and smiled weakly.

"Are you writing notes about the train?" he pressed. "It would be better if you did not write while on the train." He stood there until I closed my book and tucked it away, and for the rest of the ride to Lhasa, I stared out into the deep black night.

LHASA S STATION WHERE THE TRAIN ARRIVED, ON TIME, AT 10:30 P.M. IS NOT a terminus at all. Rather, its half dozen platforms and mammoth reception hall are a metropolitan waypoint. When the train finally reached Lhasa in 2006, Beijing announced the tracks would go farther—to Shigatze, with its copper, by 2010, and then with additional branches back east, south, and to the border of Nepal shortly thereafter. From Nagqu, a line would be extended east to reach a major copper mine, and further north, inside Qinghai Province, a spur was being planned that would provide access to large coal mines. The map of all the future railroad lines that officials hoped would leave Lhasa would place the city at the center of a web of shattered glass, with routes arching to points in every direction. Disembarking passengers were released onto graciously wide swaths of pavement and marble, sheltered under two great swooping roofs shaped like aircraft wings. The cavernous terminal was a departure not only from everything familiar about Tibet but from the graceless architecture of most new Chinese development. Clean, spacious, and stylish, with ornate woodworking, massive wooden beams, and modern escalators, it was wholly impressive.

Outside, what had been the isolated construction site at N'eu was a new city in itself. Taxis queued in a roundabout, and their drivers swarmed the arriving passengers with all the aggression, annoyance, and spirit of the worst touts of Delhi. They tugged at jackets and grabbed at bags and shouted prices: fifty yuan, thirty yuan. Lhasa had always been subdued, and a year earlier a taxi from the station area had cost ten yuan.

Adjacent to the station entrance, paved avenues were lined with large fluorescent lights. Buildings, four- to eight-story structures, stood everywhere: new hotels, a police compound, some sort of staff dormitory housing. An illuminated billboard was pasted with a school bus–sized photograph of a model, head propped on her hand, selling her skimpy underwear. Another plugged Motorola's RAZR cell phones. A highway sign in English, Tibetan, and Mandarin pointed the way straight for Beijing Road, right for New Century Road, and hard right for the Lhasa Bridge. The Tibetan names for these places had all been replaced.

Across the river, the Potala Palace was hardly recognizable. Its red and white walls, freshly painted and bright, glimmered under the powerful spotlights that raised the venerated building from the cloaked night with the fanfare of the Bellagio tower on the Las Vegas strip. The view lasted only a few seconds before it was blocked by several new tall buildings constructed along the riverfront, their rooftops alight with the ubiquitous flickering neon of advertisements and animated ticker-tape strips.

Downtown Lhasa was lively, if no longer distinctively Lhasa, or Tibetan. Dozens of hotels were festooned with streaming lanterns and strings of lights to attract the truckers who still rolled in off the highway from the east. A fresh PetroChina station tried to compete with its own shower of glowing fluorescents. On New Century Road, the strip to the south of the Barkhor that was once the city's shadowy outskirts of ambling strays and diesel-spewing sixteen-wheelers, signs and banners for Budweiser hung in the windows of the cozy, months-old restaurants. Firecrackers snapped among a group of kids on the street. While it was a faint echo of the place it used to be, by the standard of Chinese megacities, Lhasa had become charming. The Barkhor had adopted the name "Old City," and a new gate separated it from the modern bustle of the main streets, like the Chinatown arch in San Francisco.

That night, the power went out in downtown Lhasa. It did so again the next morning and a third time the following evening. Some people had heard reports that the outages were due to the construction of a transformer station on the north end of town, but the predominant theory was that the city just didn't have the juice to support its ballooning population, with all its new lights and buildings, or the extreme demands of the mining and other new industries. There were similar complaints about other critical infrastructure issues, like sewage treatment plants, of which Lhasa had just one.

In fact, the edges of Lhasa grew considerably in 2006. On the west end, bordering the suburb of Tolung, new Kia and Toyota dealerships sat enclosed in large glass showrooms. On the east end, which industrious immigrant Han farmers had previously lined with endless rows of vegetable greenhouses, Lhasa University had built a sprawling new campus, and half a dozen villages had been resettled into ten neat four-story apartment complexes. The stories were familiar: the residents had received compensation that would last two years, maybe three, but in exchange they had lost their homes, their animals, and their land, which they thought would have carried them through a lifetime. Sons and fathers who had turned fields and corralled goats were standing outside hotel construction sites, hoping for day labor tossing stones or digging pits. It was as if the government was gathering all the small villages of the valley—and all the Tibetans who lived there—and sweeping them like errant pebbles into a towering pile in the middle.

The scene was even more stark in the sloping alluvial valley south of the new station, near where the N'eu resettlement lay. Three entire villages spread over several square miles had been moved out of their homes, and the fourth, the last in the valley, had been given its notice. The expansive fields, empty, were bisected by a four-lane stretch of pavement with arching streetlamps. It seemed not to matter that it led nowhere, that not a single building had yet been built along it, that at night the highway could be mistaken for a landing strip on the moon. Surreally, every hundred yards or so, crosswalks were painted at intersections that dropped abruptly into the ungraded pasture, and electric crosswalk signs flashed stick pedestrians—their pale green light falling flat on the rural landscape. At the end of 2007, Beijing announced that the place would become the Liuwu New District industrial park. "To help the city accommodate an influx of tourists and migrants" the $100 million "high-tech" park would have boundaries larger than all of existing Lhasa; it would house more than 110,000 residents and employ another 114,000. It was seven miles from downtown Lhasa, but that area was now part of the city—Lhasa's municipal boundary had been extended in 2006 to swallow the far reaches of its "suburbs," all the way out into the midst of the Tolung Valley, to Kalden's house.

IN KALDEN S VILLAGE, THE TRANSFORMATION HAD REACHED A STASIS, IF not a resolution. As the train construction had sped up, the dust and debris kicked off the tracks had made life there miserable, if not impossible. Kalden's family, along with their neighbors, fought for compensation, arguing that their homes beside the rumbling tracks were unlivable. In the spring of 2005, the government agreed to move them across the highway to a flat steppe of unremarkable, though arable, land. But their compensation, twenty thousand yuan, was just a fraction of what was originally promised when the railway project was announced, and it would be paid out in installments conditioned on the new home meeting certain zoning requirements set up by local officials. The idea seemed to be to maintain a degree of uniformity in new construction across the rural areas and, ironically, to install certain Tibetan cultural characteristics. Tibet had to start looking developed, but *feel* Tibetan— at least so far as it could be seen out the windows of the train. Taken broadly, the trend was the result of a set of laws that had been passed to subsidize the local construction industry, which accounted for an increasing chunk of all economic growth in the TAR that year.

Kalden's new house had been one of its cookie-cutter projects. A padded bench ran the length of the poured concrete floor of the main room, and a wall of single-paned glass faced east, but failed to capture much of the morning sun because the house was tucked into the shadow of the mountainside. The room was mostly empty—his family didn't own enough things to fill it—and it was freezing. New materials, besides being costly, didn't have the insulation properties of indigenous architecture. "The old house was built from river stone and mud," Kalden said. "It was so cheap. Everything in the new house had to be bought." Chinese law mandated that the new homes be built of stone quarried by one of the large local Chinese-owned businesses machining the hillsides of the Lhasa Valley and that they use wooden beams—much of which had to be shipped in from eastern Tibet or over the plateau from Golmud and eastern China. The beams, according to local law, should be "painted colorfully with flowers and animals," Kalden explained. "But we've run out of money, so we can't afford to paint."

Kalden and his brothers had to finance the construction themselves, then apply for reimbursement later. The house had cost them twenty thousand yuan, but by August of 2006 they had only received about sixteen thousand yuan from the government. The four thousand yuan they were still owed was being withheld until finishing touches, like the decorative painting, had been completed. Paying for the move required each working family member's savings—an amount equal to about four years' worth of income. They saved, they sold animals, and they found day labor on the railroad, or wherever they could. Yet they never had enough. "It's not fair," Kalden said. "We work just to pay for the change the railroad forced."

That summer he and his brother Gyatso had torn down the old house with their own hands, and walking through the rubble ignited intimate memories of their father and of the past. "This was our front gate." Kalden pointed to a flat spot of earth between two sunken stones. "This was our storage shed"—a shell of old walls of river stones, hand positioned in the mud mortar to hold them in place— "our kitchen"—a small rise or step up onto another dirt platform, a smattering of stones, garbage, and broken woven baskets on the floor, the walls erased entirely. "And this was our prayer room." He gestured toward an open expanse at the back of the property, near where an aqueduct still ran with cold emerald water before the terraced hill dropped to another gorgeous farm field and then to the river.

A train rushed by and broke the stillness, not a crashing noise but a steady high-pitched scream. The stiff draft blew Kalden's bangs off his face, and the ground shook violently underfoot. "They told us that when it opened, things would become cheaper," Gyatso said. "Things would get easier." So far this had not been the case, but Gyatso stuck to his optimistic if not helpless view. "We have to believe them. They said so, and we have to believe them," Gyatso insisted, almost frustrated. "We have no choice."

Kalden was quiet for some time, unsure, it seemed, of how to speak. He massaged his brow and bit his lip. He folded a one-yuan bill into tiny triangles until it was the size of a penny, and he stared at his older brother, as if asking for permission. "I don't believe anything they've said," he said finally, softly. "We used to eat *tsampa*. We still eat *tsampa*. It's not like after the train opened, we started to eat rice—I'd rather have rice," he said. "It's better for officials, for those who work for the government. For me, the train does not bring anything good."

I asked Kalden what he wanted. "I don't know. I hadn't ever thought about it before," he said. "I guess I want money."

MOST DRIVERS IN TIBET, LIKE THE REST OF CHINA, HAVE LESS EXPERIENCE behind the wheel than a newly permitted American teenager. And so I was particularly nervous when Pemba insisted on picking me up. No sooner had I jumped into the seat of his little white Mitsubishi hatchback than he skidded into the wheel of a large, pedaled cart, reversed back into a shouting crowd of frightened shoppers, and sped awkwardly into the face of oncoming traffic. "This is the universal trend," he said, taking a hand off the wheel to point to the development and metropolitan chaos he was swerving to avoid. "It would be happening whether China was doing it or Tibetans were doing it. But assuming that Tibet was an open country, where there was access to resources including health care, education, and a global network, and if we had a good system to run it, then I believe we could achieve the same results. It could be even greater." He had bought the car a week before for five thousand dollars and was eager to show it off.

He pulled up to a trendy local restaurant, a Chinese version of

Applebee's, on the west end of Lhasa—an odd choice for a young Tibetan. Pemba was twenty-seven and, with a leather coat, jeans, a sweater, and eyeglasses, looked studious, and his intellect was a geyser of ideas. He had been educated in Beijing, lived there for seven years, and spoke fluent Mandarin as well as English. "I'm glad there have been a lot of improvements, but I am so sad for what has been lost. I wish we could do better than that." For Pemba, globalization was assaulting Tibet's culture and morally eroding the society, as it had done in the rest of China. "Development is not just a matter of how much money you have, how well off society is. It's also about people's attitudes and values and beliefs," he said. China had grown its own GDP and embraced capitalism at the expense of its cultural and religious soul, Pemba argued, a sentiment that was becoming more common among mainland Chinese, as well. "It's been replaced by materialism," he said, "but a lot of people don't care. They feel it is more important to be rich so they can be powerful."

Pemba smoked constantly, talking over beer and a bowl of Chinese dumplings. There was opportunity in what was taking place in Tibet, but Tibetans were being excluded from it. "Everything you hear about unemployable Tibetans is that they aren't skilled or don't speak the language," he said. "But I can't get a job here either." A few weeks earlier, he had joined hundreds of other unemployed Tibetan college graduates in a walled TAR government compound near the Potala Palace to protest the institutional bias against hiring Tibetans for official positions—positions that comprise an estimated quarter of Lhasa's working class and most of its upper strata.

The skewed system was all the more disheartening to Pemba because he felt that engaging Tibetans in the modern economy was the best way to preserve Tibetan culture in the face of such massive change. "I was speaking with a friend of mine—she just turned twenty-four and has graduated from college," Pemba noted sadly. "But she couldn't speak 'Sunday to Saturday' in Tibetan, which is unbelievable." A lot of the Tibetan youth, who aren't taught Tibetan language in schools after around fifth grade, can't speak Tibetan purely, he said, echoing the whispered complaints of Renzin and others from the older generation in Lhasa. Instead, they mix partial Tibetan and Chinese. Tibetan culture, at its most fundamental levels, was slipping away. Lhasa University had begun teaching its Tibetan history courses in Chinese; then it closed its Tibetan language department altogether. Pemba felt sure that soon Tibetan culture would be found only in the countryside or preserved in the museum atmosphere of the monasteries and the Potala Palace, where a hefty twelve-dollar entrance fee was levied on the five thousand visitors allowed to stroll through the fragile seventh-century earthen and wood structure each day.

Pemba was not immune. He confessed that he was not too interested in Tibetan Buddhism, though many Tibetans consider their culture and religion to be synonymous. For instance, in Tibetan homes, there is a small temple for worship of the Buddhas, at which, Pemba explained, "you have to present a lot of stuff in front of the statues." There are fourteen cups of water, seven on each side of the Buddha, and one ritual involves filling them. "You have to change each one; that indicates your gratefulness to your belief," he said. "I remember the morning my father asked me to change the water. He used a specific term—*yonchap*. I just couldn't get it. What the heck was *yonchap*?" Pemba stared dumbfounded at his father, who just kept repeating it angrily. "In his mind, *yonchap* is a very straightforward point that, as a Tibetan, you should get. I was embarrassed. I tried to excuse myself, but there was nothing I could say."

For centuries, the secular aspects of Tibetan society have been balanced by the monastic system, which served as the loci of higher education and reliably injected spiritual discipline and values back into the community. But as Pemba decried the Sinofication of Tibet, his own story pointed to the frailty of that long-standing cultural conduit, which had so often drawn the heat of the Chinese government's political crackdowns since the 1950s. Across Tibet, the government has severely restricted enrollment in the monasteries to a symbolic trickle. More than a few monks recounted stories of being forced out or excluded from monasteries because of government quotas. Religiousness bred nationalism. And monkhood, the Chinese thinking went, was an economically unproductive endeavor; it removed capable participants from the economy, a wholly ironic position given the difficulties Tibetans like Pemba had in finding work.

At the same time, the political manipulation of the monasteries continued. A monk studying at Sera, one of the two great monasteries in the Lhasa Valley, described an escalating "reeducation" campaign during the fall of 2006 through which Chinese officials mandated that the monks study five textbooks versed in Chinese communist theory and ideology. Monks were regularly interrogated by Chinese officials as to the status of their political views and made to repeatedly disavow allegiance to the Dalai Lama in sessions that could be arduous and often violent, just like in the days of the Cultural Revolution. A few weeks earlier, the monk told me, a lama at the Drepung Monastery had committed suicide in protest. In general, teaching positions had been gutted and Tibet's independent education system cannibalized by the central government.

Viewed in the context of the rural land-use policies and tax laws, Pemba said, it was hard not to think these religious policies were part of a larger campaign to dilute Tibetan identity. As he began to delve into more delicate topics, a close friend of his, a Chinese man who worked for a government bank in Shigatze, arrived. They shook hands and laughed warmly.

"I should explain what we're talking about," I said to Pemba, hoping he would translate. "No," Pemba said. "You shouldn't." And that was the end of the conversation.

THE MAJOR. THAT WAS WHAT FRIENDS CALLED LI DUO LONG, A HIGH-ranking People's Liberation Army officer and the only Chinese army official willing to socialize with an American in the autumn of 2006. We first met in an east Lhasa Sichuan kitchen, Third Team, named for Mao Zedong's systematic numbering of Tibetan villages during the collectivization years of the Great Leap Forward, and two large posters of Mao hung on the wall. The Major, a gregarious man in his early thirties, was bedecked in a tightly fitted green wool uniform with metal gold stars on formal red shoulder bands. He looked like he was playing dress-up, but he had lived in Tibet, stationed as a doctor in a PLA hospital, since 1996.

The Major was fond of hosting social dinners at one of the upscale Chinese seafood restaurants that crowded the west end. On such occasions, he might wear jeans and a casual button-down and nearly be mistaken for a Westerner. One night in late October, after a case of Budweiser bottles had been emptied, he stumbled down the block with his guests to one of the recently opened clubs, Babila, that provided a baptism in the new paradigm of Lhasa. At the door a bouncer, a big Chinese man decked head to toe in black, patted each person down. Tibetan men like to carry knives, he explained apologetically.

Inside, fiber-optic strands of plastic beads drizzled like rain to a long and sleek stainless steel bar. Disco balls spun from the ceiling, refracting a rainbow of dancing spotlights. On the stage several women, stripped to stiletto heels and a revealing pair of underwear, gyrated to thumping music, a Mandarin version of 50 Cent. Anheuser-Busch appeared to be in the throes of a major product push in Tibet—a neon Bud sign, more red banners, and stacks of cans were everywhere. At Babila, a Bud cost twenty-five yuan, a little more than four dollars. A traditional hotel room in Lhasa cost eight.

Babila was owned, at least in part, by its thirty-two-year-old general manager, Yang Wei, a pudgy man from Chengdu whose preferred look consisted of a warm-up jacket, designer jeans, jogging shoes, and hair slicked back with a thick layer of gel. Yang owned two bars and a liquor store back home—he had been in the entertainment business since 1997—and when a group of investors approached him about opening a business in Lhasa, he was eager to enlist in the venture. He came for a preliminary visit in March 2005, and by October had invested a million yuan in the west side and was already pouring drinks. "I'm very optimistic about the consumption capacity of Lhasa," Yang said, expressing his enthusiasm in sober, clinical terms. "It will become a very modern city." The average tab at his bar, he explained, could run from four hundred to two thousand dollars, exquisite sums in Tibet. Less than half his customers were tourists; the majority were officials—men like the Major—or wealthy business speculators checking out the opportunities for grabbing a piece of the TAR's explosive growth. Their money came from Guanzhou, Chengdu, Xi'an, or Hong Kong. Twenty new hotels had opened in the month of July alone, he said, and their owners as well as their guests regularly filtered down to spend some cash at Babila.

Like many investors in Tibet, Yang aimed to build a private empire and do it fast. He had a lease on a property on the second ring road surrounding Lhasa, where construction for his new hotel would begin later in the year. But the richer opportunities, he said, lay in the ground, which was why he had been spending his weekends driving his BMW 530i six hours north to Nagqu, signing deals and looking for a stake in a big mineral play. Yang readily admitted he knew nothing about mining—"I can manage the business side"— and so he paid an engineer to find a good investment. Within months this hired gun had uncovered a small start-up that needed more money in order to mine a rich iron seam it had claimed early on. Yang got in without hesitation, and the mine would break ground in May 2007. "First of all, we're businessmen, so the first thing we think about is profit," Yang said. "Tibet has a very rich potential for mines, but because most places are very remote it is impossible to explore them. The reason why we bought in Nagqu now is because of the railroad."

But Yang had always seen two opportunities in Tibet, and his bar had in part been an investment in the very uniqueness of the land and its people. Babila sprawled over four floors, one housing a cabaret, another had private room after private room of KTV karaoke. "Before I came to Lhasa, I thought it was an exotic and mysterious place," he recalled. "Tibetan culture is so deeply rooted here, I don't think it will be diluted—it's important for business." Yang was sanguine. "But it is also very Han friendly. There are so many Sichuanese people now, I feel more comfortable." Cozied up to the edge of a stage, a bunch of lonely-looking men sat at tables as dancers swung bare legs over their heads in wide, sweeping arcs.

At the first-floor bar, the Major was slurring his speech and talking loosely. He clucked about how the Japanese were rumored to have offered to pay the cost of railway construction in the early 1990s for a guaranteed stake in mineral discoveries, and he said that army officials considered the railway primarily a strategic defense push and that the economic development was a sideshow. He and a couple of dangerous drinking buddies were quickly engaged in a serious game of shit-talking. The subject turned to the Olympics: "What would American athletes bring to Beijing?"

A waiter came by the table with the club's latest promotion—bottles of Chivas—and the group was thirsty. It was my turn to pick up the tab of 480 yuan, or sixty dollars—half a year's farming income for a typical Tibetan villager living on the edge of Lhasa. The bottle was opened, and the Major and I had our tumblers filled with ice cubes and a heavy pour, while the rest of the table opted for the more traditional Chinese way of enjoying a glass of scotch: add it to bottled green tea as a mixer and drink the concoction in shots. The waiter filled a pitcher with the stuff, and everyone got down to playing dice, a drinking game that was a combination of poker skill and chance that somehow always resulted in my glass being raised to my lips. The waiters swung by every few moments—dropping a couple extra ice cubes in the glasses, topping them off, and soon the bottle of Chivas was empty and the table was ordering another.

AS THIS GREAT PROJECT HAD FINISHED, IT HAD BROUGHT MANY THINGS to Tibet, not all of which had been expected, at least not by Zhang Luxin. With the train open for service, Zhang's offices at the Qinghai-Tibet Railway Company headquarters in Golmud were full of boxes, and the unit was preparing to move back east, so he had ventured to a hotel a few blocks down the road. His eyes a bit watery behind his large eyeglasses, Zhang seemed nostalgic and deep in thought. We had been talking about his son—about the disappointment caused by his decision not to continue in Zhang's career and how, with the railroad project, Zhang had never had time to be much of a father. "You have respect for the decisions I have made and the kind of person I am, don't you?"

It was a striking question, full of sudden vulnerability. This man who had driven a monumental project through a combination of conviction and desperation was seeking validation, and from, of all sources, an American journalist. "I mean, I think you believe, with me, that it takes dedication and sacrifice to make something of yourself," he continued, without prompting. "My wife has always complained about our separateness, about my not being a father. But she had no power to change that situation. I understand from a human point of view this is something that shouldn't happen; it may be very hard for people to understand. So I will pay back to my family by working even harder, and making more money, and giving the money to my family," he said, remorseful and almost whispering. "Nothing is perfect in the world. There are many families in China like mine, very unstable. But I have a town house in Beijing. I bought a car this year—a new Volkswagen Passat. We live very well now. So this is like an old Chinese thing—the sweet after the bitterness."

We live well now. That seemed to be the predominant theme in everything that had happened. It was what the World Trade Organization wanted for China, what Hu Jintao professed to want for its west, what the World Bank had aimed for in Qinghai, and what Tibetans—especially those able to embrace the accoutrements of a new world—wanted for themselves. Yet the world is one of opposites and balance, and at some point there are costs to bear. "One of my criticisms of international economic institutions is that they try to pretend there are not trade-offs—a single set of policies made everyone better off—while the essence of economics is choice," Joseph Stiglitz explained in his book *Making Globalization Work*. "There are alternatives, some of which benefit some groups at the expense of others, some of which impose risks on some groups to the advantage of others." Kalden, like most Tibetans snared in China's fifty-year campaign to remake Tibet, learned that the hard way. Zhang's son experienced it in a lesser way. And Zhang too paid a price for the credit and recognition he had finally claimed. It may be increasingly unrealistic in an age of plundered resources and a warming environment to think that true globalization can happen equitably. "Globalization, as it has been pushed, has often made it more difficult to maintain the requisite balance," Stiglitz wrote. China, more than any other country on Earth, knows that now.

But Zhang could afford the Passat.

By the number of new cars each day hitting the streets of Beijing, or Lhasa for that matter, it seemed that the Go West campaign was, at least for some, a success. But after the subsidization stops, and after the expansion of China slows, as it must someday, Lhasa, traded of its heritage and land and architecture, will be left to compete with the other identical boomtowns of China's new west, a capitalist version of Mao Zedong's plan for Tibet's future.

As Pemba had put it a few days earlier, "Sooner or later they'll have to cope with that." It was inevitable that someday the boom would be over.

EPILOGUE

CHINA—ITS MARQUEE PROJECT FINALLY SUCCESSFULLY built and its ears ringing with criticism about ethnic migration and the train's potential impact on Tibetan culture—could have exhibited increased modesty in perpetuating its further plans for Tibet. But, in December 2007, the state-controlled China Railways, the state-owned parent company of sorts to the Qinghai-Tibet Railway Company, raised an astonishing $4 billion in IPOs on the Hong Kong and Shanghai stock exchanges. Along with the announcement in November 2007 that PetroChina had succeeded ExxonMobil as the world's most valued company—based in part on the irrational exuberance of investors on the "casino-like" Chinese exchanges and also on the big hopes of massive new oil fields in Tibet—it appeared China had seized its prize and had no intention of releasing any bit of it.

Construction and expansion have continued in full force, and in addition to the Liuwu Industrial Park, which authorities reported will be the future base of seventeen high-tech and industrial companies, a freight railway depot has had its groundbreaking in the Tolung suburb of the city, west of Lhasa terminal. The largest logistics center in Tibet, the $200 million project is intended to manage the comings and goings of more than 3 million tons of minerals, construction materials, and industrial imports each year. Another similar facility is being planned for Nagqu. The railway extension to Shigatze, along the Yarlung Tsangpo River, is scheduled to be operational by the end of 2012, and plans are evolving not only to extend the line into eastern Tibet, but perhaps to complete several of the other major routes that were originally proposed as Tibet's first railway, including the Yunnan and Lanzhou routes. Each would be built out with the specific intention of servicing large new resource extraction projects in eastern Tibet.

In the last few years, Lhasa physically expanded by more than 60 percent and its unofficial population is now estimated to stand at more than half a million people. The constant influx of traders, migrant laborers, and tourists—whose numbers are often underestimated—has made Tibet more vulnerable to the kind of problems already common in eastern China. For example, food-borne illnesses prevalent in eastern industrialized agriculture have reached Lhasa. In early 2006, bovine growth injections were being pushed on China's herding communities to increase meat production. Soon afterward, cattle in rural areas of Tibet began suffering from a strange virus that is believed to be connected to the hormones. Thousands of animals had to be exterminated, devastating the farmers' livelihoods. In March 2007, after some 8,000 chickens had been transported to Lhasa's markets from other provinces, inspectors announced that a bird had tested positive for the H5 strain of bird flu. In a rush, more than 7,500 chickens were slaughtered across the city.

Meanwhile, tight controls on religious expression and Tibetan culture have continued unabated. In May 2007, the seventy-year-old abbot of Dungkyab Monastery was forced to step down after he refused to denounce the Dalai Lama in an ongoing series of intense reeducation sessions. In August, the central government's lawmakers, in one of its strangest gestures yet toward total religious control of Tibet, waded into the afterlife to demand that lamas returning as sentient beings gain government endorsement of their reincarnation. Then, in early September, dozens of young school boys were arrested near Labrang Monastery after officials found graffiti calling for the Dalai Lama's return to China and "Free Tibet" on one of the walls; while they were in detention, many were assigned to hard labor, and four of the boys, some of whom were still being held at press time, were reported to have been badly beaten, including with electric cattle prods. In Lhasa, residents reported that fifth graders have been queried by officials in schools about their thinking around the idea of a "free Tibet" in apparent hopes it would yield insight into the political standpoints of their parents. And when the Dalai Lama was honored with the U.S. Congressional Medal of Honor in October 2007, Chinese police responded by tightening down Lhasa; they strictly outlawed any celebration and surrounded nearby Drepung Monastery with armed soldiers before temporarily closing the monastery altogether.

Environmentally, literal and figurative cracks have begun to form in Tibet's facade. By late 2007 news reports were mentioning increasing levels of industrial air pollution in Lhasa, and the government enacted a tax on private vehicles—of which they counted more than seventy thousand—in the hopes of cutting exhaust. On the railway, problems began to be discovered almost immediately. State press reported that the permafrost foundation was sinking and cracking in places and that cracks had been observed in the concrete— developments that Ministry of Railways spokesman Wang Yongpin, quoted by Beijing News, said were "making the railway unstable in some places," and posed "a hidden danger to the railway line quality."

In June 2007 the Chinese central government enraged the international environmental community with plans to pave a highway to the base camp of Mount Everest, an extraordinarily sensitive area. The construction, which flies in the face of development guidelines set by the International Olympic Committee, was so far advanced by the time of its disclosure that it was obvious to observers that the central government had long been developing the road in secret. Though Beijing eventually backed off that project, Chinese athletes will carry the Olympic torch to the summit of Everest.

Then on November 30, 2007, two years after the tracks were finished, the Qinghai-Tibet Railway was, for the first time, filled with soldiers of the People's Liberation Army en route to Tibet. The government said it had decided that transporting the troops via the railway was safer and more cost-effective than using the old highway, but news reports in the *Times of India* noted that the transport came just days after rumors that Chinese troops had destroyed Indian army outposts on the Indian side of the disputed Arunachal Pradesh border. In the paper's words, "The latest move confirms Beijing's strategic purposes."

NOTES

The reporting of this story—inspired by my early introduction to the Dalai Lama and Tibetan culture when I was a young boy—has evolved over many years. Its foundation was laid when I worked in the field as a young anthropologist in the Nepalese Himalayas in the early 1990s. Later I would travel the world, including to China, reporting on oil exploration, metals mining, and other issues that increasingly focused my attention on the confluence of international business and the environment and globalization. These disparate influences came together in the spring of 2001, when I read an early wire report about China's plans to extend its railway network to Tibet.

Over the five years that followed, I made four extended trips to Tibet, a half dozen to cities in central and eastern China, and one to Nepal. Much of the detail and description and anecdotes within these pages is based on my firsthand experiences during these visits. However, because of the sensitivity around the issue of Tibet's autonomy and history and the exceedingly restrictive journalistic environment there, the gathering of this story forced an examination of common journalistic ethics and often relied on techniques I would avoid under nornal circumstances. For one, I often could not be forthcoming about my identity as a journalist or my intentions in publishing a book, because of deep concerns that such a declaration would jeopardize the safety of the people I met, as well as my own. I was repeatedly advised to take this otherwise unorthodox approach by the trusted experts and sources who shaped my reporting and have spent much greater amounts of time inside Tibet than I have, on the grounds that less prudent projects in the past have resulted in the investigation and persecution of Tibetans after publication. I reserved a full explanation and disclosure of my intentions for those few people whom I chose to interview in greater depth, and whose characters are represented within these pages.

For the same concerns, the resident Tibetan sources in this book—including Renzin Tashi, Kalden and his family, Sonam Yeshi, and Pemba Norbu, as well as others—are not identified by their true names, and some identifying details, such as the precise locations of homes, have also been changed with the goal of truly guarding their identities. Besides those few specific identifying facts that I consider immaterial to the larger story, what lies in these pages is my best effort at a precise factual accounting and description of Lhasa, Tibet, the construction of the railway, and the changes it has brought. My historical accounts of the early decades of China's occupation of Tibet are collected from numerous respected accounts in the English language.

China's Ministry of Railways and the Press and Culture Department of the Foreign Affairs office of the People's Republic of China declined repeated formal requests for credentials, cooperation, and statements regarding all aspects of the railway project, and thus my reporting was completed without their sanction and involvement. Beneath this top strata of bureaucracy, though, I was offered generous cooperation from individuals involved in the railway project. Besides my own experiences, my reporting relied on extended interviews and multiple visits over several years with the Chinese engineers and scientists identified in these pages and many more who are not. My assembly of the broader time line of the railway construction itself and the construction ceremonies described, as well as quotations of higher Chinese officials, come from a compilation of China state press articles and statements published on the Web site of the Qinghai-Tibet Railway, Ltd., the body of China's Ministry of Railways responsible for the project.

1. NOW IS THE TIME

5 "metastatic crisis": Bruce Gilley, *China's Democratic Future: How It Will Happen and Where It Will Lead* (New York: Columbia University Press, 2004), p. 103.

11 "We feel very bad": Quoted in Solomon M. Karmel, "Ethnic Tension and the Struggle for Order: China's Policies in Tibet," *Pacific Affairs*, vol. 68, 1995.

11 Yin had been an underling: Based on the translation by Shi Lihong, the executive director and cofounder of the Green Plateau Institute, Kunming, Yunnan Province, of contemporaneous newspaper reports as well as China Central Television International video reports, http://www.cctv.com/english/special/C16017/ 01/index.shtml.

11 "We feel now that everything": Translation by Shi Lihong.

14–15 "black hole": Quoted in John F. Avedon, *In Exile from the Land of Snows: The Dalai Lama and Tibet Since the Chinese Conquest* (New York: Vintage, 1986), p. 247.

20 "It is impossible to solve": Interview with Zhang Luxin. Zhang could not provide the person's second name, and I have not been able to confirm further details regarding the letter or its impact.

24 "break the bottleneck": Li Jingwen, a member of the CPPCC National Committee and president of the Institute of Quantitative Economics and Technology Economics, Academy of Social Sciences. China.gov press release.

2. A SOMETIME BUDDHIST

26 "Tibetan religion and culture": Tibetan Centre for Human Rights and Democracy, "Enforcing Loyalty: Annual Report, 2000," ch. 2, http://www.tchrd.org/publications/annual_reports/2000/chapter2.html.

37 "a sparsely inhabited": Peter Fleming, *Bayonets to Lhasa: The First Full Account of the British Invasion of Tibet in 1904* (New York: Harper & Brothers, 1961), p. 52.

37 "Nobody stopped us": Heinrich Harrer, *Seven Years in Tibet,* trans. Richard Graves (New York: G. P. Putnam's Sons, 1996), p. 135.

38 "Even an inch": Quoted in Tsering Shakya, *The Dragon in the Land of Snows* (New York: Columbia University Press, 1999), p. 5.

38 "If anyone should doubt": Ibid., p. 38.

39 "If we Tibetans had fought": Avedon, *In Exile from the Land of Snows,* p. 29.

43 "Tibetan autonomous" regions: Steven D. Marshall and Susette Terment Cooke, "Tibet Outside the TAR," CD-ROM (Washington, D.C.: International Campaign for Tibet, 1997).

3. A BIGGER STAGE

49 "This railway will do": Based on contemporaneous, handwritten notes from Shi Lihong's translation of Chinese news reports.

51 "It felt suffocating": As from National Library archives by Shi Lihong.

51 "The vent pipe": CCTV report, http://www.cctv.com/english/special/ C16017/01/index .shtml.

62 "allowed pilgrimages": Wieland Wagner, "Deng Xiaoping's Legacy Divides Chinese Leadership," *Spiegel,* October 12, 2007, http://www .spiegel.de/international/ world/ 0,1518,511160,00.html.

63 "The invasion focused": Melvyn C. Goldstein, *A History of Modern Tibet, 1913–1951* (Berkeley: University of California Press, 1989), p. 45.

64 the actual line of control: Shakya, *The Dragon in the Land of Snows,* p. 247.

64 ragged Indian prisoners: Ibid., p. 286.

4. STRAY DOGS

71 "conduct which shocks the civilized world": Quoted in Avedon, *In Exile from the Land of Snows,* p. 48.

72 "I felt as if I were standing": Dalai Lama, *My Land and My People: Memoirs of the Dalai Lama of Tibet* (New York: McGraw-Hill, 1962), p. 173.

73 Many Tibetans . . . armed themselves: Shakya, *The Dragon in the Land of Snows,* p. 203.

73–74 "The streets were littered": Shakya, *The Dragon in the Land of Snows,* p. 204.

74 In Lhasa's Drapchi prison: Avedon, *In Exile from the Land of Snows,* p. 232.

80 Sonam Yeshi: Pseudonym for a man interviewed upon entering exile at the UN High Commissioner for Refugees (UNHCR) Reception Center in Kathmandu, November 2006.

81 "continued to commit . . . abuses": From 1997 U.S. Senate Foreign Relations Committee testimony read by John Kerry, quoting 1966 documents, "The Situation of Tibet and Its People," May 13, 1997.

81 "In the course of the struggle": Shakya, *The Dragon in the Land of Snows,* p. 322.

87 "The effect . . . was to destroy": Shakya, *The Dragon in the Land of Snows,* pp. 322, 349.

5. MOVING HEAVEN AND EARTH

101 a unique genetic ability: S. C. Erzurum, S. Ghosh, et al., "Higher Blood Flow and Circulating NO Products Offset High-Altitude Hypoxia Among Tibetans," *Proceedings of the National Academy of Sciences,* vol. 104, no. 45, November 6, 2007, pp. 17593–98.

101 Chinese are particularly ill-equipped: Tianyi Wu, "Life on the High Tibetan Plateau," *High Altitude Medicine & Biology,* vol. 5, no. 1, 2004, pp. 1–2.

103 The doctor there . . . recently arrived: Xu Gang, *Oriental Katag: A Panorama Documentation of the Qinghai-Tibet Railway* (Nanching, China: Baihuazhou Literature & Art Publishing House, 2005).

106 "intimidation and enforced socialization": Avedon, *In Exile from the Land of Snows,* p. 44.

6. FREE TIBET

127 "Tibet is independent": Ronald D. Schwartz, *Circle of Protest: Political Ritual in the Tibetan Uprising* (New York: Columbia University Press, 1995), p. 256.

130 "all this trouble": Fleming, *Bayonets to Lhasa,* p. 232.

131 "the essence of the leaders'": Quoted in Orville Schell and David

Shambaugh, ed., *The China Reader: The Reform Era* (New York: Vintage, 1998), p. 520.

133 "China's presence and behavior": Marshall and Cooke, *Tibet Outside the TAR,* supporting materials, p. 33.

135 "The authorities, directed by President Hu": Reporters Without Borders, "Freedom of the Press Worldwide in 2007," annual report, http://www.rsf.org/IMG/pdf/rapport_en_bd-4.pdf.

140 The TAR's health-care system: These economic figures come from Andrew Fischer's book, *State Growth and Social Exclusion in Tibet: Challenges of Recent Growth* (Copenhagen: Nordic Institute of Asian Studies Press, 2005).

142 "the vast panorama of the holy city": L. Austine Waddell, *Lhasa and Its Mysteries: With a Record of the Expedition of 1903–1904* (London: Methuen & Co., 1906), p. 329.

7. UNDER A HAN SUN

147 "can hardly be described as a policy": Heiki Holbig, "The Emergence of the Campaign to Open Up the West: Ideological Formation, Central Decision Making and the Role of the Provinces," in David S. G. Goodman, ed., *China's Campaign to "Open Up the West": National, Provincial and Local Perspectives,* The China Quarterly Special Issues New Series, no. 5 (Cambridge: Cambridge University Press, 2004), p. 33.

148 "strengthening of national unity": Zhu Rongji, "Government Work Report for 2000 to the Third Session of the Ninth National Peoples' Congress," quoted in *China Daily,* March 6, 2000.

148 "barely coded phrases": David S. G. Goodman, "The Campaign to 'Open Up the West': National, Provincial-level and Local Perspectives," in Goodman, ed., *China's Campaign,* p. 11.

148–49 The ethnic preferences underlying . . . goals: Li Dezhu, "Large-Scale Development of Western China and China's Nationality Problem," *Qiushi* (Seeking Truth), June 1, 2000, trans. in Foreign Broadcast Information Service, June 15, 2000.

150 Factions totaling as many as: Emily T. Yeh, "Tibetan Rage Wars: Spatial Politics and Authority on the Grasslands of Amdo," *Development and Change,* vol. 34, no. 3, 2003.

151 "Resettled herders": Human Rights Watch, "No One Has the Liberty to Refuse: Tibetan Herders Forcibly Relocated in Gansu, Qinghai, Sichuan and the Tibetan Autonomous Region," June 2007, http://hrw.org/reports/2007/tibet0607.

52–53 "There are more and more Chinese people": International Campaign for Tibet, *Devotion and Defiance,* written and directed by Kunga Palmo, DVD, 2004.

8. THE GAMBLER

167 in Tibet the permafrost extends: Cheng Guodong, "A Roadbed Cooling Approach for the Construction of the Qinghai-Tibet Railway," Powerpoint presentation, State Key Laboratory of Frozen Soils Engineering, CAREERI (Cold & Arid Regions Environmental & Engineering Research Institute), n.d.; "Construction of the Demonstration Section of the Qinghai-Xizang Railway on the Plateau," State Key Laboratory of Frozen Soils Engineering, CAREERI (Cold & Arid Regions Environmental & Engineering Research Institute), n.d..

167 Roughly one-fifth of the earth's surface: http://en.wikipedia.org/wiki/Permafrost.

181 "Due to the complexity": Qinghai-Tibet Railway Company, "Construction of Qinghai-Tibet Railway on Track," press release, June 27, 2003.

9. THE RACE TO REACH LHASA

191 The railway company paid: The estimates ranged from $12.00 to $37.50. My number is the higher, from China-Tibet Information Service press release, Dec. 2004.

196 "It's been our long-cherished dream": Qinghai-Tibet Railway Enters Hub County," Xinhua News Agency, October 10, 2004.

199 "Due to the melting permafrost": *Beijing News,* January 22, 2006, quoted in U.S. Congressional-Executive Commission on China, *Annual Report* (Washington, D.C.: U.S. Government Printing Office, December 8, 2006), http://www.cecc.gov/pages/annualRpt/annualRpt06/CECCannRpt2006.pdf.

199 "Temperature projections": J. H. Christiansen, B. Hewitson, et al., "2007: Regional Climate Projections" in S. Solomon, D. Qin, et al., eds., *Climate Change 2007: The Physical Science Basis, Contribution of Working Group I to the Fourth Assessment Report of the Intergovernmental Panel on Climate* (New York: Cambridge University Press, 2007), pp. 850, 881.

200 "The Qinghai-Tibet Railway": Cao Desheng, "Qinghai-Tibet Railway Project Steams Ahead," *China Daily,* March 8, 2005.

203 "that an expansion of the control": International Campaign for Tibet, "China's Top Leaders Meet on Eve of TAR Anniversary to Set Tibet Policy," news release, August 31, 2005, http://www.savetibet.org/news/newsitem.php?id=804.

10. PARADISE REBUILT

219 Nearly 90 percent of its . . . arms transfers: Sujit Dutta, "China's Emerging Power and Military Role: Implications for South Asia," in Jonathan D. Pollack and Richard H. Yang, ed., *In China's Shadow: Regional Perspectives on Chinese Foreign Policy and Military Development* (Santa Monica, Calif: RAND Corporation, 1998) http://www.rand.org/pubs/conf_proceedings/CF137/F137.chap5.pdf; John E. Peters, James Dickens, et al., *War and Escalation in South Asia* (Santa Monica, Calif.: RAND Corporation, 2006), http://www.rand.org/pubs/monographs/MG367-1/index.html.

220 The border: "India-China Competition Revealed in Ongoing Border Disputes," *Power and Interest News Report,* October 9, 2007, http://www.pinr.com/report.php?ac=view_report&report_id=695&langu.

220 India woke up: Rajat Pandit, "Tiger, Dragon in Telecom Race on LAC," *The Economic Times* (Mumbai), January 26, 2006, http://economictimes.indiatimes.com/articleshow/1387688.cms.

224 "unprecedented triumph": "China Completes World's Highest Railway to Tibet," Xinhua News Agency, October 15, 2005.

11. WHEN THE WANG FAMILY CAME TO TOWN

230–31 "to maintain its status quo": All from Xinhua, repeating a July 1, 2006, editorial in *People's Daily*—my version slightly edited to correct translation errors.

232 "second invasion of Tibet": Prithwish Ganguly, "In Tibet's Interest to Be Part of China," *Boston Globe* (Reuters), December 24, 2006.

240 "Lack of resources": Li Fangchao, "Mineral Finds Off Imports Tension," *China Daily,* January 25, 2007.

241 "Five years ago": Stephen Stakiw, "High on Tibet: Continental Minerals Expects Xietongmen Feasibility in Mid-2007," *The Northern Miner,* vol. 93, no. 2 (March 5–11, 2007), http://www.northernminer.com/issues/PrinterFriendly.asp?story_id=5909092544&id=184090&RType=&PC=i&issue=03052007.

248 an estimated 2,600 Tibetans fled: In addition to firsthand reporting at the UN reception center, this section is drawn from International Campaign for Tibet's 2006 report *Dangerous Crossing* and Human Rights Watch documents and interviews shared with me.

249 Dohna: Pseudonym attached to an unnamed person in the HRW interview/ICT story, who I think is the same individual.

12. HU'S WEST

255 the chiru population: Alex Chadwick, "A Resurgence of Wildlife in Northern Tibet," *NPR Radio Expeditions,* February 21, 2007, http://www.npr.org/templates/story/story .php?storyId=7316356.

257 "The tourism industry will not encourage": "China to Scenically Develop Qinghai-Tibet Plateau by 2020," ANI, July 20, 2007, http://in.news.yahoo.com/070720/139/6i93q.html.

258 From Nagqu, a line: International Campaign for Tibet, "Tracking the Steel Dragon: How China's Economic Policies and the Railroad Are

Transforming Tibet" (Washington, D.C.: International Campaign for Tibet, 2008).

261 "To help the city": Lhasa Begins Construction of New District to Protect Cultural Relics," Xinhua News Agency, November 14, 2007.

272 "One of my criticisms": Joseph E. Stiglitz, *Making Globalization Work* (New York: W. W. Norton & Co., 2006), p. xv.

EPILOGUE

275 "casino-like": Peter Engardio, Dexter Roberts, et al., "Broken China," *BusinessWeek,* July 23, 2007.

BIBLIOGRAPHY

Addy, Premen. *Tibet on the Imperial Chessboard: The Making of British Policy Towards Lhasa, 1899–1925.* Calcutta: Academic Press, 1984.

Avedon, John F. *In Exile from the Land of Snows: The Dalai Lama and Tibet Since the Chinese Conquest.* New York: Vintage, 1986.

Barnett, Robert. *Lhasa: Streets with Memories.* New York: Columbia University Press, 2006.

Boorman, Scott A. *The Protracted Game: A Wei-Ch'i Interpretation of Maoist Revolutionary Strategy.* New York: Oxford University Press, 1969.

Dalai Lama. *My Land and My People: Memoirs of the Dalai Lama of Tibet.* New York: McGraw-Hill, 1962.

Dalvi, J. P. *Himalayan Blunder: The Curtain-Raiser to the Sino-Indian War of 1962.* Bombay: Thacker, 1969.

David-Neel, Alexandra. *My Journey to Lhasa: The Personal Story of the Only White Woman Who Succeeded in Entering the Forbidden City.* New York: Harper and Brothers, 1927.

Diamond, Larry. *The Spirit of Democracy: The Struggle to Build Free Societies Throughout the World.* New York: Times Books, 2008.

Ding Lu and William A. W. Neilson, ed. *China's West Region Development: Domestic Strategies and Global Implications.* River Edge, N.J.: World Scientific, 2004.

Duval, P., ed. *Annals of Glaciology: Papers from the International Symposium on Physical and Mechanical Processes in Ice in Relation to Glacier and Ice-sheet Modelling,* vol. 37. Cambridge, U.K.: International Glaciological Society, 2003.

Fischer, Andrew Martin. *State Growth and Social Exclusion in Tibet.* Copenhagen: Nordic Institute of Asian Studies Press, 2005.

Fleming, Peter. *Bayonets to Lhasa: The First Full Account of the British Invasion of Tibet in 1904.* New York: Harper & Brothers, 1961.

————. *News from Tartary: A Journey from Peking to Kashmir.* New York: Charles Scribner's Sons, 1936.

French, Patrick. *Tibet, Tibet: A Personal History of a Lost Land.* New York: Vintage, 2003.

Gilley, Bruce. *China's Democratic Future: How It Will Happen and Where It Will Lead.* New York: Columbia University Press, 2004.

Goldstein, Melvyn. *A History of Modern Tibet, 1913–1951.* Berkeley: University of California Press, 1989.

Goodman, David S. G., ed., *China's Campaign to "Open Up the West": National, Provincial and Local Perspectives.* The China Quarterly Special Issues New Series, no. 5. Cambridge: Cambridge University Press, 2004.

Harrer, Heinrich. *Seven Years in Tibet.* Trans. by Richard Graves. New York: G. P. Putnam's Sons, 1996.

Hopkirk, Peter. *Trespassers on the Roof of the World: The Secret Exploration of Tibet.* New York: Kodansha America, 1995.

Human Rights Watch. *No One Has the Liberty to Refuse: Tibetan Herders Forcibly Relocated in Gansu, Qinghai, Sichuan and the Tibetan Autonomous Region.* New York: Human Rights Watch, June 2007. http://hrw.org/reports/2007/tibet0607.

————. *World Report, 2007.* Introduction by Kenneth Roth. New York: Human Rights Watch, 2007. http://www.hrw.org/wr2k7/wr2007master.pdf.

Intergovernmental Panel on Climate Change. "Regional Climate Projections." In *Climate Change 2007: The Physical Science Basis.* New York: Cambridge University Press, 2007.

International Campaign for Tibet. *Dangerous Crossing: Conditions Impacting the Flight of Tibetan Refugees in 2001* and annual updates for 2002, 2003, and 2006. Washington, D.C.: International Campaign for Tibet, May 2002. http://www.savetibet.org/documents/pdfs/2001RefugeeReport.pdf.

————. *Nuclear Tibet: Nuclear Weapons and Nuclear Waste on the Tibetan Plateau.* Washington, D.C.: International Campaign for Tibet, 1993.

————. "Tracking the Steel Dragon: How China's Economic Policies and the Railroad Are Transforming Tibet." Washington, D.C.: International Campaign for Tibet, 2008.

International Permafrost Association. *Frozen Ground: The News Bulletin of the International Permafrost Association,* no. 30, December 2006. http://www.ipa-permafrost.org/FG30.pdf.

Kynge, James. *China Shakes the World: A Titan's Rise and Troubled Future—and the Challenge for America.* New York: Houghton Mifflin, 2006.

Ngok Lee. *The Chinese People's Liberation Army, 1980–82: Modernisation, Strategy, and Politics.* Canberra: Strategic and Defence Studies Centre, Australian National University, 1983.

Marshall, Steven D., and Susette Terment Cooke. "Tibet Outside the TAR." CD-ROM. Washington, D.C.: International Campaign for Tibet, 1997.

Nishimura, Richard, and the International Campaign for Tibet. *Crossing the Line: China's Railway to Tibet.* Washington, D.C.: International Campaign for Tibet, 2003.

Pan, Lynn. *The New Chinese Revolution.* Chicago: Contemporary Books, 1988.

Peters, John E., James Dickens, et al. *War and Escalation in South Asia.* Santa Monica, Calif.: RAND Corporation, 2006. http://www.rand.org/pubs/monographs/MG367-1/index.html.

Schell, Orville. *Virtual Tibet: Seaching for Shangri-la from the Himalayas to Hollywood.* New York: Metropolitan Books, 2000.

Schell, Orville, and David Shambaugh, eds. *The China Reader: The Reform Era.* New York: Vintage, 1998.

Schwartz, Ronald D. *Circle of Protest: Political Ritual in the Tibetan Uprising.* New York: Columbia University Press, 1995.

Shakya Tsering. *The Dragon in the Land of Snows: A History of Modern Tibet Since 1947.* New York: Columbia University Press, 1999.

Shastri, Amita, and A. Jeyaratnam Wilson, eds. *The Post-Colonial States of South Asia: Democracy, Development and Identity.* New York: Palgrave Macmillan, 2001.

Snow, Edgar. *Red Star over China.* New York: Random House, 1968.

Stiglitz, Joseph E. *Globalization and Its Discontents.* New York: W. W. Norton and Company, 2002.

————. *Making Globalization Work.* New York: W. W. Norton and Company, 2006.

Thomas, Lowell, Jr. *The Silent War in Tibet.* Garden City, N.Y.: Doubleday, 1959.

Tibet Information Network. *Mining Tibet: Mineral Exploitation in Tibetan Areas of the People's Republic of China.* London: Tibet Information Network, 2002.

U.S. Congress. *China under the Four Modernizations: Selected Papers Submitted to the Joint Economic Committee.* Joint Congress of the United States, 97th Cong., 2nd sess. Washington, D.C.: U.S. Government Printing Office, 1982.

U.S. Congressional-Executive Commission on China. *Annual Report: Congressional-Executive Commission on China.* Washington, D.C.: U.S. Government Printing Office, October 2, 2003. http://www.cecc.gov/pages/annualRpt/2003annRpt.pdf.

————. *Annual Report: Congressional-Executive Commission on China.* Washington, D.C.: U.S. Government Printing Office, December 8, 2006. http://www.cecc.gov/pages/annualRpt/annualRpt06/CECCannRpt2006.pdf.

U.S. Senate. *The Situation of Tibet and Its People: Hearing before the Committee on Foreign Relations, United States Senate.* 150th Cong., 1st sess., May 13, 1997. Washington, D.C.: U.S. Government Printing Office, 1997.

Waddell, L. Austine. *Lhasa and Its Mysteries: With a Record of the Expedition of 1903–1904.* London: Methuen & Co., 1906.

Whymant, Neville J. *A China Manual.* London: Chinese Government Information Office, 1949.

Xing Zheng Yuan and Xin Wen Ju. *China Handbook, 1937-1944: A Comprehensive Survey of Major Developments in China in Seven Years of War.* New York: Macmillan, 1956. Originally published by the Chinese Ministry of Information, 1944.

Yeh, Emily T. "Tibetan Rage Wars: Spatial Politics and Authority on the Grasslands of Amdo." In *Development and Change,* vol. 34, no. 3 (2003).

Zhang, Andy. *Hu Jiantao: Facing China's Challenges Ahead.* San Jose, Calif.: Writer's Club Press, 2002.

ACKNOWLEDGMENTS

This book could not have been written without the generous and patient help of so many people, but first and foremost the community of engineers and scientists who opened their lives and offices and histories to me, often despite a cultural and sometimes legal status quo for not doing so. Above all, the team at the China's State Key Laboratory Cold and Arid Regions Environmental and Engineering Research Institute, based in Lanzhou, China, are owed great thanks—in particular Cheng Guodong, who spent tens of hours out of his insane travel, research, and speaking schedule to talk with me, answer e-mails, and relay documents. His colleagues, including Ma Wei, Huijun Jin, and especially Qi Jilin, who painstakingly arranged my visits, translated many of my meetings, and reviewed my work from afar, were invaluable to learning about the railway's early construction and understanding the properties and issues around permafrost construction. Of course little could have been accomplished without Zhang Luxin and Zhao Shiyun, who bravely shared much about their lives and the details of the construction period. And so much of my reporting in China was completed with the tireless assistance of Shi Lihong, who traveled across the country with me, serving as interpreter, guide, knowledge resource, and adviser, often despite disagreeing with aspects of my view of Tibet but always with dedication to journalistic integrity and a robust reporting process. I am also grateful to those American engineers and experts who introduced me to their Chinese colleagues, including Henry Posner at the Railroad Development Corporation, Ted

Vinson at Oregon State University, Doug Goering at the University of Alaska Fairbanks, and Lou Thompson.

Equally important to this project are the many wonderful, brave, and thoughtful Tibetans who also opened their lives and histories to me, and hosted me on my numerous visits to Tibet. They have, at great risk, each given a piece of themselves to this story, and I wish that they could be thanked here by name. Unfortunately, the political environment in China remains such that for their safety their identities must remain anonymous. Among those outside Tibet who shaped my understanding of Tibetan history as well as my reporting is a Western expatriate whose patient assistance, methodical explanations, translation, and heartfelt and faithful guidance helped make this book what it is. He has, however, asked not to be identified by full name in order to protect his ability to travel freely in Tibet. I am also indebted to John Ackerly and Kate Saunders at the International Campaign for Tibet, Tashi Wangdi in the New York office of the Tibetan Government in Exile, Robert Barnett at Columbia University, Andrew Fischer, Emily Yeh, and Adrian Moon.

The project would never have gotten off the ground without the generous support of the John D. and Catherine T. MacArthur Foundation, which, through a research and writing grant to study cultural migration and security issues in Tibet, enabled more than a year of independent travel and research.

The time to pursue such a project was equally important, and for that, as well as so much encouragement and mentorship and resources, I thank my editors and colleagues at *Fortune* magazine, including Eric Pooley, Hank Gilman, Cliff Leaf, and Xana Antunes. Zhang Dan guided much of my early reporting in Beijing and faithfully translated my interviews there. Brenda Cherry contributed countless hours of research, and Nancy Jo Johnson, besides providing inspiration and friendship, generously opened her address book of contacts for my benefit. Above all, Robert Friedman provided unfailing support and guidance and has been a great teacher as well as a sharp editor, relentlessly pushing me to hone my ideas and my writing.

ACKNOWLEDGMENTS

My literary agent, PJ Mark, has played the parts of coach, mentor, and editor and instilled me with the confidence to write this book. To him, and his colleagues David McCormick and Amy Williams, who believed in this project from the start, I owe thanks. I am also forever indebted to my editor, Robin Dennis, who has understood what I hoped this story could be from day one and skillfully and gently shaped my drafts into a robust manuscript. I am also grateful to Paul Golob, editorial director of Times Books, for his enthusiastic support and commitment, as well as all of those who have worked energetically on the marketing, production, and design, including Kelly Lignos, Tara Kennedy, Chris O'Connell, Meryl Levavi, Kelly Too, and Lisa Kleinholz.

Warm thanks to my friends and family, who have always supported my curious passions and oft-illogical leaps in my career, and who did so again this time as I became nearly obsessed with the building of a far-flung railway. In particular I am grateful to Chris Stewart, who convinced me the project had the makings of a book and lent invaluable instruction on how to get started, as well as to Alex Hildebrand, who edited my initial grant proposal for research funding, and Karin Carrington, who read my drafts.

And not least, I owe the deepest gratitude to my wife, Jodie, who always supports my endeavors without question, tolerated my absence for months at a time over the course of the last five years, and then put up with my manic mood swings as I struggled to put everything on the page.

INDEX

ABOUT THE AUTHOR

ABRAHM LUSTGARTEN is a contributing writer for *Fortune* magazine and the recipient of a MacArthur Foundation grant for international reporting. His articles have appeared in *Esquire, The New York Times, Outside, Sports Illustrated, National Geographic Adventure, Salon,* and many other publications, and in 2003 he was awarded the Horgan Prize for Excellence in Science Reporting. He splits his time between New York and Oregon.